D1028927

"A lively travelogue through time and space! Dr. McGovern, our amiable guide, brings us on board with the promise of good beer and well-prepared food, both of which he offers in abundance. But he also takes us much farther afield to discover ourselves and our ancestors in the near and far corners of the world"

—Roger Barth, author of *The Chemistry of Beer:*
The Science in the Suds

"McGovern's latest book is a fine history of our ancestors' infatuation with fermentation and its imbibable consequences disguised as a rollicking good account of his adventures in search of the earliest beers and wines. . . . McGovern is at once archaeologist, historian, chemist, naturalist, foodie, and raconteur."

—John S. Henderson, Professor of Anthropology at Cornell
University and author of *The World of the Ancient Maya*

"If you ever wondered what might happen when America's most adventurous brewer and a molecular archaeologist whose love of extreme beverages extends across ten millennia begin fiddling together, this is the book for you! Great storytelling, as ancient brews live again!"

—Roald Hoffman, Winner of the Nobel Prize in Chemistry

"A thrilling and brilliant book. Although each chapter is a full-fledged episode, very few readers will refrain from reading this outstanding and inspiring book from the first to the last sentence."

—Martin Zarnkow, Head of Research and Development
at the Technische Universität München

"With its ever-engrossing narrative and fascinating descriptions of the virtually boundless possibilities of scientific investigation and experimentation, this book is essential reading for anyone interested in the history of alcohol or in the trajectory of present-day craft brewing."

—Max Nelson, professor specializing in
beer history at the University of Windsor and author of
The Barbarian's Revenge: A History of Beer in Ancient Europe

"*Ancient Brews* delivers up everything we have come to expect from Dr. Pat: extraordinary new research, an incredible depth of experience, compelling stories. Excellent."

—Ken Schramm, owner of Schramm's Mead and author of
The Compleat Meadmaker

ANCIENT BREWS

OTHER BOOKS BY PATRICK E. MCGOVERN

Uncorking the Past:
The Quest for Wine, Beer, and Other Alcoholic Beverages

Ancient Wine:
The Search for the Origins of Viniculture

ANCIENT BREWS

Rediscovered and Re-created

Patrick E. McGovern

FOREWORD BY Sam Calagione

W. W. NORTON & COMPANY

INDEPENDENT PUBLISHERS SINCE 1923

NEW YORK · LONDON

This volume is intended as a general information resource for readers interested in the history and re-creation of ancient beverages, along with meals that might have accompanied them. Neither the publisher nor the author can guarantee that every reader will be able to re-create any particular beverage or meal from the instructions given or that every reader will be able to drink any re-created beverage without any adverse effects. As of press time, the URLs displayed in this book link or refer to existing websites. The publisher is not responsible for, and should not be deemed to endorse or recommend, any website other than its own or any content available on the internet (including, without limitation, any website, blog page, or information page) that is not created by W. W. Norton. The author, similarly, is not responsible for third-party material.

For *Homo imbibens,* today and in the past

"There's the story, then there's the real story, then there's the story of how the story came to be told. Then there's what you leave out of the story. Which is part of the story too."

—MARGARET ATWOOD, *MaddAddam*

CONTENTS

List of Illustrations   xiii

Foreword by Sam Calagione   xv

Preface   xxi

CHAPTER 1

The Holy Grail of Extreme Fermented Beverages   1

CHAPTER 2

Midas Touch: An Elixir Fit for a Middle Eastern King   25

    RECIPES

    Homebrew Interpretation   50

    Meal Pairing   52

CHAPTER 3

Chateau Jiahu: A Neolithic Brew to

  Settle Down with in China   55

    RECIPES

    Homebrew Interpretation   78

    Meal Pairing   80

CHAPTER 4

Ta Henket: An Herbal Bomb for

  Our Gregarious African Ancestors   85

    RECIPES

    Homebrew Interpretation   110

    Meal Pairing   114

CHAPTER 5

Etrusca: A European "Grog" before Wine Surges In   119
    RECIPES
    Homebrew Interpretation   140
    Meal Pairing   143

CHAPTER 6

Kvasir: Nordic Heat for Frigid Nights   145
    RECIPES
    Homebrew Interpretation   172
    Meal Pairing   175

CHAPTER 7

Theobroma: A Sweet Concoction to Stir Romance   177
    RECIPES
    Homebrew Interpretation   201
    Meal Pairing   204

CHAPTER 8

Chicha: Chewing Our Way to Corn Beer   207
    RECIPES
    Homebrew Interpretation   230
    Meal Pairing   234

CHAPTER 9

What Next? A Cocktail from the New World, Anyone?   237
    RECIPES
    Homebrew Interpretation   252
    Meal Pairing   256

Acknowledgments   259
Select Bibliography   261
Index   273

For mood-enhancing atmospherics and more meal suggestions, go to: http://www.penn.museum/mcgovern/ancientbrews/.

LIST OF ILLUSTRATIONS

ix   Sam Calagione (right) and "Dr. Pat" adding salivated Peruvian red corn to the kettle at the Rehoboth Beach brewpub, on their way to re-creating *Chicha*. (Photo courtesy of Dogfish Head Craft Brewery.)

xxxi   Sam Calagione and "Dr. Pat" traveling "Back to the Future." (Cartoon courtesy of Tony Kentuck, Brookvale NSW, Australia.)

1   Our Stone Age ancestors gathered around the "watering hole." (Cartoon courtesy of Tony Kentuck, Brookvale NSW, Australia.)

25   Original bottle label for *Midas Touch*. (Photo courtesy of Dogfish Head Craft Brewery.)

55   Bottle label for *Chateau Jiahu*. (Photo courtesy of Dogfish Head Craft Brewery.)

85   Bottle label for *Ta Henket*. (Photo courtesy of Dogfish Head Craft Brewery.)

119   Bottle label for *Etrusca*. (Photo courtesy of Dogfish Head Craft Brewery.)

145   Bottle label for *Kvasir*. (Photo courtesy of Dogfish Head Craft Brewery.)

177   Bottle label for *Theobroma*. (Photo courtesy of Dogfish Head Craft Brewery.)

207   Sam, Clark Erickson, and "Dr. Pat" salivating red Peruvian corn, in advance of re-creating *Chicha*. (Photo courtesy of Ryan Collerd.)

237   An ancient Aztec *pulque* "party." (After Codex Magliabechiano.)

FOREWORD

Sam Calagione

I met Dr. Pat McGovern at a beer festival in 1999, on his home turf of the University of Pennsylvania's museum. We were introduced to each other over pints of beer by the British writer Michael Jackson—the patriarch of the modern beer journalism world. When we first started working together on *Midas Touch*, he came to our brew pub early in the morning to make the first starter batch. We had our coffee, we chatted, and we started questioning where the honey should come from for the batch. Should it come from Turkey or Italy? And then, without asking, Dr. Pat walked behind the bar and at 9:00 in the morning he filled up his coffee cup with our Chicory Stout. At that moment, listening to him passionately talk about which honey they would've used historically and arguing back about which honey would contribute the most nuanced and delectable aromas to the beer, I realized, "this is going to be a fun journey with this guy. He knows his shit but he's also not afraid to have a breakfast beer." And we have been great friends ever since. I think the reason that we hit it off so well is that our perspectives and personalities are more complimentary than they are overlapping. Dr. Pat sums up this reality very well when he says that his focus is on the past and mine is on the present.

Even though our daily work at Dogfish Head is on the present, and indeed the future, of craft brewing, looking to the past with Dr. Pat has proven personally and professionally rewarding to me. I think my invaluable and inventive colleagues at Dogfish Head, like Mark Safarik, Leader of the Dogfish Head Brewing Team, and Chef Kevin

Downing, as well as Doug Griffith of Extreme Brewing, all of whom have had the chance to work with Dr. Pat, would say the same thing. And I believe any homebrewer, commercial brewer, or beer lover can find as much or more opportunity for creative inspiration by looking backwards to how our ancestors approached producing and consuming fermented beverages as by relying on their own forward-looking creativity.

I began homebrewing one month after graduating from college, and months after producing my first batch I began writing a business plan to open my own brewery. As a 24-year-old kid, I knew I'd be starting my brewery very small. And as an English major, my experience was limited to bartending and waiting tables, so I knew I needed a unique and well-differentiated business model to stand out against the more established first-generation craft brewers—then called microbrewers—that had popped up across America throughout the 80s. This was the early 90s, the dawn of the Internet era, but I did my research the old-fashioned way at the New York City Public Library. I researched the beginning phases of the American locavore food movements, studying everyone from Alice Waters at Chez Panisse to James Beard, the great East Coast local food evangelist.

In researching the contemporary locavore movements in America, I also stumbled upon the concept of the *Reinheitsgebot*, a German beer purity law—which, ironically, is celebrating its 500th anniversary as I write this—that declared only water, barley, and hops could be used in the production of beer (later, when the role of yeast was better understood, the rules were revised to include it). When I read that, I decided that it would be my call to arms and Dogfish Head's great source of differentiation: we would be the first brewery committed to brewing the majority of its beer outside of the *Reinheitsgebot* conventions, using culinary ingredients from around the world. In 1995, our initial beers were a *Chicory Stout* and *Raison D'Etre*, made with raisins and beet sugars. Then we branched out with some beers I like to think of as "historical," such as an Ethiopian *Tej*, made with honey and tree leaves, and a medieval British *Braggot*, made by fermenting honey and barley together. Originally, people thought that Dogfish Head was being disrespectful to brewing traditions by making beers with culinary ingredients instead of just yeast, hops, and barley. Which is why it was so fortuitous that I got to meet Dr. Pat. As it turns out—and as you'll read in this book—the idea behind that 500-year-old law is actually a comparatively modern limitation.

Once Dr. Pat and I began doing work together, brewing these, as we call them, "liquid time capsules" and bringing these traditions back to life; I could finally hold my head up high. History and science were on my side to prove that the *Reinheitsgebot* is nothing more than a relatively recent attempt at censorship. Through my work with Dr. Pat, I've learned that so many different civilizations, in so many different parts of this world, have long made beers limited only by their creativity and the range of natural ingredients that grew in the lands that they called home. By using science and the physical remains of these ancient brews when creating our recipes, Dr. Pat brought a much higher level of authenticity to a process that I had already begun by making my own historic beers or making beers with culinary ingredients that had no historic touch to them and just came from my imagination.

That's not to say that re-creating the ancient recipes didn't involve an element of creativity. Dr. Pat's research gave us laundry lists of ingredients, but it was on us to evolve that into a modern interpretation of an ancient recipe. As a contemporary brewer, I had to balance being faithful to Dr. Pat's findings with being faithful to the expectations of modern beer drinkers. In most of the homebrew recipes in this book there is at least one liberty that we intentionally took for the sake of the modern beer drinker—for nearly everything we suggested using a single, pure strain of yeast and boiling the beer to create a sterile environment. It's highly probable that every recipe in this book, when enjoyed in the era it was first produced, would've been fermented by bacteria and wild yeast. They almost certainly all tasted most similar to modern Belgian lambics, which are intentionally sour and acidic because they're brewed with wild yeast and bacteria to this day. Beyond taking that one liberty, we work really hard to be as authentic as possible.

Our times drinking the test batches together are as important and as informative as any other part of the process. Dr. Pat is not only a great scientist, but also a great beer drinker. He has developed a very acute palate and he's very involved with me and my Dogfish Head coworkers in developing the reimagined recipes. As you might expect, our styles of work are inherently different. As an entrepreneur, I get an endorphin rush from facing risks and taking chances. I like to just throw stuff at the wall to see what sticks, what works best in combination. Dr. Pat, on the other hand, uses the scientific method. His inclination is to change one variable at a time, and to study the minutiae of the data that comes out of his research. Fortunately for us, these two very different approaches work beautifully together when implemented in a collaborative spirit. We didn't always agree with each other when working on these recipes, but we would always hear each other out. As an entrepreneur, when I can spend time with someone whose knowledge pool is so deep and somewhat separate from my own knowledge pool, that's incredibly valuable. I think my favorite thing about this book is that it brings our pools of knowledge together into one vessel, which then has something to offer historians, scientists, and home-brewing fanatics alike. And our process of listening to each other and reflecting on each of our areas of expertise before making a decision makes the integrity of the recipes that much richer. The homebrewers reading this book—or the readers who go out and buy Dogfish Head's *Midas Touch* at a liquor store—should know that hundreds of emails and multiple debates over innumerable pints of beers went into each of these recipes. Our different perspectives, woven together, make the recipes way stronger from both a historical and a contemporary perspective.

Until I started working with Dr. Pat, I would never have guessed that human saliva contains enzymes that convert starch to sugar, and that many different indigenous beers produced in different regions of the world were made by humans chewing the starchy grains and vegetation in order to begin the process of the starch-sugar conversion. So that first time ever that we made such a beer, we spent a whole afternoon sitting around on buckets in a brewhouse, chewing corn and spitting it out with the saliva, I remember having a moment, sitting there, thinking, "this is so awesome"—in the truest sense of the word—"and so unorthodox. We're sitting here making a beer not only from corn but from our saliva." Saliva as an ingredient in the production of beer—this is nothing new or crazy—it's just history coming back to life.

The existential moment for me was being with Dr. Pat in the tomb of Ti in Egypt, an archeological dig site that had, on its wall, the oldest known artistic representation of the brewing process (see Chapter 4). Beer making is how I make my livelihood. Being confronted with that, having my raison d'être inscribed on a wall, was pretty profound. The fact that that wall and that image and the art of brewing are still around today—and that I can connect myself to the oldest brewers—shows the power and the durability of storytelling. Whether you're a scientist trying to articulate your discoveries in a published article or an entrepreneur trying to establish a brand-new product in a crowded marketplace, the success of your endeavor really hinges on how well you can articulate yourself as a storyteller. I think homebrewers coming to this book will first have their minds blown about how integral alcohol is to our human experience, from the gaseous clouds of alcohol that existed in the galaxy before animals were on this planet, to the alcohol we create and consume today. Dr. Pat's great storytelling traces the through line between those two points, and I hope that, if you're reading this as a homebrewer, you continue on that path as a fellow storyteller. My dream is that you become an evangelist to spread the word that beer deserves to be defined as something much broader, much more exciting, and much richer than what many of the world's biggest breweries want consumers to believe.

At the moment there is tremendous pressure to homogenize and commodify the global drinking experience. And so it's up to the homebrewers who recreate the recipes in this book to continue in perpetuity the same line that includes those ancient Egyptian brewers on the cave wall all the way up to Dr. Pat and me. Now, I recommend that the homebrewers hone their skills first by trying to perfectly reproduce the recipes that are included in the book. Start there, but on future batches homebrewers should feel free to follow their own creative impulses. In addition to serving as a rulebook for re-creating the individual recipes as authentically as possible, this book can also be used as sort of a brewer's Rubik's cube. Why not pull the culinary ingredients from the food pairing recipes contained within the book and add them to the beer recipes? Or why not take an ingredient from the Americas and introduce it to a Scandinavian brew? We as home-brewers now have access to the best ingredients from around the world at our fingertips. We have the opportunity to go *really* ancient and symbolically reunite Pangea in one homebrewed recipe by combining several of them. Don't be afraid to use the different ingredients refer-enced in this book to make your own new beverages and new dishes. Try every ingredient.

I'm happy to say that I'm as excited to be a creative craft brewer today as I was when I first wrote that business plan over 22 years ago. There has never been a more exciting moment in history to be a beer maker—whether a homebrewer or a professional—or to be a beer drinker! The diversity of beer styles and beer traditions throughout the world is at an all-time high. It's heartwarming to see that this work we've done together fires people up to actually do their own inter-pretations of ancient beverages. Even though it also means that other commercial breweries are now doing their interpretations of differ-ent ancient or historic beverages, making it more of a crowded field, it really only serves to underline Dr. Pat's leadership in pioneering the revival of ancient fermented beverages.

At the same moment, the world's biggest breweries are working hard to recapture the consumers that they've lost to the smaller, most creative breweries. So, on behalf of creative commercial breweries throughout the globe, I urge the readers of this book to take their own versions of the recipes included here and share them over meals and great conversations with your friends and families. And, in this way, collectively retain the ancient traditions that Dr. Pat has bravely devoted his career to keeping alive. My hope is that this book, by bring-ing together such an amazing breadth of information—the worlds of science, history, archeology, sociology—in a package that is fun to read and accessible, can galvanize brewers to carry Dr. Pat's and my torch of brewing creatively in a way that honors the ancient past.

PREFACE

S am Calagione, founder of Dogfish Head Craft Brewery, and I are often asked how we met, got the idea to re-create ancient fermented beverages based on scientific evidence, and began making them for the *Ancient Ales and Spirits* series at Dogfish Head Craft Brewery. I provide some of the answers to these questions in this book.

Our story is still very much a work in progress. Just like an archaeological excavation, I have sorted through and analyzed the tattered remains of our species' brewing past, which are an infinitesimal fraction of what our ancestors made and drank. I have scoured the literature on alcoholic beverages, past and present. Together, Sam and I have devised and tested reasonable hypotheses of what went into an ancient drink and how it was made. We have not always agreed, but then that's to be expected. Human beings see the world through the prism of their own experiences, perceptions, and emotions.

We may agree on the broad outlines of our story, but we continue to add more and sometimes quite different details. To give you one example, in the second chapter on *Midas Touch*, which launched us on our adventures, I recount a tear-gassing incident in a restaurant in Ankara, Turkey. In the heat and confusion of the moment, one of our filming team left a satchel full of cash on a chair. Of course, it was gone after we filed back into the restaurant. Later, when we shared stories, I had only a vague recollection of the missing pouch. Sam remembered the incident in minute detail, perhaps because of his astute business acumen.

My focus is the past, Sam's is the present. Together, we make great re-created beverages together.

DISCOVERING ANCIENT FERMENTED
BEVERAGES IN THE FIELD

THE READER MIGHT think that reconstructing an ancient fermented beverage is straightforward. You just need to scrape out the residues inside what you believe to be an ancient beverage container, one that might have been used to make, store, serve or drink a beer, wine, mead, or extreme beverage (more about that in Chapter 1). You lay your hands on the highest-power analytical tools you can and then test the residues. Voilà, you have the answers for making a re-created fermented beverage!

I wish it were that simple. That point was driven home to me as I pioneered the field of organic residue analysis in archaeology, beginning in the 1980s. Despite many false starts and failed experiments, the past 30 years have been full of discoveries, including the earliest chemically attested grape wine, barley beer, chocolate "wine" (*Theobroma*: Chapter 7), and extreme fermented beverage (*Chateau Jiahu*: Chapter 3) from China. I started with grape wine and barley beer, whose stories are recounted in my other books, *Ancient Wine* and *Uncorking the Past*. I ended up with extreme fermented beverages, which can combine all and sundry from your environment—high-sugar fruits, honey, roots and cereals, herbs and tree resins—into a palatable and very powerful drink. They are the most challenging to my mind.

I am a combination archaeologist and chemist, which is sometimes called a biomolecular archaeologist or an archaeological chemist. The process of discovering and re-creating an ancient fermented beverage starts with archaeology. If you don't have the best samples you can get—the best dated, the most well-preserved, and the least contaminated—then you're wasting everyone's time and money.

Well-excavated archaeological sites are the be-all and end-all. Forget about any vessels bought on the antiquities market, which could well be fakes or lack verifiable provenances. What you need are organic samples in association with other well-dated finds. You might be fortunate enough to uncover a silo of grain, a workshop for making a fermented beverage, a temple, tomb or house where the beverage was enjoyed by everyday people, or perhaps a shrine or temple where it was served up to the gods.

It's icing on the cake if your samples have *not* been exposed to water and oxygen, which will degrade and destroy them. Your best option is an undisturbed tomb or habitation in the desert. Intact shipwrecks, which have sunk hundreds (ideally, thousands) of feet to oxygen-free levels beneath the surface, can also be good. Likewise, bogs and glaciers can be kind to organic remains but generally yield only the isolated body or object from an uncertain time and circumstance. For example, the Ice Man named Ötzi, found in the Italian Alps, is fascinating and very well-preserved, but without a larger archaeological context, it is anyone's guess whether he was traveling north or south and whether or not he was murdered or lost his way in a storm. Moreover, any canteen of fermented beverage, which he might well have been carrying to see him on his way, is yet to be recovered from the ice. Such a vessel might lay thousands of feet away from the body in a deep crevasse.

I am in the enviable position of being based at the University of Pennsylvania Museum, one of the best archaeological museums in the United States. Its collections of well-excavated finds span the world. I have my pick of the best samples. Many of the collections are dominated by putative fermented beverage vessels, such as the numerous Greek vases adorned with Dionysiac scenes and the standardized jars for drinking corn *chicha* (Chapter 8) in Peru from antiquity up to the present.

Despite the excellent proveniences of many of these artifacts, you must still proceed cautiously. I once noticed some early wine jars in the museum's Egyptian storeroom. They dated to the Early Dynastic period, about 3100 to 2700 B.C., when the royal winemaking industry began in the Nile River Delta (Chapter 4). They appeared very promising. One look inside convinced me otherwise: their interior bottoms were littered with cigarette butts. They had been convenient ashtrays for interns registering articles during the WPA (Works Progress Administration) days of the Depression.

I am also frequently invited into the field as a consultant on organic residue analysis. It is the ideal arrangement because I can watch the artifacts come out of the ground, assess contamination by ground-water, and examine other remains associated with a specific artifact (a humanly contrived object) or ecofact (a natural object, especially plant material, when dealing with ancient fermented beverages). I can monitor how well the excavation is being carried out, and whether the artifacts and ecofacts are being properly handled. The best samples come from *in situ* (Latin, literally "in place") contexts such as intact tombs or habitation floors, which have been sealed beneath destruction levels. Ideally, any burning was minimal, since that destroys organic materials.

Artifacts or ecofacts of interest should *not* be overly washed in water or conserved with any chemical that might interfere with analysis. Soil samples are collected at the same time to assess the background environmental chemistry, which can be heavily influenced by microorganisms churning out the same compounds for which we are searching. All the samples are wrapped in aluminum foil and packaged in polyethylene plastic bags for the trip back to the States. The plastic should be very high quality and free of plasticizers (such as the omnipresent phthalates) and other contaminants, which can interfere with the detection of ancient organic compounds.

Archaeologists can be their own worst enemies in overprocessing what they have discovered before there's a chance to ferret out the invisible chemical compounds. Fortunately, word has gotten out that organics comprise much of what we are as humans—from the clothes we wear and the houses in which we live to the food and drink that we consume. Indeed, our very bodies belong to the organic world.

Even after selecting the best samples, you still need to obtain the requisite permissions from the local departments of antiquities to export the samples, which is often a major hurdle. You can imagine the reluctance of officials to hand over a gold or silver drinking-horn. It helps to be an archaeologist. The growing interest in ancient fermented beverages, which have often played major cultural roles in nearly every country's heritage, has often been another point in my favor.

As my area of research has become better known, I have also had many archaeologists arrive on the doorstep of our laboratory, samples in hand. Drawing on their knowledge of parts of the world with which I was less familiar, I could decide whether to move forward on an analysis.

IN THE LAB

THE SECOND HALF of my job title involves doing the chemistry that will shed light on the contents of the vessels. Working in a relatively poorly funded laboratory of a private museum, our staff has been limited to using the most basic analytical instruments. Fourier-transform infrared spectrometry (FT-IR) has been the mainstay of our operation from the beginning, and it has the advantage of providing an initial assessment of how rich in organics a sample from an artifact or ecofact is. The technique can sometimes precisely identify the chemical "fingerprint" compound of interest or biomarker.

By far, my greatest asset over the years has been the dedicated and enthusiastic cadre of Ph.D. analytical chemists from industry, all volunteers, who decided to take up a second career in archaeological chemistry. Equally intelligent and committed students, both undergraduate and graduate, have worked alongside us. You can image how passionate they can be when it comes to archaeology and fermented beverages! Many have gone on to make their own mark in the field.

Our wet chemical bench is where we start with any sample. Even if we have what appear to be uncontaminated physical residues, we have learned that an extraction with organic solvents will usually help to release the compounds from their matrices and to make them more concentrated. Many of our "residues" are invisible to the naked eye as well, having been absorbed into the pores of pottery wares, whose ionic or polar properties retain and preserve some organics for thousands of years. Boiling in methanol and chloroform, which are relatively more and less polar with respect to the absorbed compounds, enables recovery of the suite of preserved organics.

Based on the FT-IR results of the extracted residues, we then move forward with increasingly more precise chemical analyses, including gas chromatography-mass spectrometry (GC-MS), liquid chromatography tandem mass spectrometry (LC-MS-MS), and headspace solid-phase microextraction (SPME) coupled to GC-MS. For the chemically challenged, these techniques separate the various compounds of an unknown sample by their boiling points. As the compounds come off the chromatographic column at different times, they are fed into a mass spectrometer and successively fragmented to measure the masses of the parent and daughter ions. From these data, we are able to determine which compounds are present in our sample.

Over the years, our laboratory has built up a network of collaborators, who are so highly motivated by the prospect of reconstructing ancient fermented beverages that they donate their state-of-the-art instruments and all-important expertise in running them and interpreting the data. Among the many governmental, industrial, university, and private institutions that have filled in the analytical gaps in our museum laboratory, we have most recently worked with NASA's Goddard Space Flight Center, the Scientific Services Division of the Alcohol and Tobacco Tax and Trade Bureau (TTB), the Scientific Research and Analysis Laboratory of Winterthur Museum, and the Monell Chemical Senses Center.

EXPANDING OUR PERSPECTIVE

FT-IR AND GC-MS analyses of our samples are about as close as we get to a "shotgun" approach to identifying as many compounds as possible in a sample. Usually, we already have working hypotheses for what the vessels might have originally contained, which are based on auxiliary scientific data. I have already mentioned the importance of the archaeological context of the artifact or ecofact, which often provides clues as to what kinds of fermented beverages were available.

Since fermented beverages are essentially processed plant materials, archaeobotanical findings can provide valuable clues for what we might expect to discover chemically. Sieving soil samples using a range of mesh sizes helps in the recovery of tiny seeds and larger plant parts. Wet flotation methods, using different density liquids, enable other botanical remains to float to the surface of the liquid so they can be collected and analyzed. Pollen can be identified microscopically, as can phytoliths (characteristic silica particles in plant tissues) and starch remnants. The latter have much to tell, especially if they are embedded in a grinding stone, incorporated into dental calculus (tartar), or mixed into the residue itself.

In this interdisciplinary endeavor, you also need to be something of an art and textual critic. Ancient artwork and inscriptions can bring the mute scientific data to life, as it were, by illustrating and describing how the fermented beverages were made and drunk. Yet we cannot assume that they represent reality; they might be selective or even wrong. They are human creations likely made after the fact—unlike our samples that are contemporaneous with the drink.

Ancient Egypt stands out as the premier instance of how illuminating iconographical and textual evidence can be. As early as 3000 B.C., thousands of years before anything comparable appeared in other parts of the ancient world, Egypt's tombs, temples, and palaces show wine and beer being made—step by step—and enjoyed by men and women alike. If you have any doubts about what is depicted, accompanying inscriptions provide commentary. The problem is that once a motif had established itself in the Egyptian artistic repertoire, it was repeated through the ages. What might have started out as an eyewitness rendition thus became a hackneyed idiom of the past, perhaps with little relevance to the present. For Egyptians, though, such stock images assured them a safe passage across the Nile into eternity.

Anthropological accounts of premodern and modern peoples making and enjoying their fermented beverages add another dimension. Native drinks are usually central to their societies and, as such, are highly conserved through time. Although we might be stymied by an unusual archaeological feature or scientific result, the puzzle is often solved by an ethnographic or ethnohistorical study.

Bringing all the various clues from the different disciplines together, archaeological chemists must make educated guesses as to what plants and processing methods were involved in making an ancient fermented beverage. They must search through the available chemical literature for a given region to decide what distinctive biomarkers of specific natural products to look for. Modern search engines can speed up the process, although pertinent articles may be in other languages. For example, we turned to native Chinese and Japanese students and museum staff to help us to "decipher" chemical reports in these languages when we reconstructed *Chateau Jiahu* (Chapter 3).

Once we have a grocery list of compounds, we work out the best extraction methods. We decide on the technique or combination of techniques that is most sensitive for detecting the given compound. Finally, we interpret the data, not just chemically (which can be challenging), but also in terms of how the results affect our working hypotheses. We may need to analyze additional samples or process them differently. As new, more sensitive techniques become available, we can retest previous samples.

Obviously, such research does not occur overnight but goes in fits and starts, perhaps for many years, before meaningful results emerge. Those who want to learn more should consult "Charting a Future Course for Organic Residue Analysis in Archaeology" (McGovern and Hall 2015) for further information on the theoretical, scientific, and practical underpinnings of biomolecular archaeology. In this article, my colleague, Gretchen Hall, and I review the analytical methods for detecting ancient milk and cheese, beeswax, honey, and mead, with particular reference to grape wine carried aboard the oldest shipwreck in the Mediterranean at Uluburun, Turkey (Chapter 5).

As we move through the various ancient fermented beverages in the chapters to follow, you will begin to understand how the myriad strands of more or less well-substantiated archaeological, archaeobotanical, chemical, and other scientific data contribute to a reconstruction of an ancient fermented beverage.

MAKING AN AUTHENTIC
ANCIENT FERMENTED BEVERAGE

LACKING AN ANCIENT recipe book, the "leap" from the scientific reconstruction of an ancient fermented beverage to making a "recreation" is huge. We may know the essential ingredients, but what percentage of each was used? How were they processed, and do we need to replicate ancient tools and vessels to capture the original aromas, flavors, and other characteristics? Since all the alcohol has evaporated and disappeared from the ancient residues, how do we know what the alcohol content was? What yeasts and associated bacteria should we use to carry out the fermentation? If we have a complex mixture of ingredients, do we ferment them all together, or do we carry out separate fermentations and mix them together at the end of the process? When do we add in the bittering and herbal ingredients—near the beginning to fully integrate them into the drink or near the end so as to preserve more of their unique characteristics? Do we expose our ferment to the sun, keep it in the shade, or heat it up, assuming that the ancient people had fire? The questions and possibilities are nearly endless, and we can only address a limited number of them in each experimental brew. Still, slowly but surely, we gain insights into how the ancient beverage was made and tasted.

This is experimental archaeology at its best: various clues are assembled and different scenarios of the original ingredients and ancient processes are tested in the present for their practicality and, perhaps most importantly, their palatability. It proceeds on the assumption that humans worldwide, probably going back millions of years to Palaeolithic times, had a genetic, physiological, and psychological makeup similar to ours. In short, like us, our ancestors knew what smelled and tasted good and what gave them a buzz, cultural preferences aside. No doubt, they also had an appreciation for pairing special foods with fermented beverages.

The natural process of fermentation itself, described in Chapter 1, guarantees that we will be on approximately the right track from the start of our re-creation if we just let nature take its course. We begin by assembling the most likely ingredients, according to the evidence we have. We will squash the fruit, dilute the honey, chew the wild grains and tubers, gather up the herbs, and collect the tree saps we think most plausible. But once we expose these products to the environment, native yeasts and bacteria take over, and the end result, today as in the past, should be a transformed liquid with a plethora of aromatic compounds that combines sweetness, sourness, and alcoholic bite, perhaps a backbone of bitterness, and some carbonation. Before airtight containers became common, however, people had to drink their beverages quickly before the carbon dioxide was lost.

Homebrewers who aspire to make an interpretation of an ancient brew needn't be overly concerned about whether their brew kettle and carboys are made of stainless steel, glass, or plastic. Even if these materials were improvised by humans at relatively late dates in our history, they will realistically carry out the same fermentation process that made ancient fermented beverages possible.

You still may want to try out containers made of pottery, wood, gourd, leather, or a more exotic material in keeping with ancient times. I can attest to the meaty funkiness of a wine, fermented from native American grapes in goat skins, which I consulted on with a North Carolinian farmer. This experiment was tailored to what an early Old World wine might have tasted like, since Native Americans did not have goats until the Europeans arrived. And, as far as we know, they never produced wine despite the profusion of grape species in the Americas.

Because we usually don't know the starting amounts of each ingredient and biomarkers may degrade or be lost to groundwater percolation, we cannot calculate exact amounts or percentages of ingredients. We usually assume that the main ingredients were originally present in about equal proportions. Thus, for an extreme beverage made by combining a cereal, fruit, and honey, the contribution will be about a third each. The finished product will then be a third beer (with 4–5% alcohol produced under average fermentation conditions), a third wine (yielding about 10–12% alcohol), and a third honey mead (again, about 10–12% alcohol). Averaged out, the re-created beverage will be about 9% alcohol.

We can experiment with varying amounts of other detected ingredients, such as herbs. We may not know the absolute amounts, but we will at least have gained an appreciation for the contribution of each additive to the final drink.

As you move from one ancient re-creation to the next—starting in Africa where our species emerged and then following our ancestors around the world—you will begin to appreciate the rich tapestry of ancient fermented beverages made from ingredients and microorganisms as varied as the environments from which they come. You will see how different scientific techniques are applied to extract as much information as possible from artifacts and ecofacts and how the many variables are assessed in "re-creating" an ancient fermented beverage.

So, hop aboard our time machine, as Sam and I travel "back to the future" to discover, re-create, taste, and enjoy some liquid time capsules. Feel free to lie back in your comfortable armchair, preferably with an *Ancient Ale* or *Ancient Spirit* in hand. You will travel to remote parts of the Earth, uncover the drinking vessels of our ancestors, analyze their residues for clues to what they contained, and discover how enterprising and innovative our ancestors were in converting plants and herbs into delicious, mind-altering drinks. Our stories are as serendipitous and exciting as the alcoholic beverages we rediscovered and re-created.

ANCIENT BREWS

I

The Holy Grail of
Extreme Fermented Beverages

Our alcoholic beverage story on Earth begins in deep space, billions of years ago, with an astounding molecule: alcohol or ethanol. This simple compound of two carbon atoms, six hydrogens, and an oxygen is part and parcel of our universe as far out in space as we can see.

If you have a powerful enough telescope, you might catch sight of a gas cloud named Sagittarius B2N near the center of our galaxy, the Milky Way, in a warmer star-forming region. It's about 26,000 light-years or 240 quadrillion kilometers (150 quadrillion miles) away from Earth. This cloud contains literally billions upon billions of liters of alcohol—methanol, ethanol, and highly reactive vinyl alcohols.

Sagittarius B2N is but one of many gigantic, star-forming clouds at the center of the Milky Way and, as astrophysicist Carl Sagan was fond of saying, our galaxy is just one among 100 billion galaxies, each with 100 billion stars. We are obviously talking about a lot of alcohol. The bartenders among us will also be happy to know that, besides alcohol, these clouds contain ethyl formate, which gives raspberries their flavor and smells like rum. Talk about a cocktail, just waiting to be mined in deep space!

Alcohol is not confined to these gas clouds. In January 2015, spectroscopic measurements of Comet C/2014, otherwise known as Lovejoy, had it living up to its name. This "messenger" body between the stars was spewing out ethanol on its closest approach to our Sun. Nicolas Biver (2015), the lead author of the scientific report, rhapsodized: "We found that comet Lovejoy was releasing as much alcohol as in at least 500 bottles of wine every second during its peak activity." Talk about an open bar!

Is it possible that some of these alcohol molecules hitchhiked a ride on a comet and helped jump-start life on Earth, as the theory of Panspermia has it? A few months before we learned of Lovejoy, astrophysicists of the European Space Agency's Rosetta Project successfully landed a robotic spacecraft on the comet 67P/Churyumov-Gerasimenko. It was like picking a needle out of a haystack. The comet was only 4 kilometers (2.5 miles) wide, and the probe had to travel 10 years and about 450 million kilometers (280 million miles) to rendezvous with it.

Unfortunately, the spacecraft's solar batteries went dead soon after its robotic probe landed, but not before its instrumentation detected other essential building blocks for life on Earth: water, carbon dioxide, and a whole range of more complex "prebiotic" molecules. A GC-MS instrument, such as we employ in our ancient fermented beverage research, was part of the equipment arsenal on board the probe. Even more complex carbon molecules essential to life—such as vitamin B3 (nicotinic acid)—have now been reported from meteors within our solar system.

However tantalizing the chemical evidence from comets and meteors for the beginning of life on this planet, possibly including a role for alcohol, it is a far cry from proving the Panspermia theory. We're talking about an event that is supposed to have taken place about 4.5 billion years ago. Reconstructing an ancient fermented beverage from a mere 18,000 years ago, as we attempt to for prehistoric Africa (Chapter 4), is difficult enough as it is. Yet lack of evidence has never kept us humans from fabricating stories to explain our origins and purpose on Earth, as we will see in the following chapters when the myths and ceremonies, which swirl around and nourish the rise and use of ancient fermented beverages, are described.

COMING DOWN TO EARTH

IN STEP WITH our species' exploration of outer space, we have begun to reveal the secrets of the inner submicroscopic world of the living cell. Only within the past two decades, the entire genetic blueprints of hundreds of protists (single-celled organisms), fungi, plants, and animals have been mapped out. Some of these organisms are essential to our ancient fermented beverage story.

In 1996, the first organism to have its complete DNA sequence deciphered for its 32 nuclear chromosomes was the key player in fermentation: *Saccharomyces cerevisiae*, otherwise known as the wine, beer, or bread (baker's) yeast. Eleven years later, the genome of the first fruit—the Eurasian grape (*Vitis vinifera*)—was fully mapped. The researchers said they picked it because of our chemical attestation of the earliest grape wine in the world from Hajji Firuz in Iran, dated to about 5400–5000 B.C.

The complete DNA sequences of other players in our drama, including the honeybee (*Apis mellifera*) and fruit fly (*Drosophila melanogaster*), occurred within a year of the one for grape. Many other fruits (e.g., cacao, apple, almond, and date palm), which enter into our stories of ancient fermented beverages, have now been sequenced. For the beer-lovers among us, the same can be said for most of the world's major grains: barley, rice, wheat, millet, sorghum, and maize. We will see that these cereals were likely domesticated by our ancestors to produce more of the sudsy.

We have even turned the DNA probes back on ourselves, along with other ancient and modern primates. That is quite appropriate, since *Homo imbibens*—to use an apt phrase—has certainly earned the reputation as the consummate consumer of alcoholic beverages.

This new genetic information, together with a host of other scientific findings that illuminate Earth's geological and archaeological past, underlies our stories of ancient fermented beverages. As limited as these data may be due to the vagaries of time and degradation, they form the bases of plausible hypotheses of how such drinks came about. To start with, fermentation (glycolysis) is quite literally the basis of life on our planet. This biological process is believed to have powered the first cell. It still energizes every one of the trillions of cells in our bodies, as well as those of every living creature on the planet. Although life is vastly more complex today than at its beginning, the essential process has remained the same: sugar is taken in ("eaten") by the cell and processed into energy-rich compounds, with alcohol and carbon dioxide being produced as waste products. Thus, a kind of carbonated, alcoholic "beverage" was likely available from very early on. Its imbibers were yet to come.

Today, fermentation is associated with two species of single-celled yeasts in particular, *S. cerevisiae* and *S. bayanus*. They are members of a fungus family encompassing a large group of wild and domesticated strains like the wine and beer yeasts. Although just a single cell, a yeast shares nearly all the same biological organelles and chemical functions as the cells in our bodies and those of other multi-cellular organisms. These yeasts thrive in low-oxygen environments but not the oxygen-free atmosphere such as is thought to have existed on Earth when life began.

Yeasts consume sugars—whether the glucose of fruit, the fructose of honey, or the lactose of milk—and excrete ethanol and carbon dioxide as their end products. That's right, when we drink an alcoholic beverage, alcohol as a drug may be what we're after, but for the yeast, ethanol is only refuse to be disposed of, like it was for the hypothesized earliest living cells. In a more important sense, however, alcohol provides the means by which yeasts can survive in the extremely competitive world of microorganisms. Most microbes can tolerate alcohol levels up to 5%; above that amount, they die. By contrast, yeasts function in environments at much higher alcohol levels, usually up to a maximum of 12–15% but sometimes above 20%.

This difference in alcohol tolerance created a window of opportunity for the yeasts. If they could produce enough ethanol, they could kill off the competition. The earliest yeasts appear to have adapted to do just that. Their alcohol dehydrogenase (*Adh*) gene, which produces an enzyme of the same name (ADH), caused alcohol to accumulate in their environment. An even more effective and nuanced approach, however, came during the Cretaceous period of 145–65 million years ago when the genome of *S. cerevisiae* doubled, making it possible to selectively turn on and off the amount of ethanol it produced. Now, it had two versions of the *Adh* gene and enzyme. ADH1 could ramp up the alcohol to above 5% and wipe out other microbes. That accomplished, ADH2 could spring into action and convert excess alcohol back into acetaldehyde and ultimately generate more energy. The delayed gratification would have been worth the wait, now that the competing microbes had been destroyed.

THE DIE IS CAST

IT IS NOT YET known when alcohol, as an energy-producing compound like sugar, began to be consumed. But by the Cretaceous period, when dinosaurs roamed the Earth 125–65 million years ago, there is no question of alcohol's importance. This revolutionary era sets the stage for what was to follow, up through the present.

The first flowering fruit trees and shrubs appeared then, which our ancestors later exploited for making extreme fermented beverages. They provided sweet nectars, resins, and fruit that honeybees, appearing for the first time, converted into honey, the most concentrated source of sugar in nature. Fruit flies, which also have a love for sugar and even nourish their young with alcohol, appeared. Both insects have the same propensity for alcohol that many other animals have, including ourselves. They readily overindulge and get drunk. Fruit flies have been shown to have the same genes for inebriation as humans have—fancifully named *barfly, cheapdate, tipsy, amnesiac,* and *happyhour.*

Other animals share some of the same genes. Those of the zebra finch, for example, affect how its syrinx, analogous to the human larynx, and brain operate under the influence of alcohol. When these birds overindulge in fermented fruit, their songs become confused and more subdued. When we get drunk, we have a similar slurring of speech, which at times can be boisterous and then recede into inaudible mumblings.

In 2015, what has been described as an "addiction" gene (*Rsu1*), also present in humans, was discovered in fruit flies. It causes drunken behavior, presumably as a deterrent to excessive drinking. Flies with a malfunctioning gene showed excessive craving, because they were no longer getting the same "kick" from the same amount of alcohol.

Of course, such genes would be superfluous apart from alcohol, which yeasts and other microorganisms ferment from sugars into an alcoholic, aromatic concoction that attracts the animals that sense and happily consume it for energy and presumably enjoyment.

As new fruiting trees, new insects, new dinosaurs, and new yeasts emerged during the revolutionary Cretaceous period, they were bound together into an intricate web of ecological give-and-take. The breakup of the supercontinent of Pangaea added a new level of complexity to the mix of plants and animals during the millions of years to follow, as the seven continents gradually formed and drifted apart to take up their current arrangement. Populations of flora and fauna were separated from one another and developed along different trajectories.

Then, toward the end of the Cretaceous period, birds and placental mammals, grasses and cereals, and no doubt many new microorganisms, which are poorly represented in the fossil record, appeared for the first time. The yeasts and other microorganisms feasted on the new sugar sources and produced alcohol. A love of sugar and alcohol developed among most of the animals that benefited from the new fermented foods. In turn, the plants were fertilized by the insects, mammals, and, perhaps, the occasional flying dinosaur that also dispersed their seed. This symbiosis or mutualism—you might even call it a dance of plants, animals, and microorganisms—laid the foundations of what we see around us today.

BOTTOMS UP!

IT'S DEBATABLE WHETHER most animals are as attracted to alcohol as they are to sugar, but hardly any eschew both. Anecdotal evidence is abundant for animals not being able to hold their alcohol. One can point to the famous scene in Jamie Uys's film, *Animals Are Beautiful People* (1974), in which South African elephants knock down fermented marula fruit from their trees. Animals of all kinds—wild boars (warthogs), giraffes, impalas, ostriches, insects, and baboons—then join in the melee by grabbing up the fruit on the ground and gorging themselves on it. The animals certainly appear to be on benders as they careen back and forth, with the baboons engaging in some amorous behavior at the end. While some have claimed that Uys spiked the fruit with hard alcohol to get the animals plastered, there's no argument that these animals must have been drunk to get them to behave the way they did.

Most of us have our own list of favorite stories of drunken animals in which birds, in particular, play starring roles. There are the drunk robins and cedar waxwings that overindulge in ripe fruit and fall off their perches or sadly crash into car windows. Some make it into the news, like the story of the brown owl that was picked up on a roadside in 2011 by German police, completely oblivious of its surroundings. Two empty schnapps bottles lay beside the bird. The animal was clearly drunk, although the police didn't breathalyze it. It was taken to a local bird rehabilitation center and given lots of water. It finally sobered up and was released. If dinosaurs were as susceptible to the mind-altering effects of alcohol as their modern descendants, the birds, we can only imagine the consequences.

THE THIRSTY TREE SHREW

THESE STORIES HAVE begun to be bolstered by more systematic research. In a word, taking a nip has a long precedent among our family of placental mammals, the primates. Indeed, what might well be the earliest primate on the planet, the Malaysian pen-tailed tree shrew that traces its origins to the end of the Mesozoic period, some 55 million years ago, elegantly demonstrates an overweening penchant for alcohol. About the size of a flying squirrel with bulging eyes for nocturnal vision, this animal's principal diet—believe it or not—is palm wine.

The tree shrew exploits the flowers of bertam palm trees (*Eugeissona tristis*), which serve as fermenting vessels for the high-sugar nectar that accumulates in them year-round. In the warm tropical climate, the resident yeasts rapidly convert nectar to a frothy, strongly scented palm wine with an alcoholic content as high as 3.8%. Over the course of a night, the tree shrew laps up the equivalent of nine glasses of 12%

alcoholic grape wine, which is well above the legal blood-alcohol limit in our world.

Inexplicably, the tree shrew shows no signs of intoxication, as it makes its way deftly through the sharp spines of the tree from one oozing flower bud after another, pollinating them as it goes. We humans are not so well-endowed genetically, although we continue on in the tree shrew's tradition of enjoying palm wine wherever we find it. Other primates, including chimpanzees, also have a fondness for the beverage.

THE DRUNKEN MONKEY MAKES ITS APPEARANCE

MY COLLEAGUE ROBERT Dudley (2014) in his book, *The Drunken Monkey*, makes a strong and convincing case that howler monkeys really like alcohol. When the fruit of a palm tree (*Astrocaryum standley-anum*) ripens in the remote jungles of Panama, they can't get enough. They put away the equivalent of about two bottles of grape wine in 20 minutes.

Dudley hypothesizes that consuming alcohol is much more than a way to get drunk. The pungent aroma of alcohol plumes attracts the monkeys from afar to the fruit, which is nutritious in more ways than one. For example, when the monkeys drink, they become more sociable, as shown by their sharing food and working as a team. We can't get inside the minds of monkeys, but with their comparable genomes and physiologies to humans, they might be experiencing heightened emotions due to a "pleasure cascade" of neurotransmitters in their brains, which is well documented for our species.

The howler monkeys eventually curtailed their binges when the high-sugar fruits went out of season. According to Dudley, they have a relatively low intake of alcohol for most of the year, so they are not at risk for alcohol poisoning. (In fact, alcohol is as safe as sugar; it is the accumulation of acetaldehyde, a product of glycolysis, which kills liver and other cells.) Dudley argues that moderate consumption of a substance, which might be dangerous when taken to excess, can be good for you; besides alcohol, think of plant alkaloids, such as caffeine in coffee, theobromine in cacao, or capsaicin in chiles. These compounds help fend off disease-causing microorganisms, act as antioxidants against cancers and other diseases, and contribute to heightened awareness or, conversely, to sedation. Biologically speaking, this is the hormetic effect. Dudley argues that the swings between consuming excessive amounts of alcohol by early primates and hominids when a food source is available, against a backdrop of generally low-level intake during most of the year, helps to explain alcoholism in our species. Some humans today are not genetically equipped to handle a world with unlimited access to the drug all of the time.

Howler monkeys are not unique in the primate world. Most modern primates have diets comprised of 75 percent or more fruit, and are known to eat as much fermented fruit as possible when given the chance. For example, in 2015, researchers reported how wild chimpanzees in west African Guinea improvised a "tool" made from leaves to soak up palm wine from containers that humans set at the top of the trees to collect the high-sugar nectar. Precise records were kept of how many dips per minute were made, along with the alcohol content at different times of the day, which varied between about 3% during midday and up to 6% during the heat of the late afternoon. Whether male or female, individual chimpanzees consumed moderately throughout the day, drinking a total of about one bottle of wine. Assuming humans were kept at bay, they drank from morning to night. Only one male got drunk in 17 years, downing three times the daily amount of alcohol in just over 30 minutes. Since we share about 96 percent of our genome with chimpanzees, it's fair to ask: Would most of us be as moderate in our drinking as the vast majority of chimpanzees were in this experiment?

Other studies of African chimpanzees over the past several decades, especially in the Congo River basin, document the use of a range of tools (chisel-like tree branches, sharpened sticks, flexible vines, and heavy wooden clubs), sometimes used sequentially, to knock open beehives or swish out the honey in a more refined fashion. The honeycombs are usually quickly licked clean, but if a passing rainstorm comes before the chimps have had time to sate their appetites, some honey might be left in the hive. If it fills with water, resident yeasts take over and ferment the honey to mead. Any returning chimps might well be surprised by the result when they take a sip. The returning honeybees, too, might imbibe more than their usual amount of alcohol, gleaned mainly from ripe fruit, with unpredictable outcomes. Research has shown that their motor abilities can be impaired by alcohol so that they cannot do their waggle dances as well to communicate the location of nectar to their fellow workers.

EARLY HOMINIDS JOIN IN

OUR AFRICAN ANCESTORS shared a set of physiological proclivities—imperatives, you might say—that likely made them avid fermented-beverage drinkers. Available evidence from the Palaeolithic period is slim. Our ancestors' soft tissues have disappeared. But inferences about what our forebears were eating and drinking can be made from their fossil skeletons, especially their teeth.

Primate and hominid dentitions are marked by relatively small molars and canines, starting as early as the primate Proconsul, 24 million years ago, and continuing on until we reach that most famous of female hominids, Lucy. She was a short-statured *Australopithecus afarensis* from about 3.2 million years ago who was found largely intact in the Great Rift Valley of Ethiopia. Well-adapted for soft foods, not to mention liquid refreshment, such teeth are generally interpreted as those of fruit-eaters, which we know is how they're used by most modern primates.

The primate predilection for fruits and other soft foods is not to diminish the gradually growing importance of meat and cereal grains in the hominid diet, especially once the forests had thinned out about 2.5 million years ago and the grasslands expanded to accommodate large herds of herbivores. You might argue, as Richard Wrangham (2009) does in *Catching Fire*, that the controlled use of fire for cooking and softening meat might explain primate dentition just as well as a fruit diet. But fireplaces are very rare in the archaeological record thus far, possibly going back only 400,000 years. Cooking does expand the range of culinary and nutritional possibilities, but it probably did not divert early hominid diet away from its frugivorous ways and from its dependence on that other method of softening, flavoring, and enriching food and drink: the age-old process of fermentation.

We can take the skeletal evidence a step further by peering inside fossil crania for distinctive markings left in the bone by the outermost protuberances and grooves of the brain's gray matter. So-called endocasts record these features by making impressions with a soft material, such as rubber. They show that early hominids, although less so for other primates, had brains like ours. Those brains presumably worked like ours and coordinated the myriad bodily functions that keep us alive and perpetuate the species.

Our senses provide the means for our survival. In an uncertain and dangerous world, our ancestors would have been on the lookout for any plants or other natural products that might extend their lives beyond the usual 30 years or less or helped cure disease. As primarily visually oriented creatures, they would have been attracted to brightly colored fruit, such as fig, date, baobab and others, that abound in Africa. Such fruits are often brimming over with fermentable sugars. Other unusually colored or shaped objects might well have caught their attention, too, such as deeply tinted yellow honey oozing from a beehive, a strange-looking flower or herb, convoluted roots, or grass savannahs. They were all fodder for closer examination and culinary experimentation.

It took some daring to put these things in your mouth, but fortunately, there was more to go on than just taste. Our ancestors certainly would have known what a fermented beverage smelled like, since they could have detected the sharp scent of alcohol combined with the distinctive bouquet of the natural products that were fermenting. Such olfactory compounds evoke a kind of clarion call for most animals that a delicious, nutritious fermented product is close at hand.

An added advantage of any fermented food or beverage is that it can be more easily digested in the gut, because it has already gone through a "predigestive" phase by yeasts and other microorganisms outside the body. Another aid in digestion is a variant of the alcohol dehydrogenase enzyme (ADH4), which converts alcohol into energy. It is present in the mouths, throats, and stomachs of many primates, including us, and is estimated to have existed as far back as 10 million years ago. This enzyme would have increased our ancestors' ability to digest alcoholic foods and beverages, as would the many beneficial and symbiotic microorganisms that inhabit our gastrointestinal tracts.

Most alcohol is converted into energy in the liver. There, ADH1 and ADH2, related to the same enzymes in yeast and comprising 10% of this organ's metabolic enzymes, take over. They provide sustenance in our eternal quest for food (and fermented beverage).

Beyond the role of fermentation in keeping us alive and its sensory enhancement and preservation of food and drink, the trump card of an alcoholic beverage is its mind-altering effects. From our modern perspective in which drugs abound, we are apt to minimize just how powerful an effect alcohol probably had on human consciousness in antiquity. When we take a drink, major neurotransmitters—dopamine, serotonin, and opioid compounds like the β-endorphins and enkephalins—are released in our brains and course through our bodies. They unleash a "pleasure cascade," which begins as a mildly stimulating impulse at first. Individual experiences differ, but we generally feel as if ideas come more easily and we can communicate them more facilely with others, whether true or not in reality. But as we imbibe more, the depressant effects of alcohol take over. Thinking becomes more muddled, sometimes leading to hallucinations, and our apparent physical ease at the start gradually deteriorates into muscular incoordination. The end result can be a catatonic state, even death.

We can anticipate that our ancient ancestors, with their limited understanding of how the world worked and with far less available alcohol, would have been impressed by alcohol's mind-altering and physical effects. A fermented beverage to them might well have seemed extremely mysterious and alluring, especially as it tapped into the hidden realms of the human psyche.

WHY DO WE DRINK?

WHAT I AM proposing is that the place of fermented beverages in early hominid existence and society probably went far beyond simply liking them for their taste or some minor psychoactive properties. We need to step back and take a much broader approach to alcohol's role in early human society.

Building on the "Drunken Monkey Hypothesis," let's begin with the "Palaeolithic Hypothesis." According to this reconstruction of the limited body of Palaeolithic data, alcoholic beverages should be considered as the universal medicine and elixir of humankind, available around the world and effective long before we invented synthetic medicines. Alcohol acted as an antiseptic (how about a mouthwash for those ragged dentitions of early hominids?). At moderate levels, we now know that it could have served as an anticancer and anticholesterol agent. Moreover, if our ancestors needed a medicinal balm, they could have dissolved their herbs and other botanicals more readily in alcohol than in water. These potions—essentially, extreme fermented beverages—could easily have been administered by drinking or applying them to the skin.

Such alcoholic panaceas abound in ancient pharmacopeias and modern traditional medicines. They probably harken back to the medical approach of our Palaeolithic ancestors, who might have observed that people who drank a fermented beverage, rather than raw water in which harmful microorganisms lurked, lived longer and reproduced more.

Fermented beverages probably also served as "social lubricants" that knitted together the first hunter-gatherer groups by breaking down inhibitions and encouraging communication and cooperation. Fermented beverages eased the difficulties of everyday life, after a hard day, say, of hunting down that woolly mammoth or of gathering up enough berries and nuts to stay alive. They contributed to a joyful exhilaration in being alive, much like the congenial atmospheres of today's neighborhood bar or a shared meal or celebration.

The success of this prehistoric experiment in social living and drinking only went so far. Ideally, humans needed a means by which to assure adequate food supplies year-round, including fermentable natural products for alcoholic beverages. Fruits and cereal grasses were obvious candidates to target for increased and reliable production by larger-scale plantings. Grains also had the advantage that their seeds could easily be dried and kept for later use.

But to become horticulturalists and farmers and successfully plant, care for, process, and store their produce, our ancestors needed to settle down into permanent, year-round communities. By being close to their orchards and fields, they could protect and tend their plants. We will see in the following chapters that excess food production was the result of this new subsistence strategy, and led to ever larger and more complex communities. We will see that extreme fermented beverages played a major role in these developments. These drinks fueled the building of cities and temples, and even more profoundly, they fired our creative juices, likely contributing to the creation and development of language and story-telling, music, dance and the other arts, and religion—all uniquely human creations.

Early humans were probably also amazed by the process of fermentation itself. Once the fruits, honey, resins, chewed carbohydrates, and all manner of sweet substances were converted into liquids, an almost magical process ensued. The liquids were a perfect medium for yeasts to carry out their fermentation. These microorganisms were invisible to the naked eye. Yet their activity was obvious to any observer as carbon dioxide gas violently roiled the surface of the liquid for no apparent reason.

Our ancestors' eyes might have grown wider still if they carried out their fermentation in a primitive container, perhaps made of wood, woven grass, gourd, or animal hide. The buildup of gas inside the container might have caused the vessel to shake and roll back and forth. This unexplained movement might have suggested that an outside agency or supernatural force was at work, a phenomenon further reinforced by the mind-altering effects when they drank the finished product.

In fact, a proper scientific understanding of yeast's role in fermentation has been a very long time coming. Antonie van Leeuwenhoek only first observed yeast under a microscope in the 17th century A.D., millions of years after our ancestors began to roam the Earth. Even at so late a date, its central role in converting sugar into alcohol and carbon dioxide was challenged by the chemists of the day, who fervently argued for an abiotic explanation.

While fermented beverages are often painted in negative terms today, wherever we look in the ancient world and continuing up to the present, humans have shown remarkable ingenuity in discovering how to make fermented beverages and incorporating them into their cultures and religions. In these "fermented-beverage cultures," everyday meals, social events, and special celebrations, including rites of passage and major festivals, revolved around an alcoholic beverage from birth to death. Later we will see how grape wine won out over wheat and barley beers in Western religions, how rice and millet beers held court in ancient China, and how the elite's beverage of choice in pre-Columbian America was a fermented cacao drink.

In Africa, where our species began, modern cultures are still awash in sorghum and millet beers, honey mead, and banana and palm wines. Fermented beverages are more than just a part of everyday life. They are central to religions all over the continent, which can be broadly characterized as shamanistic. The office or persona of the shaman, which embodied religious and political power, probably goes far back into the Palaeolithic period. These "mystics" might well have been the most avid makers and imbibers of fermented beverages, since alcohol was needed to induce mind-altering experiences. They would have been the doctors, who could prescribe just the right herb for an ailment and tell you how to prepare it in an alcoholic medium and apply it. They would have been the priests, who invoked the ancestors and other unseen forces, and they would have been the ones overseeing the rituals that guaranteed the success and perpetuation of the community and spurred creative activities. I often say that Sam Calagione is a good example of a prehistoric brewer-shaman come to life.

To explain the universality of fermented-beverage cultures and the similarities between us and our prehistoric forebears, I believe that the "Palaeolithic Hypothesis" will eventually be shown to be a prime force in making us what we are today, physically and culturally. In other words, fermented beverages are fundamental to the human condition. Unfortunately, obtaining convincing evidence for this very early period has so far eluded archaeologists, chemists, and other scientists for a very simple reason: not a single container for a fermented beverage has been recovered from the Palaeolithic period. Since they were likely made of perishable, organic materials, they have degraded and disappeared. We have not given up hope that more exacting scientific techniques will eventually break through the impasse and lead to a major discovery.

Drinking alcohol must have been quite literally "in our genes" from the beginning to explain such a range of physiological parallels between us and our hominid ancestors, together with its preservative, nutritional, socioreligious, and medicinal benefits. Is it any wonder then that in time our ancestors would have harnessed fermentation to their own purposes, likely making it our first biotechnology?

Intentional fermented beverage-making probably started with an accidental observation, followed by an intuitive flash of imagination that brought it to reality. Early hominids might have piled ripe fruit into a primitive container and observed after several days that the liquid that collected at the bottom developed a different aroma and taste than the fruit above and, when drunk, this wine caused a change in mood and perception.

Or, perhaps, a rotten tree, which held a beehive, fell over; it then rained, and yeast in the diluted honey became active and converted it to mead. Along came our ancient hominid, who took a taste and was impressed by the result. Or he or she (more likely the latter, as we will see later) chewed some wild grain and spit it out. Meandering microorganisms sought out the sweet liquid, due to enzymes in human saliva breaking down the carbohydrates into sugar, and fermented it. Again, an enterprising human might have tasted this liquid after it had fermented to beer and was suitably impressed by the result.

The creative individual could have taken the process one step further by intentionally gathering up fruit, honey, masticated roots, and so on, prepared special containers to better control the fermentation, and hoped for the best. There was never a guarantee that the gods (read yeasts) would get the fermentation going and keep it going.

WHAT IS AN EXTREME FERMENTED BEVERAGE?

IT DOESN'T TAKE a great leap of imagination to posit that our early hominid ancestors in Africa were probably making wines, beers, meads, and, most importantly, extreme beverages from wild fruits, honey, chewed grains and roots, and every kind of herb and spice culled from their environments.

But what is an extreme fermented beverage, and why is this concept so important to our story? Extreme fermented beverages are made by mixing and fermenting together the ingredients at hand, no holds barred. These beverages push the boundaries of our current definition of an alcoholic beverage, including what ingredients to use and how to make it. For an ancient hominid, you might well want to up the alcohol content by increasing the sugar and yeast levels. What better way to do this than to mix a variety of natural resources together (some special herbs, honey, fruit, and chewed grain, say); after all, you'd have no idea what sugar and yeast were, but you might discover empirically that certain ingredients in certain amounts were most effective. Perhaps you were impressed by the taste and aroma of a particular mixture or observed that another seemed to thwart some disease. Whatever the reason—and it could be completely unsubstantiated or supposed to be magical—you were not content to make a one-dimensional wine, beer, or mead from a single substrate like only figs, one wild cereal, or palm nectar.

The development of narrowly defined fermented beverages is relatively recent, as we settled down into year-round towns and then cities, and specializations began to emerge. Fermented beverage-makers were no different, and they narrowed their focus to specific drinks. For beer-makers, the most drastic expression of this trend was the Bavarian *Reinheitsgebot* (German, "purity law"), whose original concept was first promulgated on November 30, 1487. It stated that beer could only be made from water, barley, and hops. Yeast was later included, after it was discovered. Gone were the wild, exotic herbs of medieval times on the European continent—the bog myrtle, meadowsweet, wild rosemary, and other native herbs—to make a "gruit beer" (Chapter 6).

MAKING AN EXTREME FERMENTED BEVERAGE

EXTREME FERMENTED BEVERAGES have become all the rage today in the United States, and the movement is now picking up steam elsewhere around the world. In 2000, American beers were uniformly thin and bland when Sam and I started out on our odyssey in making and releasing *Midas Touch* (Chapter 2). A revolution has occurred in the past 15 years, with more than two new breweries opening every day in the United States in 2016. Many of these breweries are headed by homebrewers, who cut their teeth on high-octane IPAs, sour Belgians, and ultradark stouts. They venture beyond the mainstream beers, which might be good for liquid refreshment but have none of the pizzazz and excitement of extreme brews. They are ready to throw anything into the brew kettle.

Sam was right at the cutting edge of this renaissance. Since 1995, when Dogfish Head first opened, he's used nearly every kind of ingredient you can think of in his beers—fruits, grains, herbs, and spices. He's tried ageing in different kinds of wood. He's even tried his hand at re-creating what he calls ancient fermented beverages, including an Ethiopian *tej* and a Finnish *sahti* (Chapter 6), before we got together. His imagination and experimentation show no bounds, which is the essential definition of an extreme fermented beverage-maker.

Any attempt at making a truly ancient extreme fermented beverage faces many challenges. Besides articulating the scientific rationale for the ancient ingredients and process, an authentic re-creation or reasonable facsimile thereof faces a great conundrum: What microorganisms were active in the brew? Yeasts and other microbes provide much of the flavor and aroma of a fermented beverage. Yet precisely identifying them in ancient drinks by ultrasensitive microscopic and chemical techniques, such as DNA technology, is a work in progress.

Every part of the globe has its native microflora living in happy (and sometimes bellicose) symbiosis (and conflict) with one another. Even the colors of rice beers in China (Chapter 3) are influenced by their ecological niches. The scientific sampling and description of the current range of microorganisms from each region has hardly begun to be enumerated, let alone for those buried in the deep past. Would-be brewers of ancient fermented beverages must improvise by sometimes collecting their own "native" yeasts (Chapter 4), retroengineering a likely candidate (Chapter 5), or approximating the microbe community in the ancient landscape with modern strains. When we wanted to re-create a sourer version of *Kvasir* (Chapter 6), for example, we turned to the assemblage of microbes in Belgian lambic beers. We had nothing comparable from the far northern reaches of Scotland and Scandinavia from where the evidence for the drink came.

Lambic beers illustrate what can be done to zero in on the ancient microorganisms, assuming that you have a dedicated cadre of scientists pursuing research on the subject. No one knows how old lambic beer-making is, but some of its ingredients (native European berries and cherries), its barley and wheat, and especially the more than 2000 microbes, many found only along the Zenne River flowing through Brussels, set it apart from most other European brews in the *Reinheitsgebot* mold. Their Asian spices, brown sugar, and fruits such as banana, apricot, and lemon, however, are of more recent vintage.

Like Chinese rice beer, lambics are spontaneously inoculated by those microorganisms that inhabit the vicinity. They can grow and drop down from the rafters of the old breweries into the open wood fermentation tanks during the cold months of the year when the brewing is done, or insects can bring the microbes in on their bodies when they are attracted to the sweet wort, the sugary liquid that results from the enzymatic breakdown of cereal carbohydrates during the malting and mashing processes. What happens next, over two to three years and going from tank to oak fermentation and ageing barrels, is nothing short of amazing. It is more like a carefully choreographed dance of microbes rather than a fight to the death, which it also is. *Enterobacter* spp., whose name points to their main activity in animal guts, proliferate at first. They are quickly succeeded by *Pediococcus damnosus*, followed by a host of other bacterial species, *Saccharomyces uvarum*, and *Dekkera bruxellensis*. *S. cerevisiae* and *S. bayanus* (*pastorianus*) fill the breach, as the alcohol level rises. *Brettanomyces*, *Pedioccus*, and *Lactobacillus* spp. then proliferate during the rest of the first year's fermentation. Finally, *Acetobacter* spp. make their appearance to give the brew a marked sour character. From start to finish, numerous aromatic compounds are generated and regenerated, yielding a beverage full of natural flavors and aromas.

Such a complicated process and diverse array of microorganisms in one region speak well for a greater antiquity of the beverage, although other yeasts and bacteria might be introduced from the outside from time to time, to find their place in the dance.

IN SEARCH OF THE HOLY GRAIL OF EXTREME FERMENTED BEVERAGES

IF I WERE asked what is the ultimate re-creation of an extreme fermented beverage, my answer would be a Dino-Brew, drawing upon the available evidence from the Cretaceous period, or a Palaeo-Brew from our hunter-gatherer days.

Recently, what is thought to be the ancestral alcohol dehydrogenase (*AdhA*) gene was discovered in *S. cerevisiae*. Once the DNA researchers knew the ancient DNA sequence, they retroengineered what can be called a "Dino"-yeast by replacing the modern *S. cerevisiae* versions of the gene (duplicated as *Adh1* and *Adh2*) with the ancient one. They even made some beer with it with moderate success. They also sent us a sample of their reconstructed yeast, in the hope that Sam and I would have a go at using it. That yeast now sits frozen in Dogfish Head's yeast library, awaiting the day when we might resuscitate it to make a truly *Ancient Ale*.

But before we get too excited, we should first ponder what the ingredient list or the grain bill—the technical phase used by modern beer-makers for the starting sugar formula—might have been for an extreme fermented beverage during Cretaceous times, which even a dinosaur might have appreciated. We would need to base our ingredient list on what was available in Africa at the time, since no samples of such a beverage have been found and analyzed and may never be. Dinosaurs were presumably attracted to similar fruits, herbs, flowers, and other plants as their descendants, the birds, are today. We can then examine the available fossil record, as well as later archaeobotanical evidence, for clues to the flora that emerged in the Cretaceous period, which are ancestral to prehistoric and modern species.

We would have to make educated guesses as to what ingredients might have been found in the same locale and could have been accidentally mixed together to be fermented by a yeast comparable to our reconstructed Dino-yeast. The process might have been similar to the scene in *Animals Are Beautiful People*. Dinosaurs, instead of elephants, might have knocked ripe fruit onto the ground, where liquid collected. Sap from a nearby tree might have oozed into the puddle. Some herbal ground cover might have been trampled down to spice up the concoction. Investigating insects might have inoculated the mix with microorganisms and started its fermentation. Curious proto-primates, related to tree shrews, might even have happened by and been surprised by the result. For the time being, any fermentation and drinking scenario for the Cretaceous period will remain highly conjectural and a far cry from reality.

A Palaeo-Brew would be equally challenging to re-create but would represent a major breakthrough. After all, more than 99 percent of our species' time on Earth was during the Palaeolithic period. Sam and I have taken a partial stab at such a beverage with our *Ta Henket* (Chapter 4). We need much more definitive archaeological and scientific data to bring a full-fledged version of the beverage to life.

The prospects for re-creating an ancient fermented beverage improve exponentially as we fast-forward to the recent past. My French and German colleagues in Burgundy, Champagne, and Munich (Jeandet et al., 2015) elegantly demonstrated this in their landmark article on very well-aged Champagne, a preferred fermented beverage of Napoleon, among others. The liquid samples, which they analyzed by state-of-the-art chemical techniques, came from corked bottles of several major producers (Veuve Clicquot Ponsardin, Heidsieck, and Juglar). They were carried on board a ship that went down in 1841 off the coast of Åland in the Baltic Sea.

My colleagues demonstrated in detail that our 19th-century ancestors had a marked preference for very sweet Champagnes, quite different from our modern bent toward drier ones. They also showed that, amazingly, very little of the wine inside the 168 bottles, which had been lying on the seafloor for 170 years, had turned to vinegar. Sulfite had been added to preserve the Champagne, as done today, and at approximately the same levels.

My colleagues then applied the ultimate test to the Champagne: they tasted it. One can complain that they destroyed a valuable sample, but when you have such a treasure trove and only taste minute quantities (30 microliters or about a thousandth of an ounce), then you can justify the loss by the new information gleaned. They learned that the wine had "animal notes," "wet hair," "reduction," and sometimes "cheesy" aromas and tastes, which could be attributed to a range of aromatic compounds that they had identified chemically. The "cheesiness" was probably due to incomplete malo-lactic fermentation, which most white wines undergo today. Lactones attested to aging in oak barrels.

Such a detailed scientific picture of a very old, if not an ancient, fermented beverage had never been assembled before. One of the co-authors on the article, Philippe Schmitt-Kopplin, at the Technical University of Munich, has promised me a "Doppeldrop" ("double-shot" or 60 microliters) of the elixir when I next visit him. His instruments have also been put to good use in our study of the earliest wine from Egypt, dating to about 3250 B.C. (Chapter 4). Now, we just need to find a really ancient sample of a fermented liquid from the Cretaceous or Palaeolithic period and put it through its scientific paces.

Since we are yet to re-create a Dino-Brew or a Palaeo-Brew, I will only suggest a single food pairing: Anyone for some velociraptor stew?

Midas Touch: An Elixir Fit for a Middle Eastern King

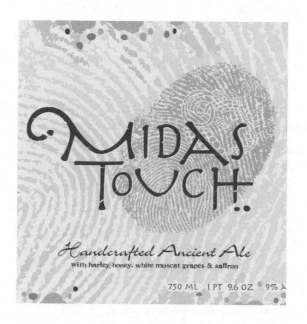

MIDAS TOUCH

Handcrafted Ancient Ale
with barley, honey, white muscat grapes & saffron

750 ML   1 PT 9.6 OZ   9% A

My adventures in extreme fermented beverage discovery and making began with a tomb: the Midas Tumulus (Latin, "mound"), in central Turkey, 76 kilometers (47 miles) southwest of the capital of Ankara, at the ancient site of Gordion. Beginning in 1957 and up to the present, the Penn Museum has intensively explored and excavated Gordion, like few other archaeological sites in the world. As its name suggests, Alexander the Great is said to have cut the Gordion knot here, making him ruler of all Asia. According to legend, the complex knot had been tied by King Midas—indeed, there was a real monarch of this name—nearly four centuries earlier.

Before the Greeks came on the scene, the city was the capital of the Phrygians, an Indo-European people believed to be of northern Greek or Balkan descent. They would have entered Anatolia from the northwest during the turbulent times of the early 1st millennium B.C., following the collapse of the great Bronze Age empires of the Hittites, who controlled much of Turkey at the time, Egyptians, and Kassites in Mesopotamia. Other peoples, including the "Sea Peoples" and the Phrygians, swept in to fill the power vacuum. What we see happening in the Middle East today as the Turks, Kurds, Syrians, Islamic State, and many other religious and political groups fight over territory is a replay of what has been going on for millennia. It's the same story with a different set of characters.

The Phrygians, who joined the fight to defend Troy against the Greeks as told in Homer's *Iliad*, settled down on the high plateau of central Turkey. Gradually, over the course of the early 1st millennium B.C., they consolidated their kingdom, which reached its acme under two of their kings, Gordias and Midas. At the same time, they were challenged on all sides by the Greeks, Assyrians, Urartians, and the wild, horse-riding nomads of Central Asia, known as the Cimmerians and Scythians. A story of Roman times, likely apocryphal, was that Midas committed suicide during a Cimmerian attack by drinking bull's blood.

The Phrygian kingdom was gradually stripped of its territory in the aftermath of defeats by the Persians, Greeks, and Romans. Still, the Phrygians continued to be renowned for their fermented beverages, especially mead, up until the 1st century of our era.

THE TOMB IS OPENED

THE PENN MUSEUM has uncovered large parts of Gordion and its environs over the past 60 years of excavation, including the Phrygian palace, fortification walls and gate, and numerous tombs. The most spectacular tomb at the site is the Midas Tumulus, which is a stone's throw away from the palace. Fittingly, it is also the most prominent feature at the site, rising to a height of about 45 meters (150 feet). You might mistake it for a naturally formed hill, but it was artificially constructed out of layer upon layer of soil and stones. Like an Egyptian pyramid, it ostentatiously announced the burial of a prominent person.

The Penn expedition discovered the tomb by digging a trench into the hillside. Near the center of the mound, they hit into a hermetically sealed log chamber, which is the oldest intact wooden structure in the world.

When the Penn Museum excavators cut through the double wall of logs, they came face-to-face with an amazing sight, not unlike Howard Carter's first glimpse into Tutankamun's tomb. The excavators saw the body of a 60- to 65-year-old male, who showed normal signs of aging. He lay on a thick pile of felt and blue-and-purple dyed textiles, the colors of royalty in the ancient Near East. He was accompanied to his grave, to my amazement, by the largest comprehensive Iron Age drinking set ever found. Some 160 bronze vessels—including large and small cauldrons, jugs and juglets, and 1- and 2-liter (approximately 1- and 2-quart) drinking-bowls (the latter perhaps for those higher in status or with greater thirsts)—were used to serve up a very special beverage, as we will see, in a final farewell dinner to the king.

But who was the occupant of the tomb? The grandeur of the tomb and its rich burial deposits could only be those of a royal personage, likely a king. The styles of the drinking vessels and other artifacts pointed to the late 8th century B.C. as the date of interment. This was the time when Midas ruled Phrygia. Referred to as Mita in the contemporaneous Assyrian records, he was a constant thorn in the side of Assyria as the two powers vied for influence in the region. The excavators were naturally inclined to believe that they had found the tomb of the legendary king. More recent dendrochronological dating of the logs, however, suggests that the tomb dates to earlier in the 8th century and may be that of Midas's father, Gordias, famous in his own right.

Whether the body was that of Midas or Gordias, various lines of evidence, including the residues that we were later to analyze, implied that he was royally ushered into the afterlife. As the body lay in state near the tomb, people gathered from all over the kingdom to pay their respects to the celebrated king. A royal funerary banquet with drinking and feasting concluded the festivities, like an Irish wake. The body was then lowered into the tomb, along with the remains of the food and drink, to sustain the king for eternity (or at least the next 2700 years).

Strangely, if the tomb were that of Midas, none of the 160 vessels were made of gold. How could the ruler with the "golden touch" be buried without some gold artifacts? As told in Ovid's *Metamorphoses*, Midas had kindly cared for Silenus, the old satyr and companion of the wine-god, Dionysus, when Silenus had gone on one of his frequent drunken benders. In return, Dionysus granted Midas one wish. Midas, in his greed, opted for turning anything he touched into gold. After nearly starving himself to death because his food and drink were also converted to the indigestible precious metal, Midas prayed to Dionysus for a reprieve. Dionysus relented, and told Midas to wash in the Pactolus River, to the west of Gordion, and he was miraculously cured.

Actual gold might have been missing from the Midas Tumulus. Yet the high-zinc bronze or brass vessels, which included spectacular lion-headed and ram-headed *situlae* (Latin, "buckets") for serving the beverage at the feast, gleamed just like gold once the copper corrosion was removed. Could it be that a wandering Greek traveler during the early 1st millennium B.C. caught a glimpse of the "golden-like" drinking-vessels and returned with the tale to his homeland, where it was later embellished into the famous legend?

The real gold, as far as I was concerned, was what these vessels contained. Nearly a quarter of the vessels held the evaporated remains of an ancient beverage. These residues were intensely yellow, just like gold. The art historian Elizabeth Simpson, who has made it her life's work to study the furniture from the tomb—said to be the finest collection from antiquity—asked me in 1997 if I would be interested in carrying out chemical analyses of the residues.

She didn't have to ask twice. It was the easiest excavation I was ever on. I just had to walk up two flights of stairs from my laboratory, turn to the left, enter the Gordion archives room, and there were the residues in their original paper bags. They had been collected in 1957, 40 years earlier, brought back to the museum thanks to the excavators' foresight and attention to detail, and had patiently awaited my "re-excavation." Together with colleagues, my laboratory could begin analyses immediately.

PROBING THE EXTREME FERMENTED BEVERAGE

WE HAD POUNDS of residues, an unbelievable trove for testing, an amount we had never had before or since. The conditions for organic preservation in the tomb had been ideal, since the atmosphere inside the tomb had been dry and depleted of oxygen. Microbial activity had been cut down to the minimum.

Besides the organic residues, the wooden furniture with its intricate inlaid geometric designs in juniper was extremely well preserved. Two collapsible serving tables with circular recesses for holding three small bronze cauldrons each, from which the beverage at the funeral feast was served using nearby ladles, stood to one side. The "Pagoda Table," so named because of its exotic appearance, lay on the floor in front of these tables, surrounded by other plain tables and some 100 drinking bowls. It was as if the scene of the funerary feast, which had probably taken place outside but close to the tomb, had been moved piece by piece indoors and reassembled. The occasional earthquake probably explained the disarray of the artifacts.

After the tomb's excavation in the late 1950s, some rudimentary chemical analyses had been carried out. For example, sample material was ignited to determine the carbon content of the residue before and after burning by the difference in weight. The sample was destroyed, something we try to avoid at all costs today, but it did show that the residues were largely organic. Our chemical analyses were to provide a much more definitive answer about their chemical makeup because instrumentation had progressed in the interim.

The Kaplan Fund of New York gave us its first "New Technologies" grant, enabling us to throw every kind of state-of-the-art technique at our samples from 1997 to 1999. We began with our workhorse technique, FT-IR (see Preface), and followed up with high-performance liquid chromatography (HPLC) with an ultraviolet-visible spectrophotometer detector. Very sensitive wet chemical tests, targeting fingerprint compounds, followed. Altogether, we put 16 residue samples from a range of vessel types through their scientific paces with our standard three complementary techniques. Already, we had done a lot more than was typical of a biomolecular archaeological investigation of the late 1990s, when the discipline was still in its infancy.

We then took the field in new directions by applying LC-MS-MS for the first time (Preface) through our collaboration with the Eastern Regional Research Center of the U.S. Department of Agriculture. Other colleagues at Vassar College and Scientific Instrument Services stepped in with GC-MS, in particular using a thermal-desorption unit that captured low-molecular-weight volatile compounds on a resin before they were passed through the chromatographic column, another first.

We used these techniques not only because they were novel to the emergent field but also because of their increased sensitivity and the range of compounds that they could detect. They enabled us to tease out the ancient molecules and identify the biomarkers of the natural ingredients that comprised the residues in the tomb's vessels.

Our tests showed that tartaric acid was present. While this compound occurs in several other fruits elsewhere, fortunately for us, it is found in large amounts in Turkey only in the Eurasian grape (*Vitis vinifera*). Some kind of grape product was attested, and it had to be liquid, because many of the vessels were clearly intended for pouring and drinking.

We had little doubt that grape juice would quickly become wine in central Turkey's warm climate because yeast would have been present on the skins of some grapes. Yeast will naturally ferment the juice to wine in a day or two. Of course, wine can easily turn to vinegar, but any royal winemaker would have known how to avoid letting it go that far and assure that the mind-altering properties of the precious alcohol were not lost. We could not test directly for alcohol, as it had long since evaporated and disappeared, but we were sure that an alcoholic beverage was the intended product because of its social and cultural importance at the time.

Our tests also showed the presence of honey, whose presence was marked by specific, well-preserved beeswax compounds. These compounds reliably marked the presence of honey in the residues, because it is impossible to completely filter them out during the processing of honey. Yeasts, which can tolerate a high sugar content, are also found in honey. When the viscous semisolid honey is diluted down to a liquid by adding about 7 parts water to 3 parts honey, these yeasts become active and convert the honey to mead.

Our final fingerprint compound was calcium oxalate, or beerstone. Aptly named, it collects as a solid precipitate along the sides and on the bottom of brewing vessels for making barley beer and is quite bitter, even poisonous. Ancient brewers, just like their modern counterparts, needed to remove as much of it as possible before reusing the same vessel.

We already knew a lot about beerstone, since we had identified it in the interior grooves of what is so far the earliest chemically attested brewing jar for making barley beer in the Middle East. The jar, which conveniently had a hole for inserting a drinking-tube or straw, was found in a proto-urban trading post, high up in the Zagros Mountains of Iran. Beer made from cereals was drunk this way around the world, because of the ease of using the same jar for making and drinking the beverage. A straw was needed to penetrate through the accumulation of spent grains and yeast on the surface to the precious beverage below. We do not usually think of Iran as a hotbed of fermented beverage experimentation, but around 3500 B.C., they were producing large quantities of grape wine and barley beer for lowland traders from Mesopotamia—and no doubt for themselves.

We were very much taken aback when we saw the final chemical results for the intense yellowish residues inside the drinking-vessels from the Midas Tumulus. Since we obtained nearly identical chemical results for a range of vessel types from the tomb, we concluded that all the main ingredients had been fermented together to make a single extreme fermented beverage. In other words, the beverages—wine, beer, and mead—had not been served separately one after another in the vessels; doing that would have resulted in highly variable chemical results. The auspiciousness of the occasion further argued for a one-time use of the vessels for a mixed drink or what might be called a Phrygian grog or a cocktail.

Our stomachs turned as we cringed at the thought of mixing wine, beer, and mead together. Such extreme beverages are common enough now, especially among micro- and nano-brewers who enthusiastically experiment with multiple ingredients. Back in 2000, before craft brewing had taken hold in the United States, extreme beverages were only a glimmer in Sam's eye, or perhaps in that of a medievalist, who studied gruit (Chapter 6), the bitter herbs that offset the sugars in beers of the Middle Ages, long before hops took over. The drink attested in the Midas Tumulus was an extreme fermented beverage, if ever there was one! I wanted to find out more about it.

EXPERIMENTAL ARCHAEOLOGY TO THE RESCUE

THE PHRYGIAN EXTREME beverage gave me the idea to do some experimental archaeology. I've already touched on the essential ideas, rationale, and goals of what is involved in re-creating an ancient fermented beverage in the Preface. It entails trying to replicate the way it was made by taking the available evidence for the beverage ingredients and trying out various production scenarios in the present. In the process, you hope to learn more about how the ancient beverage was made and how it tasted.

If there were ever a group of archaeological samples that could be taken from a hypothetical reconstruction of an ancient beverage to a reasonably accurate replication, this was it. Our samples were some of the best you could imagine—well-preserved, well-dated, uncontaminated, and undisturbed. The chemical evidence from all 16 samples lined up, giving the same formulation. Moreover, artwork from just a few years before Midas's death provided corroborating evidence for the use of the vessels to serve and drink a beverage.

For example, at the Assyrian palace of Sargon II at Khorsabad (ancient Dur Shurrukin), northeast of modern Mosul in Iraq, numerous lion-headed *situlae*, like the one in the Midas Tumulus, are depicted on sculptural reliefs. They are shown being filled in celebration of the king's military sack of the Urartian city of Musasir in eastern Anatolia in 714 B.C. Lion-headed "drinking horns" (Greek, *rhyta*) are also raised high in the banquet scene.

Another relief in the palace depicted large cauldrons, again similar to the three in the Midas Tumulus. Most of the drinking-bowls in this scene were identical to a well-known Assyrian type, marked by *omphalos* (Greek, "belly-button") bases, intended for easy holding since they lacked handles. You just wrapped your hand around the outside of the bowl and inserted your middle finger in the concavity. The Midas Tumulus examples were plain, ribbed, grooved, or decorated with a petal design.

I had already been exposed to experimental archaeology during my studies at Penn. If one wanted to know whether Stonehenge or the Egyptian pyramids, for instance, were made by humans rather than extraterrestrial aliens with advanced technology, then you could try doing it yourself using ancient methods. You could cut multiton stones with primitive saws, and try moving them on rollers and up earthen ramps under human or animal power, and putting them in place with simple pivots and rope hoists. Various possibilities can then be ruled out and others shown to be more likely. Any human technology can be tested by experimental archaeology, but what about possibly the oldest biotechnology of all: making a fermented beverage?

I was fortunate to be on hand when Fritz Maytag of Anchor Steam Brewery and my colleague in the Penn anthropology department, Sol Katz, teamed up to re-create an ancient Sumerian beer. They based their experiment on an early "recipe" contained in a poetic "hymn" to the beer goddess of Mesopotamia, Ninkasi. Two versions of the beverage were ultimately produced, and I tasted both. According to my palate, the first in 1990 at the Penn Museum was an effervescent, almost champagne-like drink with the hint of added dates. The second in 1991, served up at a special event for the Archaeological Institute of America, was more ale-like, with a heavy dose of baked bread.

The Ninkasi re-created beverages were intriguing, and others have since followed, including a recent version made by the Great Lakes Brewing Company. But there were problems: the evidence for the beverage was based largely on an ancient literary text, and a poetic one at that. To what extent was the Ninkasi hymn derived from eyewitness testimony for the ingredients and brewing process? How much of the composition existed only in the realm of the gods, as writers exercised their poetic license through the ages? Many words, especially technical ones about the ingredients and brewing process, could not be translated exactly. Dates, grapes, and honey did appear to be mentioned in the poem, yet their precise roles in making the beverage were unclear. Were they intended to start the fermentation, because they were likely to contain yeasts, or were they added for their sugar content or to impart flavor? Depending on one's interpretation of the hymn, different amounts of the fruit or honey might go into the experimental brew.

The hymn has Ninkasi baking bread (Sumerian, *bappir*) and adding it to the beer wort (the sweet liquid that results from breaking down cereal carbohydrates into sugar). The poem does not specify the cereal used to make the bread, but barley seems most likely. It might have been combined with wheat or another grain. The consensus has been that the bread was lightly baked, to leave a moist, yeast-rich center to aid in starting the fermentation. More intensive toasting cannot be ruled out, since "amber" and "dark" beers are mentioned in other texts.

The "sweet aromatics" in the hymn presented another interpretative challenge. Like hops today, it might refer to "bitter" herbs that offset the sweet cereal malt, fruits, or honey. So far, no ancient herb has yet been confirmed and used in a re-creation.

The Phrygian grog was worlds apart from the Ninkasi re-creations. The residues we analyzed from inside the drinking-vessels in the Midas Tumulus were of this world, from the same time as the funeral of the king. Their contents had not been doctored, and their chemical composition allowed much less wiggle room for different interpretations.

Certainly, questions remained. We knew that a grape wine, barley beer, and honey mead were mixed together, but we could not be sure about their proportions. Why did the residues have an intensely yellowish color? Perhaps it was due to the honey, barley malt, or a yellowish botanical for flavor or bittering. So far, our chemical analyses have come up empty-handed.

Moreover, how had the Phrygian beverage been made? Could it be that batches of beer, wine, and mead were prepared separately and then mixed together? Or were the combined ingredients fermented as a single batch? It was even possible that the extreme fermented beverage was fermented in a beehive and later filtered and transferred to three large cauldrons for the finishing touches and presentation at the funerary ceremony. Beehives are relatively airtight containers, excellent for fermentation, and they are full of nutrients in addition to the honey, including propolis, gums, and resins for nourishing the yeasts and other microbes.

There are many other questions. Was the yeast sourced locally? If so, could we find and propagate it today? What was the most likely grape varietal in central Turkey 2700 years ago? Were the grapes added as raisins or fresh fruit? Knowing the time of year that the king had died might provide some answers; if it was in the fall, then fresh grapes might have been available. Was the barley 2- or 6-row (referring to how the kernels are arranged when the grain head is viewed on end)? That can make a difference in protein, enzyme, and carbohydrate content. What kind of honey did the ancient beverage-maker add to the mixture? Turkey is famed for its honeys today, ranging from intense citrusy ones on the Aegean coast to dark peppery varieties and delicate herbal and wildflower types inland. An especially sought-after and lus-

cious Turkish honey is made from pine "honeydew," a sugar-rich product produced by an insect that feeds exclusively on the resin of the red
pine tree.

A final question, yet by no means the last: Was the beverage
carbonated?

A YOUTHFUL SOJOURN IN BEER HEAVEN

HOW SHOULD I proceed with my experimental archaeological program? I was not a homebrewer myself, although I had an early initia-
tion into beer drinking at age 16 when I traveled in 1961 to Bavaria, a
region nearly synonymous with beer. No parents were along to monitor the travels of six high school companions as we biked through the
German, Austrian, and French Alps for a month. A second month was
spent working on a Bavarian farm in the idyllic town of Breitbrunn am
Chiemsee, with a magnificent view of the Alps.

The trip started out on a high note. On the first night, Cornell
Chemistry Nobelist, Peter Debye, grandfather to two of my fellow
travelers, treated us to dinner at a downtown Munich restaurant. That
was followed by a wild night at the Hofbräuhaus, where buxom women
carried a pair of liter-sized beer steins on each arm and hand. Despite
the temptation, I still had not tasted any Bavarian beer. That came
when I discovered that beer was less expensive than Coca-Cola. I
then quickly transitioned over to two liters of beer with my dinner.
The first liter whetted our appetites while we waited for the food to
be served. When the meal arrived, it was time for *noch ein Liter Helles
oder Dunkles* ("another liter of light or dark beer"). Those were the days
when the U.S. dollar was nearly worth its weight in gold, and we could
order anything on the menu.

The real measure of your beer prowess came at the end of the meal.
Then our waiter returned to draw up the bill. We had to tell him what
we had to eat, but after two liters of beer, that could be a challenge.
Finally, we floated into the night on our bicycles in search of an empty
barn full of straw to comfortably sleep upon for the night.

After a month of such frolicking, I was ready for working on a

Bavarian farm, where technology was still back in the Middle Ages. We rose at the crack of dawn to scythe the grass, which we then piled high with a pitchfork onto a horse-drawn wooden cart and transported back to the barn where we fed it to the cows.

The food and drink carried us through. On the first night, I was served *Radler* (appropriately, German for "cyclist"), which is made from equal parts of beer and lemonade, in one huge drinking-stein. It went around the table from person to person. Even the five-year-old daughter of my hosts indulged.

When my stay was over, my family asked what I wanted to eat and drink for a farewell meal. On this occasion, I changed my liquid refreshment from beer to coffee. (I had also begun drinking coffee on this trip, and the bean blend—*Bohnenkaffee*—was so unbelievably delicious that I have spent my whole life trying to duplicate it and have yet to succeed.) The coffee went extremely well with a breakfast of sour-milk cheesecake with raisins. The culinary skills of my host family turned out to be far above the average; when I returned more than 10 years later, the barn I had worked in had become a gourmet restaurant.

It was hard to give up such delectables when I returned home to the States, though I did finally muster the courage to don my Bavarian cycling outfit of *Lederhosen* ("leather shorts") with suspenders and a green Tyrolian *Hut* ("hat") adorned with a feather and an abundance of *Schmuck* ("jewelry") pins showing the coats of arms for the Bavarian towns we had passed through on our trip. I bravely entered a nearby watering hole, the Bushnell Basin Inn outside of Rochester, New York, and demanded a beer in German: "Ich muss ein Bier haben." The underage ploy worked.

Another 30 years passed before Bavarian beer raised its sumptuous "head" again. I was asked to give a lecture at Weihenstephan, the oldest continuously operating brewery in the world (dating from A.D. 1040), in Freising, a suburb of Munich, where the sojourn of my younger years had begun. My host was Martin Zarnkow, who has identified beerstone inside large vats at the late 2nd millennium B.C. site of Tell Bazi in northern Mesopotamia, the earliest chemical evidence for beer thus far from this region. Today, whenever I pass through Munich on my way to the Middle East, we have a meal together at the brewery's Ratskeller, and catch up on our latest research. We share a common interest in what may turn out to be the earliest beer vessels in the world: gigantic stone vats associated with monumental architecture at another site in Turkey: 11,000-year-old Göbekli Tepe.

Martin recently co-authored a book on beer with his colleague, Franz Meussdoerffer. Believe it or not, Franz lives in the same farming village that I once called home, Breitbrunn am Chiemsee. Small world indeed!

A TOAST TO MICHAEL JACKSON AND MIDAS

MY SOJOURN INTO Bavarian beer culture put me on the path to recreating the Midas beverage. With our chemical formulation in hand, I turned to Michael Jackson—not the entertainer, but the preeminent beer and scotch maven. Every year starting in 1971, Michael had visited the Penn Museum in the spring to do a beer tasting. The night before the all-day tasting on Saturday, a special dinner was held in the Upper Egyptian gallery of the museum, surrounded by statues of pharaohs and mummies.

In 2000, Michael was feted at the dinner. The assembled craft brewers, who were to show off their wares the following day, roasted and toasted him. I took the opportunity to join in the fun and described to him and the audience the very unusual, seemingly repellent, drink served at the funerary feast for King Midas or his father. Michael, as it turned out, wasn't surprised by our results, and we began emailing about how Ninkasi's "bread-beer" might have traveled overland from Mesopotamia to Russia, eventually morphing into the commoner's *kvass* there (possibly related to *Kvasir*, Chapter 6). The Russian beverage is also made from bread (usually, black rye) and whatever else is available to throw in the mix (fruits, honey, birch resin, herbs, etc.).

I found out later that Michael had confided in Sam about my experimental archaeological project and encouraged him to resuscitate the ancient drink. I still had not met Sam, but I had met his beer. When, by chance, I drove through the small town of Centreville in Delaware, I happened upon Buckley's Tavern. I ordered a Shelter Pale Ale from a strange-sounding brewery I hadn't heard of before: Dogfish Head. When I tasted the brew, I was thrown for a loop—it was easily the best beer I had ever tasted, apart from some Bavarian lagers and Hefeweisen ("wheat beer"). It stood head and shoulders above the usual "piss light" (in my opinion) of the large mainstream American producers.

Slowly but surely, I began to be won over from grape wine, which I had long studied, to aromatic beers. Shelter Pale Ale was one step in the process. The coup de grâce came when Tom Peters, the owner of Monk's Café in Philadelphia, served me a three-year-old aged Chimay Grande Réserve (Blue) from Belgium. Although a different style than Dogfish's pale ale, it exhibited the same exceptional taste.

These serendipitous tastings presaged the re-creation of the Phrygian extreme beverage. My toast to Michael Jackson at the dinner in March 2000 was a challenge to the assembled craft brewers: Who could make the finest interpretation of this ancient drink and have it ready to be served at a special re-creation of the "Midas" funerary feast to be held at the museum in September? Was it even possible to make something drinkable from such a weird concoction of ingredients? I was only able to give the briefest description at the dinner. If anyone was seriously interested, I invited them to my laboratory the next morning at 9 a.m. for more details about how best to reverse-engineer such a beverage.

Before the evening ended, however, something remarkable happened. Another of Sam's experimental creations—a medieval plum *Braggot*—was served as the dessert wine at the dinner. Braggots combine a honey mead with a cereal beer and were often heavily spiced in the Middle Ages. In his *Canterbury Tales* of the late 14th century A.D., Geoffrey Chaucer compared the sweet and wanton mouth of the carpenter's wife in the Miller's Tale to this drink. Sam's version was similarly enticing and delicious. What struck me immediately as I sipped his *Braggot* was that if you switched out the plums for some grapes, you were on your way to re-creating the Phrygian beverage.

The next day, nearly 20 brewers showed up at my lab. I would have thought that their discussions and drinking had gone long into the night, and they would not be able to pull themselves out of bed. But there they were, anxious to learn as much as possible, and I happily complied. They went back to their breweries, and soon experimental brews started arriving on my doorstep in nondescript boxes for me to taste. My job was to decide which was the best interpretation and most tasty rendition. Not a bad job, if you can get it, but I should add that some of the entries challenged the senses.

Some re-creations stood out. I especially remember those of Tess and Mark Szamatulski. They first made a stock ferment in which Greek wild thyme honey, barley malt, and Muscat grape juice were mixed together and fermented with an "ancient" French wine yeast. To test other possible bittering agents and ingredients, they made three more versions with saffron, anise, and Turkish figs. Using this approach, you could compare what each ingredient contributed to the mix.

It goes without saying that Sam Calagione of Dogfish Head ultimately triumphed in the competition, but not without a bit of subterfuge. When I asked him whether he had a brewery lab for testing his trial runs, he said "sure." He was not referring to an actual laboratory filled with instrumentation, but his Labrador Retriever!

BRINGING THE "MIDAS"
FUNERARY FEAST BACK TO LIFE

THE HIGH POINT of the gala funerary feast that September at the Penn Museum, apart from the extreme fermented beverage, was the entrée. It was the first time that an ancient meal had been re-created based primarily on the chemical evidence. This was no ordinary meal from the past, but presumably the favorite of an iconic king of history and legend, whether Midas or Gordias, who had enjoyed it during life and requested it for the afterlife.

The entrée served was a spicy, barbecued lamb and lentil stew, in accord with our chemical findings. For example, specific organic acids (caproic, caprylic, and capric) had originated from goat or lamb meat. Our chemical finding of the triglyceride 2-oleodistearin and chondrillasterol (a plant steroid), which are marker compounds for lentil, was borne out by the excavation of large jars of lentils (as well as cereals for the Phrygian grog) in the nearby palace kitchens, destroyed by the Assyrians around 700 B.C.

The entrée must have been a stew, because no bones were recovered from the dark brownish, congealed lumps of residue that filled 18 pottery jars deposited in the tomb after the feast. We might rather have expected some skewered meats—like modern Greek *souvlaki*—or a whole suckling lamb or kid to have been served at the feast. Homer's *Iliad*, which was written down about the same time that Gordias and Midas lived, focused on these dishes. As we found out later, lamb stews have been a great Anatolian favorite for centuries. A nearly identical stew to our ancient one is served up today at weddings in villages across Turkey.

Herbs and spices provided the finishing touches to the stew. We detected anisic acid, characteristic of anise or fennel, and α-terpineol and terpenoid compounds found in various spices. Anise and fennel grew in Turkey. My archaeobotanist colleague, Naomi Miller, also observed that some domesticated and wild legumes, including bitter vetch and wild fenugreek, which grow around Gordion today, have very bitter tastes. One or both of them might account for α-terpineol and the terpenoids.

Pam Horowitz, the museum's chef, prepared a scrumptious Phrygian lamb and lentil stew, based on the scientific evidence and her search for authentic, traditional Turkish recipes. Pam opted for a very spicy interpretation, including cumin, fennel, anise, rosemary, thyme, salt, and cayenne pepper; whether the latter was imported from the Indian subcontinent is possible but very unlikely. Olive oil, honey, and wine—all of which we had chemically confirmed—added flavor depth to the stew, which was garnished with watercress.

To round out the meal, I conferred with Pam on accompanying hors d'oeuvres, side dishes, and, most importantly, a dessert to-die-for that would be the finishing touch to the banquet. Since we had no evidence of a dessert from the tomb, we took some liberties. We knew that ancient Anatolians, including Phrygians, had a sweet tooth, like Turks today. A visit to the Grand Bazaar in Istanbul, with its mounds of marzipan, Turkish delight, and baklava, will convince you of that. Generally, I insisted on at least using native ingredients in our re-creations, but I made an exception in this case. I allowed Pam to substitute New World chocolate for Old World carob in her Midas-gold-leaf-touched white chocolate truffles. We rationalized the culinary breach by arguing that if Midas had tasted chocolate and been able to import it, he certainly would have done so.

THE PERFECT COMPLEMENT

THE STEW WAS delicious and nutritious, with its vegetable and meat proteins, but to wash it down, a similarly bracing beverage—no doubt of the extreme sort with lots of antioxidants and vitamins, flavors, and aromas, and, of course, a high alcohol content to carry you into the afterlife—was needed. How else could the king's long life and health be explained? An earlier Hittite king, Šuppliluliuma, summed up the essence of the funerary feast and beverage when he coined the phrase: "Eat, drink, and be merry!"

Sam stepped up to the plate and hit a home run with the perfect complementary drink to match the stew. Although he never submitted an experimental version of his beverage to judge in advance, I put myself in his hands. After all, he had proven his mettle with his Shelter Pale Ale. Since I was an amateur when it came to brewing, I stood by to advise on archaeological and scientific matters only. As the date of the dinner re-creation approached, I became nervous. What if Sam were not able to carry off his experimental brew? What if the taste were terrible? I have since discovered that Sam works best under pressure.

One key piece of advice that I passed along to Sam was that saffron might have been the bittering agent for the beverage. Although we had not identified saffron chemically in the residues, their intense yellowish color was highly suggestive of this richly hued spice. Moreover, Turkey was renowned for its saffron.

A major snag was that saffron is the most expensive spice in the world at $625 (or more) per ounce for the best quality. You could buy white truffles and Beluga caviar for much less. Sam went all out and made what he says was his most expensive beer ever. He also used the finest Greek thyme honey, as well as Muscat grapes, which DNA evidence suggests were among the earliest grape varietals in the Middle East, and 2-row barley. Lacking any firm details of the ancient yeast, Sam used a dry mead yeast to ferment the extreme ingredients of his extreme beverage.

One can always ask for a more realistic re-creation. If the king died in late summer or early fall, for example, fresh grapes might have been available for making the beverage. At other times of the year, raisins (which ferment easily), honey, and malted barley (especially if it were parched or toasted)—all of which keep well—would have served the purpose. Unfortunately, the time of year is yet to be inferred from the archaeological evidence.

One liberty that Sam took in his re-created beverages was using 2-row rather than 6-row barley; only the 6-row variety was recovered from the palace kitchens. Other issues could be raised. Should the grain have been baked, as was done for the Ninkasi brew, and only the central moist portions added to start the fermentation? Should brewing have been done in a bronze replica of the large cauldrons in the tomb rather than in the antiquated (but still relatively modern) stainless steel homebrewing apparatus in Sam's Rehoboth Beach brewpub? Should the honey and saffron have been sourced from Turkey? Should a native Anatolian grape varietal—say, a white Emir or Narince—have have been used in place of generic Muscat from California? Different regimens of heating, adding the ingredients, and other procedures might have been tried. Yes, you can always ask for more, but we had made a start.

Dogfish's *Midas Touch*, as it came to be called, was a success on the taste front (in my humble opinion). It was extremely aromatic, yet well-balanced. The wine, beer, and mead accented one another without dominating. If I had been quaking in my boots until the night of the dinner, I could now relax, sit back, drink, and revel in Sam's re-creation.

MIDAS TOUCH GOES OUT TO THE WORLD

SAM'S VERSION OF the Midas drink was a "one-off," as he often describes his many experimental brews that only see the light of day for a single event or at the brewpub in Rehoboth. It had cost a fortune. Could he go commercial with it, not just to recoup some of his investment costs, but to demonstrate to the world that our species had long had a flair for making audacious extreme fermented beverages that broke the bonds of the *Reinheitsgebot*? Could *Midas Touch* bring history and past human achievement alive for us moderns?

Sam's brewing facility was still in its infancy when the Midas beverage was brought to life again after 2700 years. He had very limited production capacity. His equipment threatened to break down at any time. He was overwhelmed by his combined role of chief brewer, driver, and sales agent. He had little capital to fall back on for emergencies, let alone expansion. He also faced the intense competition of the late 1990s and early 2000s when one hopeful craft brewer after another failed.

My wife, Doris, and I were of like minds in seeing this unique beverage go out to a wider public, so that people could begin to understand the enticements of ancient extreme beverages. We were so taken by the prospects that we stepped in to help Sam by advancing him a small loan.

We needed a name, and settled on "The King Midas Golden Elixir." Sam and his lawyers ran this name by the BATF (Bureau of Alcohol, Tobacco, Firearms and Explosives), which was reconstituted in 2003 as the Alcohol and Tobacco Tax and Trade Bureau (TTB), and the Food and Drug Administration (FDA). It was rejected, because the word "elixir" smacked too much of 19th-century patent medicine. Sam's lawyer argued in vain that the word had a broader, less pejorative connotation today. We settled on the name *Midas Touch*. The authorities approved it, apparently having no problem with an ancient legend that promised untold riches simply by physical contact.

As a forewarning for what was to come in getting approval for this *Ancient Ale* and the others to follow, the TTB has very specific rules on what can and cannot be called a "beer," which harken back to prohibition days. They must be adhered to precisely. For example, the Code of Federal Regulations states that only "rice, grain of any kind, bran, glucose, sugar, and molasses" can be substituted for [barley] malt in a beer. You are also allowed to use "honey, fruit, fruit juice, fruit concentrate, herbs, spices, and other food materials" as adjuncts. In other words, the honey, grape, and saffron in *Midas Touch* cleared the TTB hurdles. But things can get dicey with specific adjuncts and herbs, as we were to discover with fresh hawthorn fruit in *Chateau Jiahu* (Chapter 3) and meadowsweet in *Kvasir* (Chapter 6).

Moreover, the TTB's *Beverage Alcohol Manual* (*BAM*), in a nod to the *Reinheitsgebot*, goes on to say that malted barley must comprise "not less than 25% by weight of the total weight of fermentable ingredients." We were on safe ground here with *Midas Touch* as well because our general principle in making an extreme fermented beverage is to use equal amounts of the main ingredients (see Preface). Our ancient "recipe" called for a third each of malt, honey, and fruit.

Then, there was the matter of the hops for which we had no biomolecular archaeological evidence. *BAM*, again in keeping with the *Reinheitsgebot*, states that hops are essential to any beer worthy of the name. The minimum amount is 7.5 pounds per 100 barrels. Fortunately, although it may sound like a lot, this is a minuscule amount, on the order of 0.03% of the total weight of the ingredients. We could satisfy the requirement and still make a reasonable facsimile of the ancient brew.

Now we needed a label. Sam designed a striking, gargantuan golden thumbprint, worthy of a king, on a royal purple background. He incorporated the ram-headed *situla*, with the horns of the animal swirling back upon themselves, into the fingerprint whorls.

Midas Touch was first produced in 2001 in a large-format (750-milliliter, about 25 ounces), clear glass bottle. Because the labels were applied by hand, they slanted this way and that, and sometimes peeled off.

The bottles were sealed with champagne corks, which was the great bugaboo. Once again, Sam employed a "primitive" machine, manned single-handedly, that forced one cork at a time into a bottle. Depending on the beverage's carbonation, which was variable, some corks might start moving on their own accord and begin slipping askew out of the bottle—definitely not a sign of quality control. Fortunately, a wire cage held them in place; otherwise, they might eventually have shot out without warning. The day came, however, when an operator almost lost his thumb in the machine. There was nothing in the budget for another machine, so Sam switched to crown caps.

In those days, filling the bottles with the beer was also a hit-and-miss affair. Consumers noticed that they were getting more or less of the beverage, depending on the gap (or ullage) between the top surface of the liquid and the bottom of the closure. The clear bottle didn't help: it highlighted the golden elixir inside, but it also exposed the beverage to harmful UV radiation.

When our small loan went into arrears, we feared for the beverage and for Dogfish Head. As it turned out, *Midas Touch* had a lot going for it. First, there was Sam, who was rapidly establishing himself as the most successful experimental brewer in the country, thanks to his charismatic personality, boundless energy, and "hunk"-ness. He was on his way to becoming a brewing rock star.

Then there was *Midas Touch* itself. Starting in 2004, *Midas Touch* began winning awards at premier tasting competitions in the United States and internationally. That year, it took silver at the World Beer Cup, gold at the Great American Beer Festival, and gold again at the Colorado Mead Festival. It has gone on to be the most awarded of any Dogfish brew, having garnered many more golds (appropriately enough, given its name and pedigree), plus five silvers, and a few bronzes tossed in for good measure (and historical accuracy, because the drinking set was made only of this metal).

Midas Touch was introduced to the viewing public on the *Today Show* when Matt Lauer and a beautiful Olympic swimmer tasted it at 7:30 in the morning. We watched the episode with bated breath. After her tasting, the swimmer remarked on how delicious the beverage was. Matt concurred and began to shower praise on it. Then she piped up: "Women especially like how aromatic it is." We watched in horror as

Matt did a double take and said: "You mean I like a chick beer!?" The magic of the moment was gone.

More media coverage followed. The most detailed and ambitious was a re-creation of the funerary feast beside the tumulus in Turkey, probably near the spot where it was celebrated in antiquity. The hour-long British TV special, which aired in December 2001, spared no expense. Replicas were made of the bronze drinking-vessels by metal-smiths in Ankara's bazaar. The inhabitants of the local village, Polatli, prepared the main entrée by roasting lamb on a spit and gathering and crushing lentils with mortars and pestles. They produced an extremely tasty and spicy stew.

TV productions do not always go according to plan. It was Sam's first trip to the Middle East. On his first night there, our dinner was rudely interrupted by the police tossing tear gas into the downtown Ankara restaurant where we ate. Eyes aflame, we escaped into the streets.

Since we could not export *Midas Touch* to Turkey for the funer-ary feast re-creation at the tomb, I turned to the president of Kavak-lidere Winery, Mehmet Başman, to make a comparable beverage. He quickly agreed, and set one of his winemakers to the task. Perhaps the winemaker's heart was less enthralled by an extreme beverage than Sam's, since the resulting interpretation of the ancient bever-age was much less aromatic, even sour—not what I would consider fit for a king.

Our scientific paper on the extreme fermented beverage appeared in *Nature*, one of the leading journals in the world. A glorious color photograph adorned the cover of its Christmas issue that showed the king laid out on purple-and-blue textiles with his huge drinking set in the background. Everyone was inspired. At the British Museum, epigraphists, archaeologists, and conservators marked the season with their own version of the beverage.

YOU ONLY LIVE TWICE

AFTER THE INITIAL success of *Midas Touch*, reality set in as sales fell. Consumers wanted a more consistent product. Sam put life back into the re-created beverage by switching from the large-format bottle to a four-pack of 12-ounce bottles. It gave twice the beverage for the same price. Sales took off again.

All of this occurred while Dogfish Head went from being just another possibly bankrupt craft brewery to becoming the fastest growing one in the country. When I first mentioned Dogfish Head during a lecture, I just got blank stares. Now it is virtually a household name.

In 2014, *Midas Touch* expanded overseas. It earned a gold medal at the prestigious European Beer Star competitions, based in Munich. Distribution of Dogfish brews has now begun to Great Britain and Italy. Can Turkey and the Midas Tumulus be far behind?

Midas Touch lent itself to many more re-creations of the ancient feast here and abroad. I allowed for different interpretations of the entrée, since not every chef is comfortable doing a stew, however exotic. Some decided to do lamb chops or roast leg of lamb. But I do insist that only *Midas Touch* be served.

Tasting events of the Phrygian grog also took off, as consumers clamored to experience the historic beverage in real time. Interest has been especially high among the medical community, as you might expect, since these beverages were once the universal palliative and medicine of humankind. Modern physicians and the shamans of old, it seems, have always been able to afford the best. To date, I have lectured for and shared our *Ancient Ales* with periodontists, general surgeons, internists, pharmacogenomists, sensory scientists, and otorhinolaryngologists.

Sam and I often do a kind of "good brewer, good academic" routine centered around our re-creations of extreme beverages, especially *Midas Touch*. We play our dialogue off against one another in a spirited, extemporaneous way, with glasses in hand.

I may have started out as a youth with a taste for Bavarian lagers made according to the 16th-century *Reinheitsgebot*, but today, I am an ardent believer and practitioner in retroengineering and enjoying extreme fermented beverages. I often wonder what would have happened if I had not stopped at Buckley's Tavern and tasted Sam's Shelter Pale Ale. That palate-awakening experience led me to have Sam re-create the Midas beverage. That beer and I just happened to be in the right place at the right time. That was just the first of many propitious encounters over the past 15 years. As I was rediscovering ancient extreme fermented beverages, Sam was running alongside re-creating his modern idiosyncratic brews. We came together with *Midas Touch*, and that collaboration launched us onto a path of many more adventures in extreme fermented beverage-making around the world.

RECIPES

Homebrew Interpretation of
Midas Touch

by Doug Griffith (after Calagione, 2012a, 150–151 [per Bryan Selders]; cf. 170–171 [per Chris Wood and Eric Leypoldt])

INGREDIENTS

6 gallons	Water	Pre-boil
8 pounds	Light or extra light dry malt extract	75 minutes
2 pounds	Clover honey	75 minutes
¼ ounce	Simcoe hops	60 minutes
10	Saffron threads	End of boil
1 packet	White Labs WLP001 or Safale US-05	Fermentation
1 quart	White grape juice concentrate (preferably Muscat grape)	Day 3 fermentation
1 cup	Priming sugar	Bottling
	Bottles and caps	Bottling

Starting gravity: 1.086
Final gravity: 1.026
Final target alcohol by volume: 9%
International Bittering Units: 12
Finished volume: 5 gallons

PROCESS

1. In a brew kettle, heat the 6 gallons of water to a boil.
2. Remove from the heat, and add the malt extract and honey. Return to a boil.
3. After 15 minutes, add the Simcoe hops. Boil for 60 minutes. Remove from the heat, add the saffron threads, and swirl the contents of the kettle to create a whirlpool.
4. Cool the wort and rack to a fermenter, leaving as much of the solids behind in the kettle as possible. (It's okay to get some sediment into the fermenter; it's beneficial to yeast health.)
5. Pitch the cooled wort with a fairly neutral ale yeast and ferment at around 68°F to 71°F.
6. "Rock the baby" to aerate the wort.
7. After the most vigorous fermentation subsides (about 3 days), add the white grape juice concentrate.
8. Rock the baby yet again.
9. Ferment for 5 to 7 more days, then rack to a secondary fermenter. Allow the beer to condition in the secondary for 12 to 14 days.
10. Before bottling, clean and sanitize the bottles and caps.
11. Create a priming solution of 1 cup boiling water and the priming sugar.
12. Siphon the beer into a sterilized bottling bucket.
13. Add the water-diluted priming solution and gently stir.
14. Bottle and cap the beer.
15. The beer will be ready to drink in about 2 weeks.

MEAL PAIRING FOR *Midas Touch*

Spicy Barbecued Lamb and Lentil Stew

by Pamela Horowitz, Provence Catering; adapted by Ayşe Gürsan-Salzmann, Deputy Director, Gordion Archaelogical Project

T he original "King Midas Funerary Feast" entrée was pre-pared by Pamela Horowitz, then chef of the Penn Museum Catering Company. It was served at the first re-created dinner event at the museum in September 2000. It was the first time that chemical data provided the basis for an ancient meal.

Serves 4

INGREDIENTS

1½ pounds lamb or other stew meat cut into 1½-inch cubes
Salt and pepper to taste
4 tablespoons olive oil, divided
1 large onion, chopped
1 carrot, chopped
2 stalks celery, chopped
1 teaspoon cumin
1 tablespoon thyme
Splash of red wine or *Midas Touch* or homebrew interpretation
4 cups water or stock, divided
1½ cups green lentils, rinsed
2 tablespoons honey

PREPARATION

SEASON THE MEAT with salt and pepper. In a large Dutch oven over medium-high heat, sauté the meat in 2 tablespoons of the olive oil until browned, then remove from the pan. In the same pan, sauté the chopped onion, carrot, and celery in the remaining 2 tablespoons olive oil for about 5 minutes, then add the cumin and thyme, stirring occasionally. Use a splash of wine or, best, *Midas Touch* or homebrew interpretation to deglaze the pan. Return the stew meat to the pot with any juices and 2 cups of the water or stock and gently boil until tender, about 30 minutes. Add the lentils and the remaining 2 cups of water or stock, stir, and bring to a boil. Add more wine, homebrew, or *Midas Touch*, as desired. Simmer for 30 minutes. Add the honey and stir. Place in a 350°F oven for 40 to 45 minutes. When the meat is done, serve.

For mood-enhancing atmospherics and more meal suggestions, go to: http://www.penn.museum/mcgovern/ancientbrews/.

Chateau Jiahu:
A Neolithic Brew to Settle Down with in China

Although not especially old (only 2700 years), *Midas Touch* posed the question: Just how early were humans making and drinking extreme fermented beverages? *Chateau Jiahu* provides a partial answer. It doesn't take us as far back as a Dino-Brew or even a Palaeolithic "Beaujolais Nouveau," but it does "push the envelope" in more ways than one by going back 9000 years to the early Neolithic period.

Our ancestors were constantly on the move. They were hunters and gatherers after all, who had to follow the cycle of seasons, as trees fruited, grains matured, flowers and herbs sprang to life, and animals migrated. If climatic conditions worsened and food resources became scarce, they were motivated to move on. One never knew whether the grass was greener just beyond the next desert or mountain range. As the climate of Africa seesawed back and forth between extremes from hot and dry to cool and wet periods over the past 2 million years, our ancestors took their chances and came "out of Africa" into Asia. They might have followed the northern route through Sinai or cut across the Red Sea when it occasionally dried up. About 2 million years ago, they had gotten as far as Georgia in the Caucasus. After another million years, they had reached Flores in the Indonesian archipelago by some kind of watercraft, if the findings for 3-foot-tall "hobbits" there hold up.

Humans of our species (*Homo sapiens*) did a repeat performance of this journey through Asia, starting around 100,000 years before the present (B.P.). They had reached Australia by about 50,000 B.P. Again, they might have traversed a northern land route through the Sinai or crossed by boat the narrow strait of the Bab el-Mandeb at the southern end of the Red Sea. The journey to Australia would have entailed island-hopping about 20 kilometers (12 miles) at a time over a distance of at least 3200 kilometers (2000 miles).

NEW ASIAN WORLDS TO EXPLORE

TRAVELING TO ASIA, our ancestors were greeted by many new plants, which could have been exploited to make a fermented beverage. They might have passed through the Negev, today a desert but then well watered, and headed northward through the verdant Jordan Valley, where figs, dates, cereals, honey, and native herbs, including coriander, cumin, balm, and thyme, flourished.

Not everyone stayed put in the Jordan Valley or even in the Near East. Groups journeyed farther eastward—toward India and on to southeast Asia. By staying close to the coast, they avoided the mountains, which blocked passage from west to east across central Asia, but they also had to contend with the major rivers of India and southeast Asia, notably the Indus, Ganges, Mekong, and the great rivers of China including the Yangtze and Yellow, which run west to east, cutting off movement northward.

Some intrepid souls no doubt decided to strike out in a different direction across the center of the continent, perhaps over the course of several generations. This route has been dubbed the "Prehistoric Silk Road" or the "Eurasian Wine Road." It was about 3000 kilometers (1850 miles) from the Jordan Valley across Iran to the imposing mountains of eastern Afghanistan, the Pamirs and Hindu Kush. Yet our adventuresome ancestors were less than halfway to the Yellow Sea of China when they were confronted by this obstacle. They had another trek of 3500 kilometers (2175 miles), including oasis-hopping across the barren wastes north or south of the Taklamakan Desert or the "Desert of Death." This desert is said to be the origin for the expression: "If you go in, you won't come out." Their efforts, however, were to be amply rewarded when they reached the other side.

During the long journey, the wayfarers might have passed close to the oasis town of Dunhuang, which much later was adorned with flamboyantly painted Buddhist caves. Near here, the Great Wall starts its meandering 9000-kilometer (5600-mile) march to the Yellow Sea. Our ancestors then most likely traversed the Gansu corridor, which cuts directly eastward across the dry but fertile Loess Plateau to Xi'an in today's Shaanxi province, avoiding the large north-south loop of the Yellow River and following the Wei directly east instead. The rich loess soil is a remnant of the last Ice Age, when fine silt was formed along the margins of glaciers and blown across the land. The soil is meters deep and often gouged out into deep valleys and a patchwork of gullies.

The Yellow River eventually opens up onto rolling countryside, whose soils are excellent for growing deciduous fruits and cereals. Our early ancestors must have stood in awe when they saw peach, Asian pear, Chinese date or jujube (*Zizyphus* sp.), apricot, and plum trees for the first time. They would have gazed in wonder at the strange grasses waving over the plains, precursors to millet and rice cultivation.

One of the stopping-off points that early migrants might have been familiar with was Shizitan in Shanxi province, dating to approximately the same time (23,000–19,500 B.P.) as Ohalo II on the opposite side of Asia, on the shore of the Sea of Galilee in Israel. At both sites, people had begun experimenting with wild grasses, as shown by stone grinders impregnated with cereal starches and sickle blades whose edges gleamed with silicate glosses from harvesting wild grains. Ancestors of barley, wheat, and oats were attested in the west, while those of foxtail millet, broomcorn millet, rice, and wheat prevailed in the east. Wheat, however, was never domesticated in China but was introduced from western Asia in the late 3rd millennium B.C.

SETTING THE STAGE FOR THE WONDERS OF JIAHU

XI'AN PLAYS A key role in our fermented beverage story, and not just because the first emperor of a unified China, Shihuangdi, was buried there in 210 B.C. with great pomp and ceremony, together with his famous legions of terracotta warriors and attendants. Xi'an and its environs also have the distinction of being a seemingly endless repository of tombs in which were deposited tightly lidded bronze vessels containing fermented beverages, which were still liquid after thousands of years. The burials with these extraordinarily well-preserved contents range in date from the late Shang Dynasty (ca. 1100 B.C.) through Han times (from 206 B.C. to A.D. 220).

One of the more spectacular examples, found in 2003, was a jar containing 26 liters of liquid. When opened, it was said to have a "delicious aroma and light flavor." These tasting notes have yet to be followed up by a scientific report. Regrettably, all the other liquid samples, including those from Baoji (160 kilometers/99 miles west of Xi'an) and Baishui (100 kilometers/62 miles to the northeast), remain in similar chemical limbo.

Sometimes, the archaeobotanical and microscopic evidence at a Xi'an site provides indisputable evidence that a pottery vessel contained a fermented beverage. For example, a congealed white mass inside a jar at Taixi, a short distance to the northeast of the city, weighed a whopping 8.5 kilograms (19 pounds) and consisted solely of yeast cells that had collected as lees on the bottom of the vessel. That's a beverage that would have thrown you for a loop! Another large jar from the site was filled with peach, plum, and Chinese date pits, as well as seeds of sweet clover, jasmine, and hemp. With such details, one can put some flesh on the bare bones of a wine or beer tasting note.

Moving back in time, a recent discovery in the eastern suburbs at Mijiaya, on a tributary of the Wei River, has revealed the earliest brewery in China to date. The facility, built underground probably to offset heat produced during the process, comprised a wide-mouthed fermentation jar, a pottery funnel to transfer the finished product to a narrow-mouthed storage jar, and a pottery stove. Its date of ca. 3400–2900 B.C. coincides with the earliest chemically attested barley beer vessel from the Near East at Godin Tepe (Iran), which my lab analyzed. As at Mijiaya, a wide-mouthed jar served as the fermentation jar. Narrow-mouthed storage jars at Godin, yet to be analyzed, are also very similar to those at Mijiaya. Botanical and chemical studies of the Mijiaya jars and funnel showed that a malted barley had been fermented together with broomcorn millet, Job's tears, and various tubers (yam, lily, and snake gourd) to make an extreme fermented beverage. The barley represents the earliest instance of this cereal in China and must have been introduced from the west. Tests are yet to be done in search of possible fruit, honey, and herbal additives.

Xi'an was also home to one of the most important early Neolithic sites in China, Banpo, which is approximately contemporary with the settlement at Jiahu, which was 500 kilometers (300 miles) to the east. Banpo's large jars from the Yangshao culture, which likely held a fermented beverage—although analyses are yet to be carried out—are a study in ceramic art: swirling, hatched, and checkerboard designs, with the occasional bird and fish, in polychrome jump out at you from generations past. Jiahu has similar vessel shapes but without decoration. They make up for this lack in having contained the earliest chemically identified fermented beverage in the world.

A NEW WORLD OPENS UP

SINCE MY PRINCIPAL area of interest until the late 1990s was the Near East, you might wonder how it happened that I became involved in work on ancient China. If anyone can be held responsible, it's Anne Underhill, an archaeologist at Yale University, who initiated one of the first American expeditions to the Chinese mainland when the country opened up again to foreigners. She was convinced that fermented beverages were intimately involved in the earliest Chinese cultures and played a similar role to what they do today in social relations, religious ceremonies, and feasts and celebrations. She proposed that I take part in her excavations of the late Neolithic site of Liangchengzhen in Shandong province and chemically analyze some of their vessels. At that time this was too good an opportunity to pass up, even if I knew virtually nothing about ancient Chinese civilization and couldn't read a Chinese character to save myself. I took the leap and then began considering other sites where I might sample ancient pottery.

I was especially helped by Changsui Wang of the University of Science and Technology in China (USTC). Changsui was head of the archaeometry department there, and he set up an extensive itinerary of visits to leading archaeologists and scientists in Beijing and at key sites along the Yellow River. He even accompanied me on overnight train trips, serving as my interpreter and boon companion and introducing me to modern Chinese life, its customs, and especially its cuisine. Banquets were a daily occurrence, and as the guest of honor, I was expected to take the first bite of the barbecued or baked fish with my chopsticks. If adeptly managed, I was roundly applauded. Toasting with fermented beverages that had distant roots in the past, as I was to discover, was the high point of these meals. Good health and success for our research were constant refrains. To avoid the potent high-alcoholic distilled beverages, made from sorghum and millet, I usually requested the milder, more aromatic rice beer. My excuse was that I was studying a period when only natural fermentation was done.

As I looked into the eyes of my toasting partner, we bonded, paving the way for getting samples approved, through customs, and back to our lab at the Penn Museum. This is easier said than done in China, and it helped to have friends and colleagues in the right places, who were as enthusiastic and interested as I was in finding out more about ancient Chinese beverages by testing them with the latest scientific instruments.

In time, Changsui and I made our way to Zhengzhou, about 200 kilometers (125 miles) north of Jiahu, and home to the Institute of Cultural Relics and Archaeology of Henan Province. There I met the chief archaeologist of Jiahu, JuZhong Zhang, who took me into the inner sanctum of the Jiahu pottery collection. I could hardly believe my eyes. Vessel upon vessel stood on the shelves in perfect condition. The numerous two-handled jars especially struck my fancy, because they reminded me so much of the Canaanite Jars, which were used to transport wine and other commodities overland and by ship throughout the Near East and westward across the Mediterranean Sea (Chapter 5). Jugs, sharply angled at mid-body and polished to a deep reddish hue, were equally striking.

JuZhong then stepped up with the *pièce de résistance*. He said that the pottery was dated as early as 7000 B.C. and continued to be made until about 5500 B.C. I nearly fainted. The Near East began making pottery around 6000 B.C. and was reputed to be the "cradle of civilization." Here was extremely well-made pottery from a thousand years earlier. Indeed, it is now known that China was making pottery as early as 16,000 B.C. In 1999, word had just begun to leak out about how far advanced China was at a very early date.

I have already touched on the importance of pottery in discovering ancient fermented beverages in the Preface. As our ancestors began settling down and domesticating the various plants and animals that became the bases of their unique cuisines, the malleability of clay enabled special vessels to be made for processing, storing, serving, and consuming food and beverages, which were then fired to make pottery. This utilitarian technology was thus central to human subsistence, but it had an additional advantage: the pottery fabric, which is porous and polar, absorbs liquids, like fermented beverages, and retains and helps to preserve many of their compounds for millennia. That makes a pottery vessel the perfect medium for chemical analysis.

JuZhong was ready for me to step in immediately and begin the analysis. Before the day was out, we had chosen 16 pottery sherds, generally from the bases of the jars where solid materials settle and the greatest impregnation of the pottery by a liquid occurs. We celebrated the prospects of discovering what the vessels contained that evening at dinner with a very fragrant and flavorful rice beer.

MUCH MORE THAN A DRINKING SOCIETY

JIAHU ISN'T JUST your run-of-the-mill early Neolithic site. As ably excavated by the Chinese, it has yielded some of the earliest rice, dating back to 7000 B.C., rivaling finds made in the lower Yangtze River valley. The Jiahu rice is about equally divided between domesticated and wild varieties, implying that it is in the process of being domesticated.

JuZhong and his team have made other exciting scientific discoveries, including pottery fired as high as 900°C that points to the use of a kiln, stone sickles with silicate gloss, turquoise artifacts evidencing long-distance trade, ceremonial dog burials, and tortoise shells buried in house foundations (quite appropriate since they represented long life and stability in later Chinese tradition).

By 2013, when I attended the 25th anniversary of excavations at Jiahu, the expedition had recently uncovered more burials to go with some 200 already excavated. The tombs, cut as shallow pits into the ground, generally held completely articulated skeletons of single individuals, except in the few instances where the head had been severed postmortem. One or more jars had been placed close to the heads or mouths of the deceased (perhaps, for easy drinking in the afterlife?).

In his lecture at the conference, JuZhong revealed new details about the extraordinary bone flutes found in many of the tombs, dating as early as 7000 B.C. The 33 flutes are claimed to be the earliest *playable* musical instruments ever found. Two to eight holes had been carefully drilled into them, making them capable of playing pentatonic, hexatonic, and heptatonic scales, all of which sound unusual to the Western ear. The pentatonic scale, achieved by covering all but one hole of a six-hole flute in turn, is the basis of traditional Chinese folk music.

Intriguingly, the flutes were all made from a specific bird wing bone: the ulna of the red-crowned crane. This bird, with its snow-white plumage accented by black and red, engages in an intricate mating dance, replete with bows, leaps, wing extensions, and ringing musical notes as a finale. It is still celebrated in Chinese tradition. Perhaps, the Jiahu musicians, who were buried with flutes at their sides, decided that human music could only properly be rendered by this bird's bone.

Jiahu has also produced what are arguably the earliest Chinese characters ever found, which were incised on tortoise shells. Thousands of years later at the fabulous Shang Dynasty capital cities, such as Anyang, similarly inscribed tortoise shells are believed to have been used by shaman-like priests to predict and assure a good future. We don't know if the Jiahu shells, assuming they bear a form of early Chinese writing, have the same significance. The hypothesis gains credibility from their association with the musical instruments and especially the mixed fermented beverage, which were all-important in later Chinese religious and funerary ceremonies. Moreover, many of the unincised Jiahu tortoise shells were filled with pebbles, which was a popular divination technique in the later Shang Dynasty.

We might also consider the importance of the tortoise elsewhere in Asia about the same time. For example, at the site of Hilazon Tachtit in the hills of Galilee of Israel, an elderly woman was buried around 12,500 B.P. with over 50 carapaces of the animal—this, in addition to marten skulls, an auroch's tail, a golden eagle's wing tip, a leopard's pelvis, a male gazelle horn, a wild boar's foreleg, and a yet-to-be-explained articulated human foot. Animals, which might be symbolically represented by body parts, have been gatekeepers of spiritual realms in many cultures. The excavators of Hilazon Tachtit make a good case that the woman, who was physically handicapped, was especially revered in the community and possibly a shaman. Whether she made and dispensed any extreme fermented beverages is still uncertain, but a grinder that she took to her grave might have been used to crush cereals and botanicals that went into one.

From later texts of the 1st century B.C. through the 1st century A.D., specifically, the *Li Ji* or *Book of Records*, and the *I Li* or *Book of Conduct*, whose traditions go back to the Shang and Western Zhou dynasties of the late 2nd to early 1st millennia B.C., we know that when a family member died, a *shi* (Chinese, "descendant") was chosen to communicate with the ancestors. The *shi* was to drink nine goblets of millet or rice beer in preparation for the ceremony. The consequences were predictable. If the vessel were an elegant bronze goblet (Chinese, *gu*) of the Shang Dynasty, it might have held as much as half a liter (half a quart) when filled to the brim. If the *shi* were to drink nine rounds, which adds up to 4.5 liters (over 1 gallon), he or she would almost certainly become inebriated. The same can be said for the *shi*'s Neolithic counterpart if such a ceremony existed then. A Neolithic jar was about the same volume as a *gu*, and, as we will see, a 10% alcoholic beverage is not beyond the realm of possibility then.

But drunkenness in such rites was the whole idea and in keeping with the extraordinary antiquity of Chinese tradition. Like the shamans of the northern tundra, an altered state of consciousness enabled one to enter the spirit world. In the process of the *shi* getting drunk, it is said that "the spirits are all drunk." Music and drums signaled the end of the ceremony in later times, and we might imagine a Jiahu shaman doing likewise by playing on a flute.

THE ANALYSIS BEGINS

WHEN I GOT back to Philadelphia, everything was ready to begin our analyses of the Jiahu jars. The Midas beverage study had wound down, and we were set to use the techniques that we had pioneered for that project. We also added two new techniques to our analytical arsenal: the detection of volatile compounds by purge-and-trap thermal desorption GC-MS, which operates similarly to SPME (Preface), and isotope studies to identify plants, which preferentially take in and metabolize carbon, nitrogen, and oxygen atoms of different atomic weights from the atmosphere.

We had little doubt that the jars had once contained some kind of liquid, since they were ideally shaped to hold and serve a beverage, with their high necks, narrow mouths, and flaring rims. The question was: What was the beverage?

As we analyzed the extracts from one pottery vessel after another, the same chemical compounds kept showing up. There were beeswax compounds, which we had also detected in the Midas drink, showing that one of the constituents was high-sugar honey. We also found tartaric acid, the biomarker of grape and wine in the Middle East. In China, however, it could also mark the presence of hawthorn tree fruit (*Crataegus pinnatifida* and *cuneata*), which contains three times the amount of the acid as in grapes. Finally, close chemical matches with phytosterol ferulate esters pointed to rice as the third main ingredient. Yeasts associated with the high-sugar fruits and honey would have assured the liquid's fermentation.

You could call this extreme fermented beverage a "Neolithic grog or cocktail." It combined honey mead, a rice beer, and a grape and/or hawthorn fruit wine. Such a hybrid fermented beverage might sound strange and unappetizing, as had the Phrygian grog. As we've learned over the past 15 years, mixed fermented drinks were generally the rule in antiquity, especially during Neolithic times when plants were first domesticated and fermented beverages began to be "mass-produced." By combining multiple sugar sources, our ancestors appear to have accidentally hit upon a solution to a never-ending quest: upping the alcohol content as much as possible.

A GRAPE AND/OR HAWTHORN WINE
REIMAGINED

WE DON'T KNOW as yet whether only grape or hawthorn fruit, or both, went into the Jiahu beverage. After we published our chemical results, an archaeobotanical study showed that only those two fruits were present at the site. While nicely corroborating our findings, we were still left uncertain.

If grapes were used, wine-lovers will appreciate the fact that the Jiahu extreme beverage lays claim to being the earliest chemically attested grape wine in the world. Of course, it is more than a wine because of the drink's other ingredients. The potential use of grape this early in time—likely a wild Chinese species such as *Vitis amurensis* with up to 20% simple sugar by weight—took us by surprise. As far as we know—but continued exploration may change the picture— none of the estimated 40–60 grape species found in China were ever domesticated.

Similarly, no evidence yet exists that native North Americans domesticated any of the 25–30 species of grape on that continent, let alone made wine from them. To date, only the Eurasian grapevine (*Vitis vinifera vinifera*) is known to have been domesticated by humans. It accounts for up to 10,000 varietals and 99 percent of the world's wine today.

Consensus had it that grape wine only came to China in 138 B.C. when General Zhang Qian was sent on a fact-finding mission to central Asia and points west by the emperor in Xi'an (ancient Chang'an). He came back with stories about monster vines with huge clusters of grapes in the Fergana Valley, not unlike the report of the Israelite spies on seeing Canaan for the first time. The grapes of the Fergana Valley, which straddles the borders of Uzbekistan, Kyrgyzstan, and Tajikistan, were put to good use. According to Zhang Qian, they made an ethereal wine, which might be aged up to 20 years or more. He brought cuttings of the Eurasian vine back to the capital. They were planted, bore fruit, and supposedly were used to make the first Chinese grape wine.

For a country as old and vast as China, Zhang Qian can be excused for not knowing what had happened at Jiahu thousands of years earlier. We now know that people there were familiar with and probably experimenting with grapes as early as 7000 B.C., presumably without any direct influence from central or western Asia. Additionally, the oracle bone and tortoiseshell inscriptions of the late Shang Dynasty, some 800 years in advance of Zhang Qian's quest for a trans-Asian route, likely refer to a fruit-based beverage (Chinese, *luo*), which might well have included grapes, whether native or the Eurasian species.

Shaanxi province, where Xi'an is located, sits on the southern edge of the Loess Plateau, which has superb conditions for growing grapes now, as it did in the past. The same can be said for regions farther north (Shanxi and Ningxia provinces) and to the west, deep into central Asia (Xinjiang province). In the last two decades, the truth of this observation has been borne out by the vast acreage brought under grape cultivation in these regions and the ever improving quality of the wines. The loess soil is the crucial factor: it retains moisture and requires minimal irrigation. The vines must struggle to reach the water table some 12–15 meters (40–50 feet) below the surface and in the process produce better, more flavorful fruit.

The Jiahu Neolithic grog probably included hawthorn fruit besides grape. Westerners are mostly unfamiliar with wines made from hawthorn, although decent ones can be produced from the European and American species of the tree. In China, this wine was and remains highly regarded, especially for its health benefits. The same can be said for "drunken date," persimmon, chrysanthemum, and fig wines, and many other exotic flower and root concoctions for which the country is known.

But why hawthorn fruit in particular? Perhaps hawthorn fruit was chosen to go into the Jiahu extreme fermented beverage because it is very sweet and its skins harbor yeast for initiating fermentation. But you could say the same about other Chinese fruits.

The answer may rather lie in hawthorn fruit's long history as a digestive and hypertensive in traditional Chinese medicine. Scientists have shown that the fruit contains medically beneficial antioxidant compounds, which, like those in grapes, are said to lower cholesterol. Today, it is administered in pills mixed with honey or as a tea. Consumed in a fermented beverage, such as the Neolithic grog, it could have been just as effective. More studies are needed to determine its health benefits.

UNVEILING THE EARLIEST RICE BEER

RICE TAKES CENTRAL stage in the Jiahu beverage as the principal source of starches to be broken down into simple sugars for making a fermented beverage. But at this early date, how was the conversion, called saccharification, done? To my mind, chewing the grain is the most obvious and direct way to produce a sweet wort, ready for fermentation. We have an enzyme (ptyalin) in our saliva, which can saccharify raw grain. You just have to resign yourself to a lot of jaw pain from excessive chewing and gum chafing by the rough edges of the grain. Once you have salivated the grain, you spit out your sugary saliva, and wait for a hungry insect to happen by with a load of yeast to get the fermentation going.

Women are the world's best chewers, as we will later argue for the corn *chicha* of the Americas (Chapter 8). In Japan and Taiwan today, marriage ceremonies are preceded by "bridal showers" of an unusual kind. A group of women will gather around a large bowl and spend the day filling the pot with salivated rice to produce enough of the traditional brew for the ceremony.

If the idea of spitting isn't to your fancy, you can spread out some rice on a shelf in a damp, warm place for a few days. The seeds will sprout using their enzymes (amylases), similar to ptyalin, to make a sweet malt. You can then dilute the malt down with water to make a mash, and wait for the passing insect with some yeast to jump-start the fermentation.

There is yet another possibility, albeit more remote, which deserves mention because we know it was uniquely employed in China. By at least Shang Dynasty times, fermented beverage-makers there had discovered that fungi or molds—principally of the genera *Aspergillus*,

Rhizopus, and *Monascus*, whose spores are airborne—could cleave carbohydrates into sugars. If you steam a cake of cereals or pulses, a thick, luxuriant mat of fungal matter, the so-called mycelium, will form on its exterior. As mold fibers penetrate into the interior of the cake, they release amylases for saccharification.

Yeasts are incorporated into the "mold cake" (Chinese, *qu*) adventitiously, either falling from ceilings and rafters of old buildings where they have established a foothold or brought in by insects that are attracted to the ever-increasing sweetness of the *qu*. Moreover, at some point in Chinese history, it was also discovered that special herbs can accelerate the process. Today, some 100 herbs are mixed into *qu*, causing as much as a sevenfold increase in yeast activity.

One of those herbs was *Artemesia argyi* in the wormwood/mugwort family. We identified its presence, along with its sister plant *A. annua*, in a remarkably well-preserved rice beer sample from 3000 years ago, which was still liquid. The beverage had been hermetically sealed inside a late Shang Dynasty bronze jar in which the vessel's tight lid had corroded onto its neck. The liquid inside, which still filled about a third of the vessel, had evaporated down until the jar became airtight.

Equally amazing, the liquid had the characteristic fragrance of a fine rice or millet beer made the traditional way, slightly oxidized like sherry but also perfumy and aromatic like an aged lambic beer. I can still remember when I first smelled these liquids in Zhengzhou and Anyang on my inaugural trip to China. I had a very difficult time believing my nose, but my Chinese colleagues, who were excellent archaeologists, assured me the liquids were ancient. They then provided me with samples to carry back to the United States for testing.

Once we knew that a wormword/mugwort herb was likely added to the ancient rice beer, we followed up with anticancer testing of one specific compound of known medicinal value—artemisinin—at the Penn Medical and Abramson Cancer centers, as part of our "Digging for Drug Discovery" (D^3) project (Chapter 4). We were able to show by testing cancer tissues *in vitro* that the compound and its main derivative, artesunate, are highly effective against all kinds of cancers, namely, lung (Lewis lung carcinoma), colon (adenocarcinoma), eye, liver, ovary, nervous system, pancreas, and blood. It is still undergoing *in vivo* testing in mice against cancers, and clinical trials are underway for cancer treatment in humans.

Artemisinin has also been shown to be a powerful antimalarial agent and often is the medication of last resort for that disease. It was isolated by Youyou Tu of the China Academy of Chinese Medical Sciences in 1972, for which she jointly received the 2015 Nobel Prize in Physiology or Medicine. The award was a long-overdue recognition by Western medicine of the potential value of traditional Chinese medicine.

Both *A. annua* and *A. argyi* have long been important in traditional Chinese medicine and are still very popular in China today. They are usually equated with the plants *qinghao* and *ai ye*. Both are used to treat hemorrhoids and as general sexual and medicinal tonics. Leaves of *ai ye* are also burned on the tips of acupuncture needles and applied to the key body points in a practice called moxibustion. The monumental *Compendium of Materia Medica* by Li Shizhen, published in A.D. 1596, attests to the long medicinal use of *Artemisia* herbs by citing the polymath Ge Hong's *Handbook of Prescriptions for Emergency Treatment* of the 4th century A.D.

The herbs are also cited in the earliest Chinese medical prescriptions, which were written on bamboo and silk strips, found in the extraordinary tomb of a noblewoman at Mawangdui in Hunan province, dating to 168 B.C. She is said to be the most well-preserved human ever discovered with the tissues of her internal organs intact and moist.

Is it possible that the use of these wormwood plants in fermented beverages goes back even earlier, perhaps to Neolithic times at Jiahu? If so, might the fermented beverage-makers of 9000 years ago have known about mold saccharification? China has tremendously long traditions, and Jiahu's prowess in fermented beverages, the arts, and religion, whose traditions carried on for millennia, is obvious. The people at the site were experimenting with the domestication of rice, so it is not beyond the realm of possibility that they explored interactions between herbs and fungi. More excavation, combined with chemical and archaeobotanical investigation, may eventually provide an answer.

Whatever was happening at Jiahu, mold saccharification (amylolysis) is today the tried-and-true method for making Chinese fermented cereal drinks. Because the microorganisms vary from one ecological niche to another, these beverages are markedly different in color, flavor, and aroma from one region of China to another. For example, you can enjoy a deep reddish-hued brew in the province of Zhejiang, whose color derives from *Monascus* fungus, or a translucent yellowish elixir in Henan province, home to Jiahu and the three-millennia-old Shang Dynasty rice beer, which has *Aspergillus* fungus to thank for its color. In a way, these ancient fermented beverages are the equivalents of today's craft beers. By contrast, Japanese sakes are made from milled rice, a single yeast species, and ultrafine control of the brewing process.

At Jiahu, any one of these methods—chewing, malting, mold saccharification—might have been in vogue or some combination thereof. No matter how the rice was broken down, fermentation in the ancient jar might well have left a lot of debris (rice hulls, yeast, etc.) floating on the surface. The best way around that was to use a drinking-tube or straw, the time-honored method to drink a beer around the world. As yet, however, not a single drinking-tube has turned up at Jiahu, which might argue for their having improvised a filtration method.

THE EARLIEST HONEY MEAD TO THE FORE

MIDAS TOUCH MAY currently be the best-selling honey-based fermented beverage in the United States, but Jiahu's Neolithic grog, based on its chemical evidence, can lay claim to being the earliest mead in the world to date. In keeping with its heritage, China today is the largest producer of honey in the world with an annual production of over 500,000 tons. Turkey, where the Midas Tumulus is located, comes in second with about 110,000 tons.

Honey held a special place in Chinese history. As early as 770 B.C. at the start of the Eastern Zhou Dynasty, honey and bee larvae were considered a special food and reserved for the royal family. Jiahu was probably a more egalitarian society, but it, too, appears to have had a predilection for the sweet stuff. Possibly, the people there went beyond simply adding it to their extreme fermented beverage and already appreciated its many nuanced flavors and fragrances, imparted by the nectar and pollen of the country's many flowering and fruiting plants. For instance, Henan province, the largest honey-producing region in China today, is famous for its lotus flower honey. Each region has its speciality honeys, depending on what plants grow wild (or are now domesticated) and are exploited by the Asiatic honeybee (*Apis cerana*).

The Jiahu inhabitants might well have had an empirical knowledge of some of honey's medicinal and nutritional benefits. Honey is still a regular part of modern Chinese diet and traditional medicine. The *Compendium of Materia Medica* claims that it can "dispel pathogenic heat, clear away toxins, relieve pain and combat dehydration." Numerous Chinese desserts and entrées with honey are legendary.

BRINGING THE JIAHU EXTREME FERMENTED BEVERAGE BACK TO LIFE

WITH SUCH A wealth of information about the main ingredients that went into the Neolithic grog from Jiahu and given its long-standing cultural backdrop, I turned to Sam and his crew to resuscitate the extreme beverage in 2006. If ever there were an experimental brewer with a Neolithic flair for the exotic, Sam was it, so why go elsewhere?

The story of the re-creation of *Chateau Jiahu* also owes much to Mike Gerhardt, who is now the brewmaster at Otter Creek Brewery in Vermont. Although he had never done anything like it before, in one iteration of the re-creation, he started with a *qu* mold cake following the directions of my close colleague, Guangsheng Cheng, a superb microbiologist. The cake was dissolved in about 20 liters of water and yielded a sour but aromatic liquid, smelling slightly of acetone. To this, Mike added rice malt of milled medium-grain rice, like that preferred by the sake brewers, together with gelatinized (steamed) rice with their flavorful hulls and bran intact. The mold cake caused an active breakdown of the rice starches to sugars. Because of the clumping of the rice, Mike struggled but managed to transfer the saccharified liquid to the boiling kettle. The final volume of liquid was about 600 liters.

About halfway through the boiling of the wort, the hawthorn fruit powder, which had been bought from an herbal outlet in the state of Washington, went into the kettle. It has a grapey taste and chalky consistency, which is strangely different but intriguing. American wildflower honey was dumped in at the same time. Near the end of the boil, Mike put in about half a pound of dried chrysanthemum flowers, which I had procured from a traditional Chinese medicine shop in Philadelphia's Chinatown.

The wort was then transferred to the fermentation tank, where we took a shortcut, probably not available to the Jiahu fermented-beverage makers. Instead of gambling on yeast in the honey or on the fruits to start and carry out the fermentation, we added some dry sake yeast. Finally, we added some Muscat grape syrup from California.

This experiment was successful in producing an alcoholic beverage, but one too heavily dominated by hawthorn and not sweet enough. Our assumption was that early humans, who had very limited sugar resources, would have preferred a sweeter beverage.

So, we moved on to other experiments. When I proposed to Sam that chewing was the most likely saccharification method in Neolithic times, he immediately agreed to have a go. When I followed up by saying that the modern world might not be ready for this method, we put that experiment on hold until we made our *Chicha* (Chapter 8).

After various experimental fits and starts, we settled on the following ingredients for our re-creation:

1) Hawthorn fruit. Rumor had it that the fresh fruit was allowed by the FDA but prohibited by the TTB, presenting us with a predicament. We ended up playing it safe and used only the dry powder, which passed muster with governmental regulations and potentially expensive legal complications.
2) Muscat grapes. We have not yet been able to obtain and import wild native grapes from China, but *Midas Touch* had taught us of the heritage and delights of this grape.
3) Orange blossom honey. We have tried in vain to import native

honey from China (whether lotus or wildflower). We do know that the genetic cross that led to the modern sweet orange was accomplished by Chinese "horticulturalists" as early as 314 B.C., according to literary sources, so we decided to use that honey.

4) Gelatinized rice malt with hulls and bran, in keeping with probable ancient practice.

We could not be sure what herbs, if any, had been added to the brew in the Neolithic period, so we kept that part simple: we didn't use any. If we discover some plant additive by future analyses, we can revisit that decision.

All the ingredients were then brewed together with an American ale yeast to a 10–12% alcohol content, the assumption being that, like *Midas Touch*, the chemical results were uniformly consistent from one vessel to the next and that the alcohol level should be the average of a combined wine, mead, and rice beer (probably higher than a barley or wheat beer). Fermentation proceeded for 12 days, followed by 50 days of ageing and conditioning in the tank and bottle at room temperature (3–4 days) and subsequently at a cold temperature of 35°F.

When you pop open a bottle and pour *Chateau Jiahu*, you are greeted with a fine carbonated mousse (head foam), almost like champagne, due to rice proteins. As you smell and taste the beverage, you will note a marked sweet-and-sour profile, which goes well with Chinese cuisine today and presumably in the distant past at Jiahu. We ended up reassured that we had a reasonable and tasty facsimile to what the ancient Jiahu fermented beverage-maker was after.

Sam came up with the image on the label, based on a dream he had. What appears to be a roaring twenties flapper of Asian heritage and with short-cropped hair, elegantly holding a champagne flute, clearly pushes the envelope visually, as does the extreme fermented beverage inside the bottle. When pressed, he has refused to provide more details of his dream.

The deep brooding yellow color of the drink is symbolic of the Chinese emperor, beginning with the legendary founder of Chinese civilization, the Yellow Emperor Huangdi. The seemingly enigmatic tattoo that graces the lower back of our celebrant on the bottle is in fact the Chinese sign for "wine" and alcoholic beverages generally. It shows a jar with three drops of liquid falling from its lip. The logogram dates back to the Shang Dynasty and has been in continuous use ever since.

Chateau Jiahu took the drinking public by storm when it went on the market. Even in China, where it hadn't been tasted, the newspaper *Xinhua* gave such prominence to the scientific finding of the Jiahu alcoholic beverage—the world's earliest—that my microbiological colleague in Beijing, Guangsheng, wrote to say that "you are now a celebrity of the CCP—the Chinese Communist Party."

My superstar status diminished when editorials began appearing that complained about an American company "stealing" the ancient recipe and making money from a Chinese invention. I pointed out that most of my co-authors on the Jiahu paper, published in the prestigious *Proceedings of the National Academy of Sciences USA*, were well-respected scholars and scientists, all famous in their own right. Nearly half, six of the co-authors, were from mainland China. Our results had been published for the world to see and marvel at early Chinese innovation. Anyone could read the paper and learn more by doing their own "experimental archaeology" to bring the ancient beverage back to life.

Any hard feelings then have now been smoothed over. At the 2013 Jiahu conference, I ceremoniously presented two bottles of *Chateau Jiahu* to the assembled scientists and political dignitaries. Perhaps someday it will be imported there. An even better solution would be for a Chinese company to produce its own version of the Jiahu Neolithic grog by experimental archaeology. Using wholly native ingredients and microorganisms, such a beverage could well surpass ours in authenticity and deliciousness. Either way, this extreme fermented beverage deserves to be served in its homeland, especially at the site of Jiahu. Our shamanistic spirits demand as much!

MY FAVORITE RE-CREATION

I AM OFTEN asked what my favorite re-created *Ancient Ale* is. I usually stammer some, and say I like them all. But if I had to choose, *Chateau*

Jiahu is my odds-on favorite. It's not just that it's the oldest chemically confirmed alcoholic beverage in the world. It's also because of something that happened at the 2009 Great American Beer Festival (GABF) in Denver, the largest and most celebrated beer gathering in the world. I was there at the invitation of my editor, Blake Edgar of the University of California press, which had published *Uncorking the Past*. Dogfish Head also happened to be serving up many of the *Ancient Ales* at its booth, including the first version of the chewed *Chicha* (Chapter 8), which I helped to pour out for the curious to taste. Spit was no deterrent to the masses, who lined up across the civic center. The crowd was so large that the Big Three brewing companies at the time, which controlled most of the beer market, complained that no one could get to their booths.

As I signed copies of my book in the authors' room, the blind tasting awards were being handed out. Word came that *Chateau Jiahu* had taken gold in the specialty honey beer category. Sam and I quickly made our way to the podium, where no less than the homebrewer incarnate, Charlie Papazian, presented us with the award. Sam, who already had numerous medals, turned to me and draped the Jiahu medal around my neck. Back in Philadelphia, I set up a small shrine in my office. The medal now adorns a bottle of *Chateau Jiahu* with the enigmatic lady of Sam's dreams on its label. Several of the 9000-year-old sherds, which we analyzed, keep her company. Every morning when I enter my lab, I bow to the shrine and gain inspiration for the day.

RECIPES

Homebrew Interpretation of
Chateau Jiahu

by Doug Griffith (based on McGovern, 2009/2010)

INGREDIENTS

5 gallons	Cool water	60 minutes
4 pounds	Extra light or light dry malt extract	60 minutes
2 pounds	Rice syrup solids	60 minutes
½ pound	Dried hawthorn berries	During boil
¼ ounce	Simcoe hops	10 minutes
½ ounce	Sweet orange peel	10 minutes
3 pounds	Honey	End of boil
1 packet	Fermentis Safbrew Abbaye, White Labs WLP530 Abbey Ale, or Wyeast 4134 Sake	Fermentation
½ quart	White grape concentrate	Day 2 of fermentation
1 cup	Priming sugar	Bottling
	Bottles and caps	Bottling

Starting gravity: 1.088
Final gravity: 1.015
Final target alcohol by volume: 8.5%
International Bittering Units: 10
Finished volume: 5 gallons

PROCESS

N.B.: IF using the liquid yeast, we recommend making a starter 24 hours before brewing to maximize yeast cell counts.

1. Fill a brewpot with the 5 gallons water and bring to a boil.
2. As the water is beginning to boil, remove the pot from the heat.
3. Add the dry malt extract and rice syrup solids. Stir to prevent clumping and scorching on the bottom of the pot. Return the pot to the heat.
4. Allow the wort to come to a boil, and boil for 30 minutes. If using defoamer to help prevent boilovers, add per instructions.
5. While the wort is boiling, put the hawthorn berries in a blender, cover with wort (liquid from the brewpot— caution: hot), and carefully purée.
6. At the 30-minute mark of the 1-hour boil, add the puréed hawthorn berries. Boil for 30 more minutes.
7. 50 minutes into the boil, add the Simcoe hops and orange peel.
8. At the 60-minute mark, turn off the heat. Add the honey. Stir the wort for 2 minutes while building up a whirlpool effect. Stop stirring and allow the wort to sit for 10 minutes.
9. Chill the wort with a wort chiller or in a cold water bath until it is under 75°F.
10. Transfer the wort into a fermenter; aerate (rock the baby) for 1 minute.
11. Pitch the yeast into the fermenter.
12. Top up the fermenter to the 5-gallon mark with cool water.
13. On the second day of fermentation, add the white grape concentrate.
14. In about 14 days, the beer should be ready to bottle. It can

be siphoned to a 5-gallon carboy to allow extra time for clearing if desired, for about 7 days.

15. Before bottling, clean and sanitize the bottles and caps and create a priming solution of 1 cup boiling water and the priming sugar.

16. Siphon the beer into a sterilized bottling bucket, add the water-diluted priming solution, and gently stir. Bottle and cap the beer.

17. Allow the beer to condition for another 10 days at 70 to 75°F; it should then be ready to drink.

MEAL PAIRING FOR *Chateau Jiahu*

Although we lack direct chemical evidence of the foods that might have accompanied *Chateau Jiahu*, my favorite Chinese dish, after many trips to China, is spicy tofu. My microbiologist colleague, Guangsheng Cheng, taught me to enjoy the delights of many kinds of tofu, including "stinky tofu" in the town of Shaoxing where legend has it rice wine was discovered. Tofu is a processed, often fermented, food made from soybeans, and one of the first domesticated plants of China.

At home, my wife makes a scrumptious spicy tofu entrée. Her recipe is based on that of *Martin Yan's Feast: The Best of Yan Can Cook* (1998). It differs from Christopher's recipe below by adding ham, which would fit with the earliest domesticated pig remains in China having been excavated at Jiahu. She omits the vegetables of Christopher's recipe, except for the black beans, and rather than preparing a sauce, she sears the tofu after cooking up the other ingredients in light oil. The spicy tofu pairs extremely well with the sweet-and-sour taste profile of the re-created beverage.

Spicy Tofu

by Christopher Ottosen

Serves 4

INGREDIENTS

14 ounces extra-firm tofu

Asian vegetables, depending on availability and amount
    desired, including Asian cabbage—such as bok choy,
    choy sum, and pei tsai—snow peas, amaranth leaves,
    Chinese leeks or garlic, parsley, baby leaf greens, broccoli,
    cucumbers, kale, spinach, and others

1 tablespoon tamari sauce

1 tablespoon rice or black vinegar

1 tablespoon fresh mandarin zest, grated

1 tablespoon cinnamon, ground

1 tablespoon fresh ginger root, grated

1 teaspoon fennel seeds, ground

1 teaspoon gentian root,[*] ground

½ teaspoon Sichuan pepper, ground

½ teaspoon cloves, ground

½ teaspoon anise seed, ground

Pinch of salt

Fermented black bean sauce (recipe follows)

PREPARATION

PRESS THE WATER out of the tofu block by placing on a sieve over a
bowl, covering with a plate, and setting a heavy object (such as a can)

---

[*] Online resource: http://www.herbco.com/p-763-gentian-root-cs-wild-crafted
.aspx

on top. Wait at least 1 hour. Slice the tofu into rectangular- or square-shaped pieces. For a standard block, three slices lengthwise and width-wise is usually best. Chop up the vegetables to the same size as the tofu pieces. In a small bowl, mix the tamari sauce and the rice or black vinegar with the mandarin zest and spices. Fry the tofu gently in canola or sunflower oil in a wok or pan. After browning the tofu on all sides, add the spice mixture, vegetables, and fermented black bean sauce to the pan. Cook until the vegetables are tender, about 5 minutes. Serve with roasted red rice (see recipe at http://www.penn.museum/mcgovern/ancientbrews/).

Fermented Black Bean Sauce

INGREDIENTS

3 heaping teaspoons (3½ ounces) fermented black beans
    (Chinese, *douche*), or make your own (recipe follows)
1 teaspoon garlic, minced
1 onion, minced
1 teaspoon fresh mandarin orange zest, grated
1 teaspoon fresh ginger, grated
1 teaspoon gentian root, ground
1 tablespoon rice wine or mirin
1 tablespoon soy or tamari sauce
1 tablespoon sweet bean or hoisin sauce
1 cup chicken stock
½ cup *Chateau Jiahu* or homebrew interpretation

PREPARATION

RINSE THE BEANS with cold water through a sieve. Sauté the garlic and onion in canola or sunflower oil, avoiding the development of any color. Add the mandarin zest, ginger, and gentian root and continue gently heating. Add the fermented black beans, rice wine, soy sauce, and sweet bean sauce. Then add the chicken stock and *Chateau Jiahu* or homebrew interpretation. Simmer for 10 to 15 minutes. Mix well with a blender or food processor, on low for 30 seconds, then at full speed for 2 minutes. Season with more soy or tamari sauce and rice wine or mirin, as desired, for more intense flavors. Strain through a fine sieve or serve as is.

Fermented Black Beans

INGREDIENTS

   7 ounces black beans, dried or canned
   1 quart water
   1 quart cultured brine from a batch of lacto-fermented
      vegetables (see Fermented Daikon or Asian Radish recipe,
      below)

PREPARATION

SOAK THE BEANS for 24 hours at room temperature (they will double in size). Change the water after 12 hours. Cook the beans in the water until tender. Strain the beans, cool, and remove their skins by hand. If you want to give the beans added taste, mix them with the same spice mixture as that for the spicy tofu (page 81). Add the beans to a sterilized jar, and pour the cultured brine to its top. Seal the jar.

   Allow to ferment at room temperature for about a week, until fermentation has ceased (i.e., no more bubbling) or at pH 3.3. Store in a cool, dark place—the longer, the better.

Fermented Daikon or Asian Radish

by Christopher Ottosen

Serves 4

INGREDIENTS

6 teaspoons salt
1 quart unchlorinated water
Chinese leeks or garlic
Daikon or Asian radish (any color), thinly sliced
1 tube lactobacillus[*]

PREPARATION

DISSOLVE THE SALT in the water at room temperature. Cover the bottom of a pint glass jar with Chinese leeks or garlic. Fill two-thirds with radish slices. Fill the jar to the top with the salt water and add the lactobacillus. Seal the jar and leave it at room temperature for about a week. Open the lid every day to relieve the pressure. When gas buildup has stopped or at pH 3.3, seal and store the jar in a cool, dark place— the longer, the better.

For mood-enhancing atmospherics and more meal suggestions, go to: http://www.penn.museum/mcgovern/ancientbrews/.

---

[*] Online resource: http://www.northernbrewer.com/white-labs-wlp677 -lactobacillus-bacteria

4

Ta Henket: An Herbal Bomb for Our Gregarious African Ancestors

L et us now return to where humankind first began making alcoholic beverages: Africa. As fate would have it, Sam and I started our extreme fermented beverage odyssey around the world in the Near East with our Iron Age *Midas Touch*. It paved the way for other *Ancient Ales*, and taught us what was possible when you had a plethora of excellent archaeological, chemical, botanical, historical, and ethnographic data from which to work. *Chateau Jiahu*, our second re-created beverage of early Neolithic date, showed us that we could go back 9000 years and still have well-preserved containers with intact organic compounds from well-excavated archaeological contexts. Yet, as I lamented earlier, we still have a long way to go in resuscitating a Dino-Brew or even a Palaeo-Brew from our ancestors' "homeland" continent. Africa deserves a closer look before we continue following our ancestors in their quest for extreme fermented beverages across the Mediterranean and northward into Europe, and then travel to the New World.

I proposed earlier that our African forebears were quite likely making every kind of extreme fermented beverage right from the start of our species' appearance on this planet, based on the inherent probability of the "Palaeolithic" and "Drunken Monkey" hypotheses. I pointed out that more sensitive scientific instruments and more archaeological investigation were needed to be certain. But how far back in time can we go in Africa at present, to get a better scientific handle on what humans were making and enjoying, and then bring it back to life?

Sam and I really pushed the envelope with our *Ta Henket* (ancient Egyptian, "bread-beer") extreme fermented beverage. We did not base our re-creation on a single archaeological site with strong scientific evidence as we have done with nearly all our drinks. We relied instead on three early sites of different time periods in southern Egypt: 18,000-year-old Wadi Kubbaniya of the Upper Palaeolithic period, 8000-year-old Nabta Playa of the Neolithic period, and the 5000-year-old tomb of King Scorpion I at Abydos. We based our reconstruction on the preserved archaeobotanical and archaeological remains at the two prehistoric sites, and these lines of evidence combined with chemical data for the Scorpion I tomb. The final ingredients for our very "mixed" beverage thus span some 13,000 years and take us back as far as we can go presently in reimagining an extreme fermented beverage for Egypt or Africa as a whole, earlier even than the Jiahu grog. The unusual genesis of this beverage took shape in our heads in the raucous, chaotic Khan el-Khalili bazaar in old Cairo during a TV show, as you will see. It came to reality in the small experimental brewing facility of Dogfish Head's Rehoboth brewpub.

ASSEMBLING THE EVIDENCE

WHEN YOU THINK of archaeology, especially for Africa, Egypt immediately springs to mind. How many children have been enthralled by mummies and dreamed of becoming archaeologists, or how many adults are Indiana Jones wannabes? I never engaged in such fantasies and came to archaeology when I was around 25 years old and in search of my "origins." The University of Pennsylvania, with its well-excavated archaeological collections from around the world in the Penn Museum, was the perfect place to pursue this goal. I could combine my love of languages, the humanities, and natural sciences in a Ph.D. program that spanned the globe—from our origins in Africa to the beginnings of civilization in the Old World and New World.

Penn has a long tradition of excavating in Egypt, going back to the 19th century, so it was quite natural for me to take a minor in Egyptology. Because of the desert climate, its archaeological remains—including detailed artwork, very early texts, and, above all, organic remains—were unparalleled and preserved like few other parts of the world. I sought to learn more about the first documented presence of humans there, about 700,000 years ago, to the end of the pharaonic period around 30 B.C., when Cleopatra stirred the passions of the Roman world.

The prehistoric sites of Wadi Kubbaniya and Nabta Playa, excavated by Fred Wendorf, are located about 200 kilometers (125 miles) apart in the southern Egyptian desert—an extension of the great Sahara Desert—near the town of Aswan.

At Wadi Kubbaniya, a seasonal Palaeolithic encampment of hunters and gatherers, Wendorf found numerous grinding stones with grains of starch embedded in their surfaces. Some kind of plant tuber had been crushed, possibly bulrush, which was a great favorite at the time and later. But to what end? Could the grinding of the tuber have been intended as a preparatory step before chewing the plant and spitting it out to make a fermented beverage, such as we have already observed and hypothesized about for prehistoric Israel and China and as we will see later was also common in the New World?

The archaeological remains at Nabta Playa are equally thought-provoking. Here, our ancestors had settled down during the Neolithic period by building 20 small huts, probably of brush, on the edge of a large lake. Nearby, what are believed to be the earliest megalithic astronomical structures in the world lie exposed in the desert. One circle of stones (structure A) looks eerily like Stonehenge in southern England but is dated 2000 years earlier. The monoliths might have marked the first light of the sun during the summer solstice, which preceded the summer monsoons and brought new life to the land. If so, we may be witnessing the beginnings of Egyptian religion.

Numerous cattle burial mounds further suggest that the goddess, Hathor, who is later depicted either as a cow or anthropomorphically with a headdress of a solar disk set between cow's horns, might have been a principal deity at Nabta Playa. We cannot be certain because we are in a preliterate period. In later periods, Hathor was celebrated in a major festival called the "Drunkenness of Hathor" at the temple of Dendera, about 300 kilometers (185 miles) north along the Nile. This annual celebration coincides with the yearly inundation of the river during summer. Its inspiration is taken from an ancient story of Hathor changing into her feline form as the lioness goddess, Sekhmet, to carry out the dictates of Ra, the sun-god, to destroy humanity.

Just in time, Ra relents and fills the Nile and its flooded fields with "red beer." Hathor lapped up the alcoholic brew, became drunk, and assumed that the red beer meant that she had already carried out her gruesome task. The story fits with the Nile becoming reddish during the inundation due to iron-rich soils being washed from upstream. Hathor was called "the mistress of drunkenness." One can conjecture that her "holy intoxication" was meant to facilitate communication between the gods, ancestors, and the living, similar to the role of the shaman in ancient Chinese ritual.

Thus far, no clear-cut chemical evidence for a fermented beverage has been obtained at Nabta Playa. Our several analyses were inconclusive. The wealth of archaeobotanical remains, however, from storage pits, fireplaces, wells, and pit floors—running into the tens of thousands of specimens—holds out promise for future testing.

The principal cereals of east Africa, sorghum and millet, are well represented at the site. Sorghum, in particular, is today the basic staple and a great favorite of the "sorghum beer belt," which follows the semi-arid Sahel across Africa from the Red Sea to the Atlantic Ocean. Nabta Playa, where the cereal might well have been domesticated, could be where brewing of sorghum began.

Sorghum beer, besides its nutritional value, was and continues to be central to the economic, social, and religious life of the eastern Sahel. You can still see women chewing the grain and spitting it out in the age-old method of making the beer; this technique, however, is unattested in pharaonic Egypt. The cereal is also made into a fermented dough, which goes into heavy porridges and dumplings. Since sorghum lacks gluten, it cannot be made into bread, thus distinguishing sub-Saharan Africa from the Middle East with its barley and wheats.

Of another 40 plants found at Nabta Playa, the following stand out as excellent substrates and/or adjuncts for a fermented beverage: bulrush (*Scirpus*), *Rumex* (a dock or sorrel herb in the buckwheat family), legumes, *Setaria* (bristlegrass), mustard, caper, fruits and seeds of *Ziziphus* (a tree in the buckthorn family, which includes Chinese date or jujube), and various unidentified tubers. Besides bulrush roots, brittlegrass, legumes, and the other tubers would have been good candidates for grinding and salivating. *Ziziphus* fruit is very sweet, so it would ferment naturally.

The much earlier site of Wadi Kubbaniya had its own suite of botanicals to add to a potential alcoholic beverage, still to be confirmed. Besides bulrush, several unidentified wild grains and tubers were noted, together with chamomile, water lily (*Nymphaea* sp.), and fruits of the dom palm (*Hyphaene thebaica*), which has an especially high sugar content that would have been ideal for fermentation. The sap of palm trees was also historically made into a fermented beverage, as is still done today in tropical Somalia and Djibouti.

WINE AND BEER FOR ETERNITY

IN 1988, WHEN the German archaeological team, under the direction of Günter Dreyer of the German Institute of Archaeology in Cairo, opened up the tomb (designated U-j) of Scorpion I of Dynasty 0 (ca. 3150 B.C.), one of the first rulers of ancient Egypt at Abydos, they must have been dumbstruck at what they had uncovered. Abydos, about 400 kilometers (250 miles) north of Aswan, was one of the first capitals of Upper Egypt and considered home to Osiris, the god of the dead, resurrection, and fertility. The site has produced more than its share of spectacular finds. Moreover, if you combine Osiris's so-called *Wag*-festival to celebrate the inundation, an orgy lasting for three days at Abydos, with Hathor's festival of "Drunkenness" a day later, you have the makings for a deluge of fermented beverages. We already know what royal funerary wakes like that of Midas or Gordias can lead to: a lot of drinking.

Scorpion I's tomb was built as a "model funerary palace" in which the chambers were interconnected by very narrow 20-centimeter (8-inch) wide slits through which only spirits of the dead were thought to pass. Its foundations had been dug about 2.5 meters (8 feet) into the desert sand, and, after the burial, its rooms were roofed and covered over with a mound of sand. The German team arrived over 5000 years later to find the tomb undisturbed. The burial goods, especially those made of organic materials, were extremely well preserved, owing to the dry, hot climate.

As the excavators opened up one room after another, it was as if they had discovered a time capsule from the very beginning of dynastic Egypt. The large burial chamber at the back of the tomb held the remains of a wooden shrine on which the king was laid out with his ivory scepter at his side. The other rooms were stacked high with goods—bread loaves and the molds from which they were made, cedar boxes filled with clothes, stone vessels for oils and fats, and, most important for our purposes, over a thousand large pottery jars containing wine and beer, to sustain the king in the afterlife.

The likely beer jars, based on their stylistic similarity to later Egyptian examples, were well represented in the corpus. Analyses remain to be carried out. As beer was the principal fermented beverage throughout Egypt's history, an adequate supply of this beverage for the afterlife was crucial to king and commoner alike. Abydos even had one of the earliest and largest beer-mashing installations of any excavated site of the time in Egypt.

The floors of some chambers in the tomb were littered with perforated plaques of bone and ivory, especially in the vicinity of the stone vessels. The plaques bore what are reputedly the earliest Egyptian hieroglyphs, including a realistic rendering of a scorpion, which designated the name of the king. They are most likely labels of the content or claims or receipts of ownership, which had once been tied by rope to the jars, since disintegrated.

I was most intrigued by the approximately 700 pottery jars of foreign type in three chambers on the northeastern side of the tomb. They were stacked from floor to ceiling, one layer above another. Each jar had a capacity of about 7–8 liters, so if the jars were originally full, they would have held about 4500 liters (1200 gallons) of liquid.

The jars had filled with sand. Slanted rings of a yellowish crusty residue were revealed on the interiors of the jars once the sand was poured out. The rings are best explained as "tide-lines" that mark the surface of a liquid. As the liquid gradually evaporated over time, it left behind solids that had been floating on the surface. If a jar had moved, its ring was slanted from the horizontal. Residue had also accumulated on the bases where other solids in the liquid had settled.

What did these vessels originally contain, and where had they come from? The director of the excavation, Günter Dreyer, and his pottery specialist, Ulrich Hartung, contacted me in 1993 to find out more about the mysterious jars.

We began by testing the yellowish residues inside three jars by our standard battery of analyses in search of biomarkers for possible natural products. Once we had the data in hand, we sat back and took another look. There was little doubt that tartaric acid, the fingerprint compound for the Eurasian grape, was present in the residues. When expressed as a liquid, grapes readily ferment to wine in the Middle East.

We were surprised by this result. The royal Egyptian winemaking industry wasn't established in the Nile Delta until several hundred years after Scorpion I, around 3000 B.C. Moreover, the wild grapevine (*Vitis vinifera sylvestris*) had never grown in the arid climate of Egypt. If our results held up, we had likely discovered the earliest grape wine in Egypt.

We needed to take our analyses a step further by retesting the residues for tartaric acid in parts per billion by the most sensitive method yet available: LC-MS-MS (Preface). But, as a poorly funded museum laboratory, we didn't have such sophisticated instrumentation. Usually, we then reach out to better endowed colleagues. This time it was different. The Scientific Services Laboratory of the TTB came calling in 2005 when its director, Abdul Mabud, and his fellow scientists invited us to their laboratory in Beltsville, Maryland. Drawing upon the tax money generated by the sale of alcoholic beverages in the United States, the TTB lab is one of the best equipped in the country, with row upon row of GC-MSs and all the latest scientific gadgetry. The TTB scientists had caught wind of our groundbreaking research on ancient fermented beverages and wanted to learn more. They were ready to help in whatever way they could.

Help they did. Soon we were on our way to rigorously retesting the Scorpion I residues and initiating many other biomolecular archaeological projects. One TTB scientist in particular, Armen Mirzoian, stepped in to coordinate and carry out the analyses. He was clearly the right person for the job, since he was from Armenia, which is known for its ancient wines and now has the distinction of having the earliest wine-making facility in the world at Areni, where its finest wine is still made today. Armen was passionate about both ancient and modern wine. He personally retested the Scorpion I samples. The result was unequivocal: tartaric acid was present. We did have the earliest wine in Egypt.

Now that we were convinced that the jars contained wine, we wanted to know where such a huge quantity of wine had been made and how it had ended up in Scorpion I's tomb. Clues to its origin were the unusual shapes, decorations, and manufacturing details of the jars that were foreign to Egypt. The beer jars of Egyptian type, for example, lacked handles and were minimally decorated. The wine jars usually had a pair of handles and were decorated in dramatic fashion in red paint on white surfaces. One swirling design called "tiger-stripes" was alien to Egypt. But this type and the others were known from sites in the Jordan Valley, near the Dead Sea, and in the vicinity of Gaza along the Mediterranean, the closest settled area in the southern Levant to Egypt.

Stylistic comparisons can be misleading, since a potter in one place may imitate the style of a potter elsewhere. Future excavations in Egypt might even yield more such wine jars from sites other than Abydos, suggesting that they were a native Egyptian product.

Chemical analysis again stepped in to provide the answer. We employed instrumental neutron activation analysis, in collaboration with colleagues at the University of Missouri Research Reactor in Columbia. By measuring as many as 35 chemical elements, especially the rare earths, and applying very powerful statistical techniques, we were able to show to a 99 percent probability that the wine jars from the Scorpion I tomb were made of the same clays as those found in the Jordan Valley, the Hill Country of the West Bank and Transjordan, and the Gaza region.

The correspondence between the stylistic and chemical findings could hardly be coincidental. At this early period, the Early Bronze Age I in the southern Levant, most pottery was being made in small, household workshops. The clay came from local beds. The conclusion was obvious: where the pottery was made was almost certainly where the wine inside the jars was made.

We were left with the question: Why had Scorpion I imported such a large quantity of wine to stock his tomb with—what might be called his "wine cellars for eternity?" He might have enjoyed the occasional good jar of Levantine wine during life, perhaps to flaunt his wealth and position, but why go to an extreme in death? Why not stick with readily available local beer, which was just as tasty and religiously important?

The answers to these questions probably have to do with "elite emulation" or, more understandably, "conspicuous consumption." Scorpion I's behavior was akin to what the wealthy do today when they order that $70,000 bottle of 1982 Pétrus from Bordeaux. Early Egyptian kings likely sought to imitate their Near Eastern counterparts, who had elevated wine above beer. Scorpion I would have known that rulers elsewhere celebrated their victories with special wine-drinking ceremonies, offered wine to the gods in their role as high priests as an evocative symbol of sacrificial blood, and stocked their palaces and tombs with the elixir. Wine and special wine-drinking sets were regularly exchanged between Near Eastern kings as gifts to seal treaties and royal marriages as well as to create goodwill and lend prestige to their rule. As a result, one king after another adopted wine, as well as associated social and religious elements, as the "wine culture" came their way.

Although it must have seemed like importing liquid gold, Scorpion I and other early Egyptian rulers followed suit and imported wine from the nearby Levant with its millennia-long experience in winemaking. Transport added to the cost because the jars of wine had to be carried overland by donkey and perhaps by boat about 700–800 kilometers (450–500 miles). Such a journey cannot have been good for the wine, which would have been jostled about, heated, and subjected to oxidation.

The Dynasty I kings who followed Scorpion I eventually solved the problems of rugged transport and the high cost of importing wine. They established a royal winemaking industry in the Nile Delta around 3000 B.C., probably by commissioning the same people who had supplied Scorpion I with his wine—the Canaanites, a Semitic people—to lay out the first vineyards in the Delta and to provide the all-important vinicultural expertise to tend the grapes and make the wine.

A homegrown industry had the advantage of providing much more wine on a regular basis at lower cost and tailored to local tastes. The Delta with its extensive tracts of irrigated land, sunny days, and short rainy season was ideal for grape-growing. Egyptian tomb reliefs of winemaking—unique in the ancient world—show how advanced the industry was at this early date, with carefully tended vines, grape-stomping installations, and pottery jars or amphoras for fermenting and storing the wine. The vessels were sealed with clay stoppers that recorded the year of the pharaoh and sometimes the location of the winery in the Delta: the world's first wine labels.

The Delta winemaking industry was still in the future, after the country was united under Pharaoh Narmer, the first king of the First Dynasty. Scorpion I, who ruled earlier in southern Egypt in Dynasty o, had to import all his wine from the Levant. As the earliest wine yet found in Egypt and a measure of the Levantine industry, it deserved a closer look.

TREE RESIN, HERB, AND FRUIT ADJUNCTS

OUR CHEMICAL ANALYSES showed that Scorpion I's wine had been resinated with pine and probably terebinth tree saps, based on characteristic diterpenoid and triterpenoid compounds (unsaturated and cyclic hydrocarbons). We have found that most ancient grape wines from Neolithic times up until the medieval period were resinated, most likely because tree resins have antioxidant properties that prevent wine from turning to vinegar, or failing that, they cover up off-aromas and off-tastes. Indeed, tree resins are so prevalent in ancient wines that their presence provides corroborative evidence that the intended product was wine. Strangely, the only carryover of the ancient practice today is Greek *retsina*, although heavily oaked wines also fall into the same category.

We took our chemical analyses one step further with Armen and the TTB laboratory by using SPME coupled to GC-MS (Preface) to analyze the Scorpion I residues. This technique is better able to detect lower molecular weight, volatile compounds. For instance, we identified various alcohols, acids, esters, and aldehydes, which are commonly found in grape wine. We were surprised that they had survived the passage of more than 5000 years.

Beyond these simpler, less definitive compounds, the Scorpion I wine was also laced with herbs, as evidenced by an array of more complex monoterpenes, including linalool, camphor, borneol, L-menthol, alpha-terpineol, carvone, thymol, geranyl acetone, and others. By extensive searching of the chemical literature to find the natural products, which explained the most monoterpenes, we were able to show that the most likely herbs included savory (*Satureja*), *Artemisia seibeni* (a member of the wormwood family), blue tansy (*Tanacetum annuum*), balm (*Melissa*), senna (*Cassia*), coriander (*Coriandrum*), germander (*Teucrium*), mint (*Mentha*), sage (*Salvia*), and thyme (*Thymus/ Thymbra*).

Significantly, most of these herbs are native to the southern Levant where we proposed that the wine in Scorpion I's tomb originated. Only three herbs (savory, senna, and sage) are possibly native to Egypt, with the emphasis on *possibly*. All the herbs in the wine could well have come from the Levant.

Whole specimens of fruit were also recovered from the jars. Remarkable in their own right in having been preserved for 5000 years, they bore out some of our chemical findings and additionally shed new light on ancient Levantine winemaking. The fruit included numerous raisins, together with seeds and skins. Apparently, the wine was not finely filtered, perhaps to further extract aromatic and bitter compounds.

The most unusual finding was that several jars contained a single desiccated fig, unique for winemaking in both the ancient and modern worlds. Each had been sliced and had a central hole. The excavators conjecture that the figs were suspended by strings from the mouths of the vessels down into the wine, allowing more contact with the fruit. The figs might well have served as a sweetening agent, special flavoring, or to provide additional yeast for fermentation. There may be another, less pragmatic reason: we read in the Old Kingdom Pyramid

Texts, "The king shall make his meal from figs and wine which are in the garden of the god." By having a wine laced with figs, the dead king was assured of a fully sanctified repast in the afterlife.

A WINE FOR ALL TIME

THE CHEMICAL AND archaeobotanical arguments for the Scorpion I jars containing wine is further buttressed by archaeological evidence. For example, the Scorpion I jars were probably fired to a high temperature, up to 700° C, which would have fused the clay particles and minimized oxygen diffusing through the walls of the vessels. Some oxygen for nourishing the yeast and mellowing out the harsh tannins of a wine is good, but too much can lead to the bane of all winemakers and drinkers—turning perfectly good wine into perfectly good vinegar.

Even more important for preserving wine is to have a tight closure in the mouth of the vessel. Remember that we're in a time before glass bottles and corks. Instead, ancient winemakers usually made do with unfired clay stoppers, sometimes stuffing grass or fabric into the neck of the vessel, then covering the opening with a pottery sherd, and sealing the top with clay. Vintners had used this technique since about 3000 B.C., as shown in tomb reliefs.

The Scorpion I wine jars, imported from the southern Levant, were likely closed in another way. Numerous clay seals were scattered around the jars. Their backs had impressions of jar rims and strings. The upper surfaces of the seals displayed finely cut cylinder seal impressions of non-Egyptian designs, including free-flowing renditions of antelope, fish, birds, snakes, and other animals combined with geometric patterns. Cylinder seals were usually made of stone, incised in reverse or mirror image, so that when they were impressed into moist clay, they produced the intended design. The cylinder seals had evidently been rolled over the clay seals when wet and after they had been pressed on a string that held down a cover, probably of leather, over the mouth of each vessel. When the strings and covers disintegrated, the seals loosened and fell to the ground.

A thorough search of the archaeological literature revealed no exact matches for the cylinder seal designs, but the closest parallels pointed again to the northern Jordan Valley and the eastern shore of the Dead Sea. Perhaps the animals signified wine estates in the southern Levant or a specific kind of wine. We may never know.

A YEAST FOR THE AGES

YET ANOTHER CHEMICAL detail—this time from the arena of molecular biology—made it virtually certain that the Scorpion I jars contained wine. If the starting grape juice in the jars had indeed been fermented, then yeast, if preserved, should be present. In a joint project, our colleagues at the universities of Florence, Harvard, and California at Berkeley took residue samples we had chemically analyzed and tested them for yeasts.

Intact strands of DNA, which were 840 base pairs in length, were recovered from the samples—some of the longest fragments of ancient DNA ever recovered. The sequence of base pairs was nearly identical to the ribosomal region of chromosome 12 of the modern wine yeast, *Saccharomyces cerevisiae*. Only five insertions or deletions of base pairs of the ancient strand differed from its modern counterpart, suggesting that this ancient Egyptian yeast could be a precursor of the principal wine yeast today. Much more research, especially of Near Eastern yeasts, is needed to reconstruct a "domesticated" yeast lineage, possibly including beer and bread (baker) yeasts. It remains a hotly contested issue.

Our colleagues estimated that the Scorpion I jars originally contained as much as 12 milligrams of yeast DNA, enough to have caused a very active fermentation. This was an important piece of evidence, because any ethanol, which might have proven that the grape juice had fermented, had long since evaporated and disappeared.

We believe that the ancestral *Saccharomyces cerevisiae*, perhaps in combination with other fungi and bacteria, was directly responsible for producing the alcohol of the wine in the Scorpion I jars. Intriguingly, one of these fungi, yet to be scientifically classified, was also recovered from the clothing of the Iceman in the Italian Alps, dating to about the same time as the Scorpion I wine.

ARCHAEOLOGICAL ONCOLOGY AND MEDICINE: DIGGING FOR DRUG DISCOVERY

THE BOTANICALS AND fruits in the Scorpion I wine had yet another story to tell about how fermented beverages were likely the universal medicine of humankind for millennia. The herbs and associated compounds that we chemically identified in the Scorpion I wine provided the earliest chemical evidence for a medicinal preparation from ancient Egypt.

We know from medical papyri and botanical remains found in tombs over a thousand years later than the tomb of Scorpion I that Egyptian doctors had an extensive *materia medica* at their disposal. This corpus was to grow into one of the most comprehensive and detailed in the world. Among more than a thousand prescriptions in the medical papyri, the most numerous are those that list alcoholic beverages—wine and beer—as the dispensing agents, whether by drinking them or applying them to the skin. The organic compounds of tree resins (terebinth, pine, frankincense, myrrh, fir, etc.) and numerous herbs (including many of those detected in the Scorpion I wine) were more easily dissolved in an alcoholic beverage than in water. The botanicals and their exudates were macerated, mixed together, and then steeped in the liquids. The medications treated ailments of all kinds, and traditional Egyptian medicine today still uses many of the same formulations. The earliest Egyptian medical papyri date to circa 1850 B.C. It is reasonable to assume that Egyptian medicine has much earlier precedents, probably drawing on Canaanite practice in which Levantine herbs were added to wine, to account for the biomolecular and archaeobotanical evidence from the Scorpion I wine jars.

We've taken this inference about very early Egyptian medicine a step further. I began a project with colleagues at Penn's Abramson Cancer Center. This initiative came about in a very fortuitous way.

While flying to California, I sat next to a woman who was assiduously reading one xeroxed article after another. I couldn't help looking over her shoulder and noticing that one article was about recent brain research. I had spent some time studying this topic at the University of Rochester and had begun Ph.D. research on the transfer of neurotransmitters across cell membranes. I couldn't resist and casually asked her what she studied. She turned out to be Caryn Lerman, a psychology professor at Penn as well as deputy director of the Abramson Center. We soon got to talking and spent the remainder of flight in animated discussion.

On returning to Philadelphia, Caryn contacted me about providing seed money from Penn to study whether any of the ancient botanicals and their associated compounds, which we had detected in our ancient samples, had anticancer or other medicinal benefits. The basic premise of the project was that our ancestors, beginning millions of years ago in the Palaeolithic period, had a huge incentive in trying to find any cure they could for a disease, so as to extend their lives in an uncertain world. Over millennia, they might well have discovered effective remedies, even if they couldn't explain them scientifically. Superstitions might also creep in, but in some periods, like the Neolithic when many plants were domesticated, they might have gone through their environments and winnowed out the most effective botanicals. Those discoveries might then have been lost when the cultures collapsed and disappeared. Biomolecular archaeology could be called in to rediscover the lost remedies and, by limiting the number of botanicals to be studied, speed up the process of drug discovery. Caryn dubbed the new project "Archaeological Oncology: Digging for Drug Discovery (D^3)."

The project had great potential. For example, ancient Peruvian knowledge of the powerful antimalarial properties of quinine, derived from the bark of South American trees and shrubs (*Cinchona* spp.), led to its "discovery." Similarly, ancient Mesopotamian, Egyptian, and Greek texts provided the impetus for the isolation and eventual modification of salicylic acid from willow tree bark (*Salix* spp.) in the 19th century; acetylsalicylic acid (aspirin) is today the most widely used pharmaceutical palliative.

Soon we had a joint project going with the labs of Wafik El-Deiry and Melpo Christofidou-Solomidou in which cancer tissues were tested *in vitro*. Besides studying the remarkable anticancer effects of artemisinin (Chapter 3), we also discovered that the triterpenoid ursolic acid in thyme, one of the herbs that probably went into the Scorpion I fermented beverage, increased the presence of a crucial cell protein (p53), in turn causing colon cancer cells to die, especially under low oxygen (hypoxic) conditions.

DESCENDING INTO THE NETHERWORLD

THE RE-CREATION OF *Ta Henket* represented a new approach and adventure for Sam and me. We had a fair amount of scientific evidence for re-creating an extreme fermented beverage from late Palaeolithic, Neolithic, and Early Bronze Egypt, but it was spread out over 13,000 years at three separate archaeological sites. Despite questions of authenticity and feasibility, we decided to have a go at it. To obtain the raw materials and work out a reasonably legitimate recipe, we traveled to Egypt in September 2010 to film an episode of the show "Brew Masters." I had been to Egypt many times before, but never as part of a TV production. It was an odd, even exhilarating feeling to fly into the country as a prospective film star. Although the preparations for the shoot were intense, a TV show does not always rise to the standards of a scientific investigation.

To start with, Sam, Dogfish's head brewmaster at the time, Floris Delee, and I were asked to walk down an old Cairo back alley to introduce us to the audience. That scene ended up on the editing floor, as did much else. As the director Bengt Anderson explained to me, this was the nature of a "docu-business, reality TV" show. I understood what he meant later when I saw the finished video: instead of focusing more on the evidence for an ancient Egyptian re-creation, an episode about dumping an expensive batch of *Chateau Jiahu* down the drain took precedence.

We then went on a crazy, daredevil excursion through the crowded, narrow streets, with an Indiana Jones look-alike (fedora and all), Ramy

Romany, at the wheel. He reminded me of Short Round, the teenage taxicab driver in *Temple of Doom*, who was also "re-created" so successfully in our short film, "Burton Baton and the Legend of the Ancient Ale." Ramy also looked like a younger version of Zahi Hawass, who attended graduate school with me and has since become a star of Egyptian stage and screen, archaeologically speaking. Of course, this segment made it through the final cut.

Ramy also "chauffeured" us to our first shoot the next day. It was a stone's throw away from our hotel and the pyramids of Giza. Zahi and co-director Mark Lehner had excavated the 4500-year-old pyramid workers' village. The numerous large vats, bread molds, and beer jars from the site pointed to a combination "brewery-and-bakery" complex. Because Zahi was away in Spain and no one was allowed on the site in his absence, we could only look down on the village from the cliff above. I would have liked to have examined more closely the evidence for beer-making, especially since tantalizing issues of the ancient process had been raised.

We were able to conclude that the ancient foremen probably knew their workers well enough to have made sure that they didn't run out of beer. After a hard day's labor under the hot Egyptian sun, that liquid refreshment was essential. Otherwise, the foremen might have an uprising on their hands and might not have completed the massive building project. The rise of Egyptian civilization was on the line, and mass-producing beer was necessary to make it happen.

Ramy followed up with a high-speed ride to the mastaba tomb of Ti at Saqqara, about 16 kilometers (10 miles) south of the Giza pyramids. Ti, who lived during the Fifth Dynasty around 2450 B.C., went by many names: "Unique Friend" of the Pharaoh, "Director of the Hairdressers of the Great House," and "Overseer of the Pyramids." If you've never been to Egypt, you have a special thrill in store when you enter a tomb or pyramid. Ti's tomb, very close to the prototypical step pyramid designed by the famous architect Imhotep, is one of Saqqara's most splendidly decorated and well preserved.

We entered along a long passageway that led to a columned courtyard with surrounding rooms. The walls of the rooms were lined with vibrantly painted reliefs from floor to ceiling showing detail after detail of Ti's estates: workers with sickles cutting barley in the fields to the accompaniment of a flute player; people butchering animals; fishermen pulling their nets through the marshes; Ti manning the boat on a hippopotamus hunt; force-feeding of geese and cranes to make the world's oldest foie gras (which turns out to be a nice accompaniment to our re-created beverage); tender familial scenes of Ti, his wife, and two chief sons; lines of porters carrying every kind of burial offering; and much more, as we were transported back nearly 5000 years. Nowhere in the ancient world can match Egyptian realism at such an early date. You have to wait until the Etruscans, Greeks, and Romans for similar attention to detail.

The main corridor led back to the chapel (Egyptian, *serdab*), where peering through a narrow slit one saw a life-sized statue of Ti, which represented his *ka* ("soul"). In this state, he could move freely around the tomb and smell the offerings.

What we had really come for was back up the corridor. There, in a dimly lit cubicle called the "storeroom" was the pictorial record of bread-making and beer-making, which we could examine at close quarters. The pictures were accompanied by hieroglyphic texts, if you could translate them, that served as a kind of comic-book narrative. At the very top of the back wall, our powerful photo lamps revealed men using turntables to shape pottery vessels to make the beer and then firing them in a kiln. Further down, we saw grain, probably barley and emmer wheat, being taken from tall cylindrical silos, measured out by a scribe, and then crushed and winnowed by standing men with long poles. Kneeling women finely ground the grain on millstones, sieved the flour, kneaded the dough, and molded it into large, round loaves, which were baked in an oven.

The next registers of the relief, moving upward, showed how the beer was made. We saw a large, horizontal jar in which malt is believed to have been prepared by moistening barley grain to germinate it. Possibly, the malt was then toasted in an adjacent oven, depicted next to the jar, after which it was shown being milled on a large, flat grinding stone. Next, we saw a man carrying a large platter, stacked high with bread. Large jars followed, in which malt and bread were likely "mashed" (i.e., the carbohydrates broken down into fermentable sugars) together and gelatinized. We then saw the liquidy wort being poured into smaller bowls, which appeared to have been heated under controlled conditions nearby on a fireplace loosely constructed of piled-up stones or pottery. After cooling and what appeared to be basket-filtering of the wort, a man was seen adding a liquid from a small jar to a wide-mouthed, open jar. Could this be a yeasty fruit juice or old beer batch to start the fermentation of the wort? The workers in the final stages of the process poured the fermenting beverage into jars and, after the fermentation gases diminished, stoppered and labeled them. A scribe duly recorded the amounts of beer produced.

My interpretation of some of these scenes can be debated. The overall process from bread to beer, however, is clear enough and explains why breweries are so often found next to bakeries in excavations. They share some of the same raw ingredients and many of the same procedures.

Nearly exact replicas of this process were repeated over and over again as three-dimensional models and artistic depictions in tombs for thousands of years. Obviously, once you have the canonical scenes worked out for producing lots of beer in the afterlife, you don't want to deviate from protocol.

A WALK IN THE CAIRO SUQ

SO MUCH FOR our day of archaeological reconnaissance. Now, we turned to getting the right yeast and ingredients for the job of re-creating an ancient Egyptian extreme beverage. We had some chemical evidence of what botanicals might have gone into such a beverage from our analyses of the Scorpion I jar residues. But we wanted to expand our palette of possibilities by drawing upon archaeobotanical evidence going back 18,000 years into the Upper Palaeolithic period when our ancestors were still roaming the land.

We took an unusual approach in reimagining this *Ancient Ale*. The next day, Sam, Ramy, and I prowled the labyrinth of the raucous, chaotic Khan el-Khalili bazaar in old Cairo. We went from spice shop to fruit stall, interspersing our adventure with cups of dark Egyptian coffee and the occasional hookah. Sam called it "the strangest picnic I've ever been on." When I picked up a handful of the famous Arab spice, za'atar, and smelled it, I knew we had a rich concoction of the same herbs that had been added to Scorpion I's wine. Every Arab family today has its own formula for the spice, which minimally includes wild thyme and savory. Some oregano, sumac seeds, coriander, plus any number of other herbs, might be added. The result is an intensely scented and flavored condiment, which Arabs use to flavor olive oil for dipping bread in or spreading on small pita breads and baking like pizza. You come to love the spice after living in the Middle East for a time. This herbal mixture would serve admirably as the bittering agent for our experimental brew.

We walked on further, and a basket of brown, dried fruit caught my eye. The shopkeeper told us it was dom palm fruit from the desert. This was the fruit that I had proposed might have been used to make a fermented beverage at Wadi Kubbaniya 18,000 years ago. We smelled and tasted its strong, molasses-like savoriness—unlike no other—and were hooked on using it in our re-creation. Moving ever deeper into the bazaar, we next encountered chamomile, again attested to at Wadi Kubbaniya. Its delicate flowery aroma was captivating.

Sam then saw a basket with some contorted, grayish roots of a sort. Ramy provided the translation: "deer penis." It was a possible additive, since deer did roam the Egyptian desert and were hunted. Deer penis, as an aphrodisiac, virility enhancer, or aid in pregnancy, does play a role in traditional Chinese medicine; combined with seal and dog penis, it makes for a "3-Penis Liquor." There is no evidence, however, of such a beverage from ancient Egypt. We bought some for oddity sake and moved on to lunch at a restaurant across the street from the Sphinx and Great Pyramid.

We brought along our goodies from the morning shopping spree. They were laid out on the table for inspection and a preliminary sniffing. They were then put into warm water to bring out their aromatics and give an approximation of what they might smell and taste like in a fermented beverage. We also put them into a modern Egyptian beer called Stella, which I had long drunk in Egypt. Although an insipid lager, it served our purpose. The herbal solutions were passed around the table, with everyone commenting on their peculiar qualities and what quantities might work in a re-created beverage. Since we have never been able to measure the precise amounts of the ingredients in an ancient beverage, this approach makes good sense. We received a good deal of inspiration from glancing every now and then across the road to the enigmatic Sphinx.

FRUIT FLIES TO THE RESCUE

SAM HAD ONE more thing up his sleeve. How about capturing some wild yeast for the fermentation in the night air of the Egyptian desert? We were off and running to the date palm groves at Dahshur, another 3 kilometers (2 miles) upriver from Saqqara. Petrie dishes with agar were set out in hopes that some yeast would drop from on high, or that at least some meandering insect, bearing yeast, would happen by. Truth be told, the orchard was infested with fruit flies, which are very much attracted to sugar and alcohol and share with us the same genes for inebriation.

These fruit flies became enmeshed in the sticky agar and were easily captured. Gathering up a mass of the insects, we sent them off to a Belgian lab where scientists isolated and cloned the yeast in sufficient numbers for us to use as our principal yeast for the re-created beverage. It could not produce above 5.5% alcohol, but we could live with that. Whether this yeast is indeed "wild" is unknown. It may be an escapee from a modern yeast population. Since its DNA is yet to be sequenced, we do not know how close it is to the Scorpion I yeast.

SAILING THE NILE

AS A PARTING gesture to our Egyptian sojourn, we hired a *felucca* (Arabic, "sailboat") to cruise the Nile. Besides carrying along sufficient liquid refreshment, cameras were at the ready to record a heated discussion about whether or not we should add bread to re-create our beverage. Nigel Hetherington of Past Preservers, an archaeology and media consulting firm, firmly believed that Egyptologist Delwen Samuel had settled the matter. Her studies of preserved beer residues from the New Kingdom site of el-Amarna, dating to about 1350 B.C., showed that no bread was present. She observed only partly saccharified and gelatinized starch grains from crushed emmer wheat and barley malt grains. Delwen went on to make her own re-creation of a New Kingdom beer under the name "Tutankhamun's tipple" or "Nefertiti's nip," and it sold out quickly.

I had my doubts that a finding from only one site and time period could be applied across the whole of Egyptian history. I was swayed by the tomb reliefs, like those of Ti, with their combination of a brewery and bakery in the same relief, as well as the archaeological evidence for their close association, such as at the Giza workers' village. It was the ideal arrangement for sharing ingredients and processes. Ancient Mesopotamian beer, reflecting broader Middle Eastern traditions, was also made from bread, and it was well known that traditional Egyptian beer, called *bouza* (no etymological relationship to English "booze") and often made by Nubian boatmen, contained mostly bread.

BACK IN DELAWARE

WE HAD WORKED out the essential recipe by the time we returned to the United States. Now, to make it a reality. As might have been expected, a major roadblock came from the FDA. It held the dom palm fruit for weeks in customs at large expense.

There were other ingredients to prepare in the meantime. Bryan Selders, who was stepping down as brewmaster, had already baked emmer wheat bread, using an old sourdough starter, in the Rehoboth brewpub oven. This Near Eastern cereal was one of the Neolithic domesticated plants and was later transplanted to Egypt. Eventually, all the other ingredients—dom fruit, za'atar, chamomile, and malt—came together, and the date palm oasis yeast was ready to go. Our first brew was in November 2010, and its commercial release followed about a year later.

The name *Ta Henket* reflects the decision to use baked bread, with its yeasty and carmelized flavors, in our formulation. On *Ta Henket's* label (at the beginning of this chapter), you can see *ta*, the bread-sign, represented by a semicircular-shaped bread loaf, right above *henket*, the beer-sign depicted by a jar.

Ta Henket is just one permutation among many possible interpretations of a prehistoric and protohistoric Egyptian extreme fermented beverage. Nothing like it has yet been found in an ancient Egyptian vessel. Still, it does justice to the available chemical, archaeobotanical, and textual evidence. We could have gone further by adding some water lily or blue lotus to give a hallucinogenic kick, as evidence also exists for these additives, but we refrained. The FDA had already given the go-ahead on the dom fruit and za'atar, and we thought better than to push our luck.

As one example of going too far with a re-creation, I was once approached by another show to re-create *tiswin*, a weak corn beer of 19th-century Apache Indians (see Chapter 8 on corn *chicha*, which originated in Mexico). The filming was to take place at the astonishing cliff dwelling site of Mesa Verde at the Four Corners in southern Colorado. Since my wife and I had been entranced by Mesa Verde in one of our cross-country VW bus excursions, this was an opportunity for me to revisit old memories, and I said yes. I should have moved more cautiously. During the filming, a *kiva*, the house of worship for the Anasazi—the Native American hunters-gatherers who had inhabited the site for more than 700 years (A.D. 550 to A.D. 1300)—was referred to as a "brewery." The archaeologically astute park ranger, who was overseeing the filming, and I couldn't believe our ears. The Anasazi had never made beer, and such a statement, if aired, might offend modern Native Americans who trace their ancestry to the Anasazi. Moreover, the concocted beverage was loaded with hops, which the Apaches never used.

NOT EVERYBODY'S CUP OF "TEA"

TA HENKET WAS unveiled at a theater near Times Square on November 18, 2010. The room had been suitably Egyptianized with massive columns and figures of the gods and pharaohs looking down. Sam and

Floris tapped a keg of the newly re-created *Ancient Ale*, and sitting on stage, we answered questions from the audience and assembled media. The beverage was tasted and roundly applauded by all, or so it seemed.

Unfortunately, *Ta Henket* never caught on with the drinking public. The beverage was taken off the market soon after its release because sales were down. The dom fruit and especially the za'atar, with its intense herbal flavors, were probably too much for the average American palate. Some people loved it, while others were repulsed by its taste. Such a brew might work better in the Middle East, where these intense flavors are widely appreciated.

Before it went off the market, I scooped up as many remaining bottles as I could around Philadelphia. I can report that the beverage has gotten better with age. After three years, the za'atar has mellowed out, and the beverage is tasting stellar, in my opinion. Let's hope that *Ta Henket* is not consigned to the dustbin of history, and, if not resurrected again by Dogfish Head, homebrewers will step into the breach.

RECIPES

Homebrew Interpretation of *Ta Henket*

by Doug Griffith (based on McGovern, 2009/2010)

INGREDIENTS

1 packet	Dry bread yeast (bread option)	Before Brew Day
1 cup	Warm water (bread option)	Before Brew Day
½ pound	Crushed wheat (bread option)	Before Brew Day

¼ cup	Light dry malt extract (bread option)	Before Brew Day
½ teaspoon	Salt (bread option)	Before Brew Day
½ pound	Whole wheat flour (bread option)	Before Brew Day
5 gallons	Water	Pre-boil
1	Grain bag	Pre-boil
½ pound	Caramel malt 40L, crushed (no bread option)	Pre-boil
1 pound	Wheat malt, crushed (no bread option)	Pre-boil
1 pound	Emmer, crushed (no bread option)	Pre-boil
1 tablespoon	Gypsum	Pre-boil
3 pounds	Light dry malt extract	65 minutes
½ ounce	Kent Golding hops pellets	60 minutes
4 ounces	Dried dates	15 minutes
1 teaspoon	Irish moss	15 minutes
1	Small muslin bag	5 minutes
½ ounce	Chamomile	5 minutes
3 level teaspoons	Za'atar (a Middle Eastern blend of spices)*	5 minutes
1 packet	Fermentis S-33, White Labs WLP400, or Wyeast 3942	Fermentation
1 cup	Priming sugar	Bottling
	Bottles and caps	Bottling

Starting gravity: 1.046
Final gravity: 1.012
Final target alcohol by volume: 4.5%
International Bittering Units: 12
Finished volume: 5 gallons

---

* On-line resource: http://tinyurl.com/z9jz568

PROCESS

Bread option

1. Add the bread yeast to the warm water (100°F). Stir to dissolve. Let sit 10 minutes.
2. Mix the dry malt extract, salt, and whole wheat flour (2 heaping cups to start) in a mixing bowl. Add the yeast and water mixture.
3. Mix and knead, adding flour as needed, to form a thick dough.
4. Cover the bowl and set in a warm place. Let the dough rise to about double in size.
5. Heat the oven to 350°F.
6. Place the bread dough on a greased bread pan or cookie sheet.
7. Bake for about 45 minutes until done. The bread will be dense and may be very moist inside.
8. Cool and slice into ½-inch cubes, or dry overnight and use a blender to coarsely grind.

Brewing

1. Fill a brewpot with the 5 gallons of water and add the gypsum.
2. Heat the water to 150°F.
3. Fill the grain bag with the crushed malts and emmer (no bread option) or bread (bread option). Tie off the top and place the bag in the brewpot when the temperature reaches 150°F.
4. Maintain the water at 150°F for 30 minutes, bobbling the grain bag every 5 minutes.
5. Turn the heat to maximum, making sure the grain bag is off the bottom of the pot. As the water reaches 170°F, pull out the grain bag using a large stirring spoon. Hold the bag above the brewpot for a minute, allowing most of the liquid to drain into the pot. Do not squeeze the grain bag.

6. As the water is beginning to boil, remove the pot from the heat.

7. Add the dry malt extract. Stir to prevent clumping and scorching on the bottom of the pot. Return the pot to the heat.

8. Once boiling, boil for 5 minutes before adding the hops.

9. Start timing a 1-hour boil when you make this hop addition. If using a defoaming agent to help prevent boilovers, add per package instructions as the foam rises from the boil.

10. Boil for 45 minutes. While boiling, purée the dates with a cup of water from the kettle, using a blender.

11. Add the Irish moss and puréed dates. Boil for 10 minutes.

12. Place the chamomile and za'atar in a small muslin bag and add. Boil for 5 minutes.

13. Swirl the contents of the kettle to create a whirlpool, and allow to rest for 15 minutes.

14. Cool the wort to 70°F and move to a fermenter, leaving as many solids behind in the kettle as possible. Top up to the 5-gallon mark in the fermenter.

15. Pitch the cooled wort with the yeast and ferment at 70°F until fermentation is complete.

16. Rack to a secondary fermenter for 1 to 2 weeks or until desired clarity.

17. Before bottling, clean and sanitize the bottles and caps.

18. Create a priming solution of 1 cup boiling water and the priming sugar.

19. Siphon the beer into a sanitized bottling bucket.

20. Add the water-diluted priming solution and gently stir.

21. Bottle and cap the beer.

22. The beer will be ready to drink in about 2 weeks.

N.B.: This beer will improve with age as the za'atar mellows.

MEAL PAIRING FOR *Ta Henket*

Whole Roasted Goose

by Christopher Ottosen

Serves 4–6

INGREDIENTS

1 domesticated goose, about 9 pounds

Roasted breast
1 breast on keel bone
Goose fat
2 tablespoons za'atar, available in Middle Eastern speciality stores

Spice mix
2 tablespoons za'atar
1 tablespoon date syrup

Giblet sauce
1 neck, 2 wings, 1 spine and rib cage, and 1 wishbone
1 tablespoon salted butter
Handful fresh savory[*] with stems, dried and ground
Handful fresh thyme with stems
Handful dried chamomile flowers[†] or 1 teaspoon pickled
    chamomile buds (see recipe at http://www.penn.museum/
    mcgovern/ancientbrews/)

---

[*] Online resources: http://tinyurl.com/zsf47sf, http://tinyurl.com/jrhnqjg, and http://tinyurl.com/jpsxj5j
[†] Online resources: http://tinyurl.com/gm2ej55, http://tinyurl.com/gns7ulm, and http://tinyurl.com/hfl30cn

1 garlic clove, whole

1 white onion, halved or quartered

1 cup *Ta Henket* or homebrew interpretation

2 tablespoons date vinegar

3 figs, cut in half

3 dried dates, cut in half

Salt

Legs

Coarse salt

Goose fat

Handful fresh savory with stems, dried and ground

Handful fresh thyme with stems

Handful dried chamomile flowers or 1 teaspoon pickled
    chamomile buds

2 cloves garlic, whole

Innards

1 tablespoon goose fat, from the roasted breast

1 heart, 1 liver, and 1 gizzard

1 garlic clove

3 tablespoons *Ta Henket* or homebrew interpretation

1 tablespoon butter

1 tablespoon parsley, minced

Pinch salt

PREPARATION

Butchering

Ideally, obtain a whole goose from your local butcher, divided up into
legs, crown of breast on keel bone, heart and liver, back, neck, ribcage
and spine, and wishbone. You can also butcher the bird yourself.[*]

---

[*] Online resource: http://tinyurl.com/zfusvoy. The step-by-step process for a
chicken is similar to that for a goose.

Roasted breast

Salt the goose crown of breast under and on top of its skin. For a crispy skin, refrigerate the breast overnight on an open tray. The next day, preheat the oven to 250°F, brush the breast with goose fat, insert a thermometer in the thickest part of the breast, and place on rack with a tray beneath. Make the spice mix: Mix together the za'atar and date syrup. When the breast reaches a core temperature of 145°F, after 3 to 4 hours, remove it from the oven. Increase the oven temperature to 275°F. Brush the breast with the spice mix and sprinkle it with extra salt. Return the breast to the oven, and bake for 10 minutes, or until the skin is crispy. Let rest for a few minutes before cutting and serving. Collect the fat from the tray.

Giblet sauce

Chop the bones into small pieces, removing any blood or waste. Roast the bones in an iron pan in the oven for 45 minutes at 380°F, or until they are dry and golden in color. Add the butter, and cook on the stove until melted. Add the savory, thyme, chamomile, garlic, and onion, and mix well on medium heat. After several minutes, add the *Ta Henket* or homebrew interpretation, date vinegar, figs, and dates. Heat on medium for several minutes. Tilt the pan to collect the fat. Barely cover the bones with cold water, then simmer for 1 hour. Strain the broth through a fine sieve into a clean saucepan. Reduce to half or more, and use room-temperature butter to thicken the sauce while it is still simmering. Salt to taste.

Legs

Day 1: Salt the legs, cover them with plastic wrap, and refrigerate for 24 hours. Day 2: Wash off the salt and dry the legs. Cover and refrigerate for another 24 hours. Day 3: Smear the legs with goose fat and mix with the herbs and garlic in a large saucepan. Simmer gently until the meat begins to detach from the bones. Remove the legs and cool. Preheat the oven to 275°F, and roast the legs for 10 minutes, or until crispy. The breast and legs can be roasted together for the final 10 minutes, and served together.

Innards

Add the goose fat to a pan and fry the innards on all sides. Add the garlic, *Ta Henket* or homebrew interpretation, and butter. Glaze the innards while reducing the giblet sauce. Add the parsley and salt before serving in the pan with the sauce.

For mood-enhancing atmospherics and more meal suggestions, go to: http://www.penn.museum/mcgovern/ancientbrews/.

5

Etrusca: A European "Grog" before Wine Surges In

BIRRA
ETRU
SCA
■■■■■■■BRONZE

An Ancient Ale brewed with honey, hazelnut flour, heirloom wheat, myrrh, gentian root, raisins, pomegranate juice & pomegranates.

1 Pint 9.4 fl. oz. | 8.5% Alc. by Vol.

Dogfish Head worked with our Birreria Brother Brewers (Birra del Borgo and Baladin) and biomolecular archeologist Dr. Patrick McGovern to create this Ancient Ale. We made a research pilgrimage together to early Etruscan womb tombs in the hills and along the coast of Tuscany. The 8th c. B.C. recipe is based on chemical and botanical evidence of tree resins, beeswax and honey; whole pomegranates; hazelnuts; grapes; and apples found inside ancient jars and drinking-bowls. It represents the prehistoric, mixed beverage of Italy before the arrival of wine. Our version is fermented with bronze, a popular material in brewing and cooking in the Etruscan era.

Brewed & Bottled by Dogfish Head Craft Brewery, Inc.
Milton, DE | 1.888.8DOGFISH | www.dogfish.com

As we have seen, the Canaanites succeeded beyond their wildest expectations in transferring their wine culture to Egypt. First, they enticed rulers like Scorpion I by supplying them with the new beverage. Not like wine that we are familiar with, it went to the extreme in its own way: besides grape, many other unusual ingredients were mixed in, including fig, Levantine herbs, and tree sap. After the Canaanites had won over the pharaohs, they then took their commercial endeavor a step further by transplanting the domesticated Eurasian grapevine to the Nile Delta, where it had never grown before. Royal vineyards and wineries were laid out, bringing with them other Canaanite technologies—winepress construction, pottery manufacture of wine-related vessels, special metal tools, irrigation techniques, and probably much more.

The profound Canaanite impact on Egyptian life generally is reflected in some Egyptian gods, such as Osiris, assuming a title ("The Lord of wine through/during the inundation") very much in keeping with the Canaanite creator-god El and the weather-god Baal. These deities were renowned in mythology for consuming prodigious amounts of wine, often leaving them drunk if not worse. Egyptian temple ceremonies and burial rites soon had elevated wine to a level on a par with beer, which had long been their staple beverage and was often combined with other ingredients to make extreme fermented beverages.

The transfer of the Canaanite wine culture to Egypt was helped along by having an overland route along the coast of the Sinai Peninsula. It was about 200 kilometers (125 miles) from the Gaza region of southern Canaan to the eastern edge of the Delta. Nevertheless, it required an arduous journey of ten days overland, moving pack animals from one watering hole to the next.

We can imagine the ancestors of the Canaanites, after coming out of Africa millennia ago, looking out from their prehistoric caves and encampments along the Mediterranean Sea, and wondering what the wider world had to offer and how to get there. For example, at Beirut, later to become an important Canaanite city-state and the capital of modern Lebanon, scatterings of lithic tools and weapons mark their presence. Perhaps, as these hunters and gatherers made toasts to the starry night with their prehistoric fermented beverages, they envisioned fashioning some kind of sea vessel to free them from their earthbound existence and carry them across the Mediterranean. It was just a matter of time until such a dream became reality, and later peoples headed out to points west, including Italy.

Italy lay over 1600 kilometers (1000 miles) away, as the crow flies, in the middle of the Mediterranean. The Canaanites and their Iron Age successors, the Phoenicians, could not reach this distant land and culture in one fell swoop. They had to follow the maritime equivalent of oasis-hopping in the desert; they went from seaside port to port and from island to island over a millennium-long process. We can follow the ancient mariners' routes to Italy imaginatively or, as my wife and I did, by taking to the sea ourselves.

THE CANAANITES: WINEMAKERS ON LAND, MERCHANTS OF THE SEA

TO TAKE FULL advantage of the commercial potential of their wine culture, the Canaanites built the first seagoing wooden ships, which sailed the Mediterranean. They no longer had to dream on its shores of going to sea; they made it happen.

Among the earliest preserved and most spectacular boats built by the Canaanites were the five "funerary ships" of pharaoh Khufu of the Fourth Dynasty, which were buried in the sand beside his Great Pyramid around 2500 B.C. One boat has been excavated, and it is almost 50 meters (165 feet) in length, some 9 meters (30 feet) longer than the *Golden Hind*, which carried Sir Frances Drake around the globe in the 16th century. Khufu's ship for the afterlife, which might have been piece-constructed on site or built abroad and sailed up the Nile, was made mostly of cedar of Lebanon. Its impressive construction, point-ing to many prior centuries of experimentation, was according to the so-called shell-first technique in which individual planks are joined to one another and to the keel by interlocking mortise-and-tenon joints.

The use of cedar in building Khufu's magnificent funerary barge is a dead-giveaway of where we should seek the earliest shipbuilding. Lebanon was renowned for its cedar forests in the ancient world, and no coastal site was more closely associated with the tree than Byblos, located 40 kilometers (25 miles) north of Beirut. One of Lebanon's most intensively excavated sites, Byblos provides a detailed sequence of occupation from the early Neolithic period through the end of the Bronze Age, from about 9500 B.C. to 1000 B.C.

Byblos, whose name probably meant "mountain city" in ancient Egyptian (*Kpn*) and Phoenician (*Gebal*), was particularly attrac-tive to aspiring sailors for its protected harbor and proximity to the cedar-covered mountains. We learn from 3rd-millennium B.C. Egyp-tian texts that gangs of woodcutters felled the trees in "God's Land" with copper axes and then transported the logs, most likely by river barges, down to Byblos. There the cedar timber was used to make the renowned "Byblos Ships" (Egyptian, *kbnwt*) that made it possi-ble to ferry huge shipments of the wood to Egypt. In one of the earli-est accounts, the Palermo Stone "Annals" of the Old Kingdom, Snefru (the first king of the Fourth Dynasty) claims to have brought 40 ship-loads of cedar and other conifers to Egypt and built 44 boats, some of which were 100 cubits (55 meters/180 feet) long.

THE WINE CULTURE SETS SAIL

THE CANAANITES TOOK another innovative step forward by developing the perfect pottery shape for transporting liquids—quintessentially wine—aboard their Byblos Ships. They invented the aptly named Canaanite Jar—later called the amphora (Latin, derived from Greek, literally "two-handled")—around 2000 B.C. It was shaped like the flat-bottomed Early Bronze jar that had already been in use for a millennium. But unlike the earlier jar, which was put together by hand, the Canaanite Jar was thrown on a fast potter's wheel to make a rounded base. This base, which evenly distributed forces from a liquid inside pressing outward, was far stronger than a flat base with its weak attachment between the base and sidewalls of the vessel. The curved base also served as a "third handle" so that a single man could grab and heft a Canaanite Jar of about 30 liters (8 gallons), weighing as much as 32 kilograms (70 pounds) when full, on and off a ship. Moreover, a ship's hold could accommodate more round-bottomed than flat-bottomed jars, because their narrow bottoms fit between their shoulders when they were piled one layer on top of another. On land, the jar was kept upright by a vertical support, such as a wall, or a jar stand.

Like they did in Egypt, the Canaanites appear to have applied a similar formula wherever they went: import wine and other luxury goods, present the rulers with speciality wine sets to entice them to adopt the wine culture, and then wait until they were asked to help in establishing native industries. Besides winemaking, the Canaanites and, later, the Phoenicians could also instruct their trading partners in purple dye production (since the mollusks from which the dye was obtained lived throughout the Mediterranean), shipbuilding (assuming that wood was available), and other crafts (especially metalworking and pottery-making).

Once they had established a foothold in a foreign land, other less tangible expressions of their wine culture—perhaps an artistic style or a mythological motif—might be adopted or merged with prevailing customs. A prime example is Dionysus, the Greek wine god who took his cues from the high gods of the Canaanites (El and Baal) in drinking heavily and encouraging orgiastic celebrations (so well depicted in Euripides' 5th-century B.C. play, *The Bacchae*). His more demure, academic side (*"In Vino, Veritas,"* as the Roman encyclopedist, Pliny the Elder, put it) is evoked in the Greek symposium, again of Near Eastern origin. An equally profound contribution to others was the Phoenician alphabet, the ancestor to both the modern Western and Semitic scripts. This revolutionary writing system wasn't just used to inventory goods or log sea journeys but also to express more profound sentiments about wine.

In fact, the earliest Greek inscription known was incised on a wine jug (*oinochoe*) in the 8th century B.C. It read: "Whoever of all dancers performs most nimbly will win this *oinochoe* as prize." Later in the same century, an even more amazing inscription was recorded on a Rhodian wine cup (*kotyle*) from Pithekoussai, an early Greek colony in the Bay of Naples. It was written in elegant dactylic hexameter poetry, like the Homeric epics that were composed about the same time. It read: "Nestor's cup was good to drink from, but anyone who drinks from this cup will soon be struck with desire for fair-crowned Aphrodite."

The gold cup of King Nestor, who played an important role in the Trojan War, is described in the *Iliad* (11.628–643) as having a pair of doves facing each other on opposite handles. An actual gold cup, identical to that in Homer's epic, was excavated from a 16th-century B.C. royal burial at the site of Mycenae in the Greek Peloponnesus.

The interweaving of artifacts and ancient stories of wine, women, song and dance, and sometimes human sacrifice, which was in large part inspired by the Canaanite and Phoenician wine culture, leaps out at us from across the centuries.

BENEATH THE WAVES

OUR EARLIEST MARITIME evidence of the Canaanite and Phoenician strategy of luring Mediterranean peoples into their wine culture comes from the earliest shipwreck that has been discovered thus far in the Mediterranean. The merchantman, which was excavated by Texas A&M's Institute of Nautical Archaeology, had gone down around 1300 B.C. off the rugged coast of southern Turkey near the cape of Uluburun. The boat was loaded to the gills with raw materials and luxury goods from the international world of the Late Bronze Age: 11 tons of copper and tin ingots, spouted "drinking-horns" (Greek, *rhyta*) made of faience (an artificial silicate material), Egyptian scarabs and Near Eastern cylinder seals, Mycenaean drinking-cups (Greek, *kylikes*), and much more. The ship likely hailed from a city-state along the Levantine coast because it was constructed of cedar of Lebanon in Canaanite fashion. Items on board for personal adornment, religious practice, and utilitarian use—including gold jewelry, a goddess figurine covered in gold leaf, oil lamps, and sets of animal-shaped stone weights—marked its officers and crew as Canaanites.

Since the Uluburun ship dates to a time of ever-increasing foreign trade and was built and operated by Canaanite wine devotees, we would expect that its cargo bays also carried some Canaanite Jars or amphoras with wine, as later ships did. Some 150 jars were indeed recovered from the wreck. Unfortunately, they became unstoppered after the ship likely went down in a violent storm and came to rest on a steep slope. Over the millennia, the contents of the jars were scattered and intermixed on the seafloor where they deteriorated.

An important clue for determining the contents of some of the jars, however, was that about half of them still contained nodules and chunks of terebinth tree (*Pistacia* sp.) sap. Several jars were a quarter to half filled with the sap, weighing as much as a kilogram (2.2 pounds), but most held less than 100 grams (3.5 ounces).

It will be recalled that ancient wines—that of Scorpion I being a case in point—were generally resinated, probably to help preserve the wine. So, wasn't it possible that many of the Uluburun jars with small amounts of terebinth resin, possibly including another 66 jars that were found "empty" of the sap, once contained wine that had spilled out and been lost? The several jars with larger amounts might have been intended for other purposes, such as medicine, use in mummification, or incense.

We put our "wine hypothesis" for the Canaanite Jars on board the Uluburun ship to the test by analyzing five terebinth samples in search of the fingerprint compound for wine, tartaric acid. If the jars had contained wine, then the terebinth sap should have absorbed and retained this compound. We would have preferred testing pottery samples from the jars themselves, but they were unavailable.

We used the most sensitive chemical method available for our analysis, namely LC-MS-MS (Chapter 3). Our results bore out the "wine hypothesis": two samples were positive and a third was borderline positive. Although the remaining two samples were negative, this result was not unexpected. Perhaps we had sampled a large chunk's interior that had not come in contact with wine. Or it could also be a true negative, implying that the jar contained something other than wine.

Archaeobotanical evidence from the ship provided corroborative evidence for our hypothesis. Uncarbonized grape seeds were the most prolific, preserved botanical remains on the ship: they were scattered everywhere and, most importantly, they were sometimes clustered inside Canaanite Jars. Unless the ship were carrying quantities of fresh fruit, the most likely explanation for such a profusion of grape remains was that they came from unfiltered wine. This was standard practice in antiquity, as we saw for the Scorpion I wine.

The capstone for our "wine hypothesis" is the centrality of wine in all things Canaanite. To argue for absolutely no wine on board the Uluburun ship, as some have done, is like having a Bavaria without beer or a Newcastle without coal. Canaanite officers or crew members worth their salt, traveling the uncertain high seas in a Byblos Ship, would have demanded and gotten their duly earned daily allotments of grape wine, like any archaeological team today expects its preferred fermented beverage or a cadre of pyramid builders did in the past.

LEAPFROGGING ACROSS THE MEDITERRANEAN

IN FITS AND starts, the Canaanite and the later Phoenician sailors, probably underwritten by individual entrepreneurs and rulers of the Levantine city-states, reached out to the greater Mediterranean. Cyprus, about 100 kilometers (62 miles) away from the Lebanese coast, was an obvious first target. Italy still lay on the far horizon.

Although a far cry from what the ancient mariners must have experienced when they first ventured forth in their Byblos Ships, my wife and I captured some of the spirit and adventure, even the taste of a fermented beverage on the way, when we traveled by boat to Cyprus in 1973. We were ultimately headed to a kibbutz in Israel to study modern Hebrew, but the overland route between Lebanon and Israel was closed. With only a couple hundred dollars to our name, we decided to try and hitch a boat ride to Cyprus from Beirut and then take the

$10 flight from Nicosia, the capital of Cyprus, to Israel's Ben Gurion airport.

We went from cargo ship to cargo ship in the Beirut harbor, calling out to their crews and captains: "Are you going to Cyprus, and if so, can we come aboard?"

After many rebuffs, we nervously approached the last ship. It turned out to be a Danish cargo ship, flying under a Swiss flag, and its captain said we were welcome on board. We only had to make it official by my signing on as first mate and my wife as assistant cook. As simply a ceremonial gesture to international maritime law, we weren't required to carry out these functions, but just to sit back and enjoy the journey. Canaanite and Phoenician sailors would have followed a similar seaway to the eastern coast of Cyprus, which we reached in a short overnight trip of about 200 kilometers (124 miles). The rub came when we arrived off the coast, and harbor traffic was so backed up that we would have to wait our turn to dock at the port of Famagusta.

Since it was December 23 and the Danes were planning a special Christmas eve dinner to which we were invited, we used the ship as our "hotel," and took a small outboard boat to shore the next day to see the well-preserved remains of Salamis where the Phoenicians had left their mark. Back on ship, where we had had an unlimited supply of Tuborg beer from the start, we enjoyed roast duck with all the fixings and fine French wine.

The Canaanites and Phoenicians, who preceded us, probably had a much harder time of it. Once they arrived, they established key port cities, including Kition on the southeastern coast of the island, from which they extended their influence and the wine culture inland. Their presence was marked by elegant "mushroom-lipped" jugs for serving wine. These were polished to a glossy red finish, imitating precious metal, and were likely part of a canonical Phoenician wine set, which included drinking-horns, bowls, goblets, and other vessels. They were accompanied by large bronze cauldrons similar to those in the Midas Tumulus (Chapter 2) and, of course, by the ubiquitous Canaanite Jar.

All good things must come to an end, and the Danish ship finally docked. We said our farewells, hitchhiked to Nicosia, and took the 30-minute flight to Tel Aviv. We arrived in the midst of a rare snowstorm, traveled up to Jerusalem, and the next day continued on to our kibbutz in the north, Ramat David in the Jezreel Valley.

ONWARD TO GREECE

THE NEXT STOP of the Canaanites on their westward journey to Italy—a kind of marine mirror image of the overland prehistoric "Silk Road" to China—was Greece, particularly the island of Crete. Nearly 1000 kilometers (600 miles) from the port cities of Lebanon and coastal Syria, this large island at the entry to the Aegean Sea lay on the threshold of the larger Greek world. The key site for early wine-making is Myrtos-Phournou Koryphe on the southern coast.

The Canaanites were likely plying these waters as early as 2200 B.C. Their ships probably came loaded down with wine to entice the locals and perhaps some domesticated grapevines to jump-start the industry there. Our analyses showed that large jars at the site contained a resinated wine.

Even before our analyses, one might have anticipated that the Myrtos jars contained wine. They had exterior designs of dark red painted splotches and "drips," which were reminiscent of the decoration on the Scorpion I jars. The Myrtos designs were more graphic, almost as if wine were spilling out. The interiors had reddish residues, which we analyzed. Some jars contained grape seeds and even preserved stems and skins, showing that the wine was unfiltered. Horizontal rope appliqués, running below loop handles placed near the wide mouths of the jars suggested, again like the Scorpion I jars, that leather or cloth covers had originally been tied down by rope over the vessels' mouths. Another peculiarity that the Myrtos jars shared with their Near Eastern counterparts from sites in the Zagros, Caucasus, and Taurus mountains was a small hole just above the base, deliberately made before firing the pottery, probably for decanting a liquid and avoiding any accumulated dregs at the bottom.

Numerous circular vats, often called "bathtubs," were also found at Myrtos. Such finds, well attested in ancient Egypt, are most often associated with industrial winemaking. The "bathtubs," outfitted with spouts for draining the grape juice into the large jars, were ideal for stomping grapes in succession by workers—as one tired, the next one would step into the vat and take over. Large-scale production was also marked by a massive funnel, the stock-in-trade of the Near Eastern winemaker, and impressions of grape leaves on the pottery pointed to vineyards in the vicinity.

The Phoenician seafarers followed in the wake of the Canaanites and carried on in this grand tradition. Their huge shipments of wine, purple textiles, and other exotic goods conveyed much more than material goods across the Mediterranean. They also brought a new way of life, based on wine, which gradually permeated the societies, religions, and the economies of the many peoples with whom they came in contact. Phoenician trade and colonization marginalized, modified, or displaced the native fermented beverages, including beers, meads, and extreme fermented beverages of all kinds.

Greece and Crete had their own extreme beverage before the Canaanites and Phoenicians arrived. The "Greek grog" was made from Pramnian wine (perhaps, a powerful herbal wine), honey and barley, topped with cheese—the so-called *kykeon* (Greek, "mixture") of the Homeric epics. It was prepared in large cauldrons and drunk from drinking-bowls and goblets, like the marvelous Nestor gold cup.

ENTER THE ETRUSCANS

MOVING EVER WESTWARD, into the central and western Mediterranean, the Phoenicians established colonies on Malta, western Sicily, Sardinia, Ibiza, Cádiz beyond Gibraltar—where sherry wine reigns supreme today—and most impressively at Carthage on the north African coast. By 800 B.C., they had come in contact with the Etruscans, the people I have been leading up to and the eponym for our re-created fermented beverage, *Etrusca*.

Greek traders appear to have entered the picture later. They operated similarly to the Phoenicians by parceling up many of the same islands (e.g., eastern Sicily and Corsica) and establishing colonies in southern Italy (Oenotria), north Africa (e.g., Cyrene), and at Massalia (modern Marseille) in southern Mediterranean France.

The intensity of sea trade is reflected in the many Iron Age ship-wrecks, loaded with amphoras and other wine-related drinking para-phernalia, which have been located and excavated all along the Sicilian, Italian, and French coasts. The Phoenician and Greek impact through-out the western Mediterranean was so pronounced that one can say that it was mediated by the wine culture itself.

The 8th century B.C. saw the climax of Phoenician influence on the hearts, minds, and palates of native peoples throughout the Med-iterranean. The Etruscans of central Italy along the Tyrrhenian Sea and inland illustrate the phenomenon and how it spread. This proto-Celtic people likely first came in contact with the Phoenicians before the Greeks arrived on their shores, as witnessed by their "Oriental-izing" industries. Artifacts in metal, pottery, ivory, and glass closely reflect Phoenician style, technology, and iconography. The Etruscans modeled their amphora after the Phoenician one. Where a similarity of form exists, it likely served a similar function, namely, to store and transport grape wine, which was first supplied by the Phoenicians and was soon to be produced by a nascent local industry.

"ETRUSCAN GROG"

THE ETRUSCANS HAD a tradition of making an extreme fermented beverage before the Phoenicians arrived with their wine. I did some armchair archaeology, combed through excavation reports, and pep-pered my colleagues at the Penn Museum with question after question. Jean Turfa was my main quarry, and she patiently explained to an "out-sider" who the Etruscans were and directed me to the key information about their fermented beverage, tucked away in obscure publications.

Jean told me of the difficulty in translating the non-Indo-European language of the Etruscans and of how they were one of the first Celtic groups to adopt the Phoenician alphabet. Their earliest text was proba-bly a wine text, like those of the Greeks and Romans, providing elegant testimony to the impact of the wine culture on them. She described the beautifully painted and realistic frescoes adorning their tombs, some of which the Penn Museum had discovered with underground periscopes and which I saw firsthand in all their glory at Tarquinia. The frescoes portray a fun-loving people, who were notorious for their banqueting, music-making, dancing, and games. Both men and women joined in the festivities. Their behavior stood in stark contrast to the more dour Romans, who after fighting them for a century were ultimately victorious.

Jean spoke of the Etruscans' loose confederacy of city-states, similar to those of the Phoenicians, which were generally situated on steep hills, surrounded by stone walls and looking out onto fertile plains, mountains, sea, or river. The territory of Etruria stretched from the coast of modern Tuscany up into the Apennine Mountains and as far north as the Po Valley. Most of the famous hilltop towns of Tuscany—Volterra, San Gimignano, Civita di Bagnoregio, Montepulciano, Montalcino, and Orvieto, to name only a few—were founded by the Etruscans. They still form the backbone of Tuscan society today, and merely to say their names elicits thoughts and tastes of delicious wines, olive oil, fruits and nuts of all kinds, truffles, cured meats, and cheeses.

Painstakingly, I assembled the available archaeobotanical, chemical, and other archaeological evidence for the Etruscans' native grog. There was a honeycomb found in a bronze cauldron at Murlo (Poggio Civitate), south of Siena en route to Montalcino. Elsewhere, large cauldrons were known to have been used to make a mixed fermented beverage of honey and other ingredients; they were similar to those found in the Midas Tumulus and at many other sites in Europe, as we will see in the next chapter.

More honeycomb was found inside what might be interpreted as a beehive-shaped bronze vessel at Casale Marittimo on the coast. It was accompanied by other vessels with hazelnuts, pomegranates, and much more. And although the domesticated grape had not yet arrived, there were inklings of the use of wild grape in a mixed beverage at Verucchio, close to the Adriatic Sea and at the farthest extent of Etruscan influence. Jars that were sharply angled at their mid-bodies—so-called biconical kraters (derived from Greek, "to mix")—had been excavated from 8th–7th century B.C. tombs there. They had yielded both grape pollen and cereal grains, possible shades of a combination wine-and-beer mixture. Could such ingredients and perhaps others have been mixed together into the Etruscan version of an extreme fermented beverage?

The evidence kept mounting for an early Iron Age "Etruscan grog." For example, I learned that a small drinking-bowl from a 6th–5th century B.C. tomb at Pombia, northwest of Milan, had equally convincing archaeobotanical and chemical evidence for an extreme fermented beverage that included barley, an oat-wheat, and rye. No beeswax was reported, but the drink might have been resinated and also spiced with a mugwort or wormwood herb (*Artemisia* sp.). One grain of hops (*Humulus* sp.), although little to go on, provided the first archaeological indication that this overwhelmingly popular botanical in modern beers might have been used as a bittering agent in Iron Age times. Although Pombia was inhabited by the Ligurians, another proto-Celtic tribe, its territory bordered on Etruria and its people shared a common cultural heritage with the Etruscans, presumably including fermented beverages.

COMING UP WITH THE RECIPE FOR OUR *ETRUSCA*

THE CANAANITES AND Phoenicians had led me across the Mediterranean to the Etruscans and Italy. Now it was time to get to work in re-creating an early Iron Age grog before the Etruscans were wholly swept into the wine culture of the Phoenicians.

Sam was eager to get started, not least because of his Calabrian ancestral ties. He had also worked closely with up-and-coming microbrewers in Italy: Leonardo di Vincenzo of Birra del Borgo in the Apennines east of Rome, and Teo Musso of Birra Baladin, south of Turin on the way to Barolo wine country. They had collaborated with Mario Batali and Joe and Lidia Bastianich in opening the La Birreria brewpub on the top floor of Eataly in New York City.

Early in March 2012, we flew into the Leonardo DaVinci-Fiumicino airport in Rome, remembering back to our Egyptian filming escapade, and took the train past the ruins of ancient Ostia, the port of Rome, to the Roma Termini station. Leo, Teo, and Leo's aide-de-campe, Luciana Squadrilli, were there to meet us.

After a quick stop at our hotel, we immediately set off on foot to our first meeting at the National Museum of Oriental Art where archaeobotanist Lorenzo Costantini conferred with us on the possibility of an early Etruscan extreme fermented beverage. He told us about an heirloom barley found at Cures, up in the mountains near Leo's brewery where we were shortly to do our experimental brewing of *Etrusca*. It had been shown to be excellent in making beer. We followed up our intellectual musings with some beer tastings at Leo's La Bottega brewpub, close to the Tiber River.

The next day, we launched off on a tour of Etruscan archaeological sites that had the best evidence for the ancient grog. Our first stop was Carmignano, high above the Arno River and only a short distance downriver from Florence. The superintendent of the town's museum came specially to open the collections to us for a private viewing. While one tumulus burial of a warrior of the 8th–7th centuries B.C. had three large biconical kraters buried with him, which had possibly once contained the grog, what truly astounded me was the sheer quantity of Phoenician-inspired artifacts from the 7th-century B.C. Montefortini Tumulus. They included intricately carved ivories, bronzes with Etruscan writing, and multicolored glass.

We then sped down the coast road to Casale Marittimo and its necropolis of Casa Nocera. Tomb A is the star of the show here, at least for an aspiring group of ancient grog brewers. It is very telling when only drinking-related vessels are buried in the same large biconical krater together with the ashes of a warrior prince. The contents of these bronze vessels were equally fascinating: fluted drinking-bowls of Phoenician type, which contained hazelnuts in one, a combination of apple and grape in another, and probably pomegranate in a third. Pomegranates and hazelnuts have long been specialities of this region. Then there were strange-looking vessels: a "wineskin" containing a tree resin (possibly myrrh or frankincense, which would have had to be imported from Yemen or Somalia, probably by the Phoenicians) and the beehive-shaped vessel with honeycomb inside.

The remains of whole fruits, honeycomb, and tree resin in the vessels could well signal that a uniquely Etruscan grog was served at the funeral celebration for the warrior prince to usher him into the afterlife. The commingling of native products, including grape (possibly already domesticated), and foreign drinking-bowls suggests that the Tomb A finds stand on the cusp of discovering the right balance between old and new beverages: the Etruscan grog and Phoenician wine. Developments in Etruria are a harbinger of what was soon to come farther north in central Europe and Scandinavia (Chapter 6).

The following day, after our successful archaeological reconnaissance, we traveled up into the Apennines to Leo's brewery in Borgorose, about 40 kilometers (25 miles) northeast of Rome. It was still March, and newly fallen snow greeted us as we entered the village. Leo guided us around, particularly showing off his newly fashioned replicas of ancient Etruscan pottery jars, made by a nearby potter from the local clay. He planned to carry out the fermentation of his version of *Etrusca* in them.

Teo was there, and he went around the room with a cup of myrrh in hot water. He invited all to smell its delicate aromas, which he rhapsodized about. His version of *Etrusca* was to be fermented and aged in oak barrels from his father's winemaking days. I demurred slightly, since no intact oak barrels have been found until the Roman period in Gaul. However, if the Etruscans had been adept enough to bend wooden boards to make seagoing vessels, a technology they likely learned from the Phoenicians, then why couldn't they have taken staves and made oak barrels?

The three microbrewers and I sat around a table, discussing the pros and cons of each ingredient. We tried to do justice to all the varied lines of ancient archaeobotanical and chemical evidence. We decided to include a 2-row barley, which has better malt extraction than the 6-row variety that developed as a mutant of the 2-row barley in the Neolithic period. Another possibility was a local heirloom durum wheat—Cappelli Senatore or Saragolla—which is first evidenced in

Tuscany around A.D. 400. I wasn't too keen on using a wheat that had probably not existed during Etruscan times but was outvoted and relented when I was told of its fragrancy.

We had no dispute about using pomegranate juice, hazelnut flour, and imported myrrh. For the raisins, we might have chosen a native wild or domesticated grape, but instead went with Muscat, which might have been introduced by the Phoenicians. Each microbrewer opted for their best, most delicious honey varieties. While the Italian chestnut was appropriate, Sam's Delawarean wildflower was a stretch. In place of a touch of hops (in keeping with the Pombia evidence), the microbrewers got their way in adding some highly astringent gentian root. The herb goes back at least to the time of King Gentius (whence the name), who ruled in the early 2nd century B.C. after the Etruscans. It is a common additive to apéritifs, liqueurs, and bitters, including Angostura (the sine qua non of modern cocktails). We might have taken a more conservative approach and confined ourselves to a handful of possible ingredients, but we wanted to take full measure of the archaeological and gustatory possibilities of ancient Etruria.

THE PIÈCE DE RÉSISTANCE

THE FINISHING TOUCH to any extreme fermented beverage is its yeast. For *Etrusca*, I turned to my longtime colleague, Duccio Cavalieri, who had a hand in sequencing the DNA of the yeast responsible for the Scorpion I wine. Duccio is professor of microbiology at the wine and agrarian institute of San Michele all'Adige (Fondazione Edmund Mach) in the Italian Tyrol. He was only too happy to drive the 500 kilometers (300 miles) to Rome and back, so he could be at our opening dinner and tasting at Leo's brewpub. He rose to his feet many times that evening, as we drank oyster stout from Birra del Borgo, a braggot or honeyed beer from Baladin, and, naturally, *Midas Touch*, to toast the group and expostulate on yeasts.

Duccio thought long and hard about what would be the best yeast to use for *Etrusca*. He finally hit upon it. He and his colleagues had already published a paper in which they crossed what they believed were primitive yeasts from Tuscany. One strain was a *Saccharomyces cerevisiae*, which came from Montalcino. The other strain was *S. bayanus*, which was isolated from a sample of Vin Santo (Italian, "Holy Wine"), which carries on the ancient Canaanite tradition of first drying the grapes before pressing and fermentation. It was from the general region of the Etruscan sites of Volterra, Fiesole (ancient Florence), and Barberino. He proposed crossing the two species once again, collecting the viable tetraploid spores, and multiplying them to make an "ancient" Etruscan yeast.

As I discussed in Chapter 1, *Saccharomyces cerevisiae* and *S. bayanus* are the two main yeast species for fermentation. They had already accidentally crossed in medieval Germany, to give the bottom-dwelling lager yeast, which was isolated and identified in the late 19th century by Emil Hansen of the Carlsberg brewery in Copenhagen and named *Saccharomyces carlsbergensis*, more properly *S. pastorianus*.

Duccio's efforts to intentionally cross the two Tuscan variants once again proved successful, and the offspring hybrid was shown to be cold tolerant and capable of producing high alcohol levels, up to 10%. Samples were sent off to the three microbrewers. Dogfish Head's yeast laboratory had no problem in multiplying it for batch production in the United States.

TASTES OF ITALY

BARELY SEVEN MONTHS later in October, we had our first sips of the two Italian versions of *Etrusca* at the premier event of the Slow Food movement in Torino: Salone del Gusto (Italian, "tasting room"). Teo had kindly invited Sam, his wife Mariah, and me to stay at his "bed-and-breakfast" at Casa Baladin in his small hometown of Piozzo, 60 kilometers (37 miles) south of the city. Besides being surrounded by Teo's eclectic mélange of primitivist and avant-garde art, we enjoyed the local Piedmontese cuisine, his many innovative brews made using a variety of herbs, and his wines produced in honor of his father, which were made at his brewery just down the street.

The Salone del Gusto itself was a feast of Italian cheeses and meats,

Alpine bitters, and even Polish meads. Our *Etrusca* tasting was part of a more wide-ranging workshop on "The Archeology of Beer." Sitting at the front table were not only Teo, Leo, Sam, and I, but also Jean van Roy of Cantillon Brewery in Belgium, maker extraordinaire of fine lambics and gueuzes, and two notable beer writers, Luca Giaconne and Lorenzo Dabove. Lorenzo, who goes by the nickname Kuaska, is the Italian equivalent of Michael Jackson, whose many books on beer styles jump-started the craft brewing revolution around the world.

We tilted glasses of the *Etruscas* and noted their colors and opacities: both were yellowish and opaque due to minimal filtering. We sniffed and tasted them. I was unable to detect any marked difference between Leo's *Etrusca Terra Cotta* and Teo's *Etrusca Wood*, but then I am not a trained taster. Others observed slight differences in acidity and fruitiness. Perhaps a longer ageing period is needed to bring out the oak or pottery's contributions to the flavor and aroma profiles. Experimentation with these materials, especially pottery, is still in the early stages.

Following Salone del Gusto, I had another special treat in store. Piozzo lies on the doorstep of the Langhe region where the great Barolo and Barbaresco wines are made. For three days, I made my way from winery to winery, the high point coming on my visit to the Gaja winery in the small town of Barbaresco. Its owner and winegrower, Angelo Gaja, is the vinicultural guru of the Nebbiolo vine and its powerful wine.

I was first taken to a waiting room off the gated courtyard on the town's main street. I had waited probably ten minutes when I heard the door hinges of the large wooden door squeak. A head looked in, and it was no other than Angelo Gaja himself, who smiled broadly and entered to shake my hand, congratulating me on my *Ancient Wine* book (translated into Italian as *L'archeologo e l'uva*). I would have been happy to see him from afar, but here he was in the flesh. He brought out some high boots, and said that I should pull them on to visit the famous vineyards of Sorì San Lorenzo and Sorì Tildin. Unfortunately, my shoe size is 14 (American), and the boots might have been 10 at best. I chose to wade through the mud in my docksiders, as Angelo described how the vines were laid out on the sorì (Italian, "hilltop") with a southern exposure to receive the greatest amount of sunlight.

We returned to the 13th-century A.D. grand fortification tower in the center of the town for a special tasting. I went away, as if floating on a cloud and holding a special wood-encased bottle of 2008 Barbaresco and memories to last a lifetime. It was a fitting memento of our journeys from the homeland of ancient wine in Phoenicia, across the Mediterranean, and to Italy with its Etruscan grog and homegrown wines.

YET ANOTHER SIP OF *ETRUSCA*

I CAN REMEMBER my first taste of the Dogfish version of *Etrusca*, which was made with long strips of bronze submerged into the brew kettle in partial imitation of an Etruscan bronze vessel. I had just finished speaking to an exuberant crowd of *Ancient Ale* devotees, and someone brought me a glass of liquid refreshment. I took one sip and was overwhelmed by the pomegranate and hazelnut aromas and tastes, which blended perfectly with one another. I said: "What is this? It's not any of the *Ancient Ales* I know of." I was told that it was *Etrusca Bronze*, which was being unveiled here for the first time.

RECIPES

Homebrew Interpretation of *Etrusca*

by Doug Griffith (based on McGovern, 2009/2010)

INGREDIENTS

5 gallons	Water	Pre-boil
8 ounces	Hazelnuts/filberts, roasted and ground	Pre-boil
1	Grain bag	Pre-boil
8 ounces	Brewers malt, crushed	Pre-boil
3 ounces	Chocolate malt, crushed	Pre-boil
1 pound	Flaked wheat	Pre-boil
3 pounds	Pilsen light dry malt extract	30 minutes
3 pounds	Wheat/barley dry malt extract	30 minutes
½ ounce	Hallertau hop pellets	10 minutes
4 ounces	Dried figs, whole or pieces	10 minutes
4 ounces	Raisins	10 minutes
1 teaspoon	Irish moss	10 minutes
¼ teaspoon	Gentian root, freshly ground	10 minutes
1½ pounds	Honey	5 minutes
2 level teaspoons	Myrrh	End of boil
1 packet	Lallemand Belle Saison, White Labs WLP566 Belgian Saison, or Wyeast 3711 Fr Saison	Fermentation

8 ounces	Pomegranate concentrate	Day 2 of
		fermentation
1 cup	Priming sugar	Bottling
	Bottles and caps	Bottling

Starting gravity: 1.080
Final gravity: 1.015
Final target alcohol by volume: 8.5%
International Bittering Units: 10
Finished volume: 5 gallons

PROCESS

1. Fill a brewpot with the 5 gallons water and heat to 150°F.
2. While the water heats, prepare the hazelnuts. Lightly toast/roast the nuts in an oven or frying pan. If whole, they can be roasted on a grill. Let cool and chop them fine in a blender.
3. Fill the grain bag with the crushed malts, ground nuts, and flaked wheat.
4. Tie off the top of the bag.
5. Add the grain bag to the water, maintain the 150°F temperature, and bobble the bag every 5 minutes. Do this for 30 minutes. Turn the heat to maximum, making sure the grain bag is not touching the bottom of the pot. As the water reaches 170°F, pull out the grain bag using a large stirring spoon. Hold the bag above the brewpot for a minute, allowing most of the liquid to drain into the pot. Do not squeeze the grain bag. Continue to heat the water.
6. As the water is beginning to boil, remove the pot from the heat.
7. Add the dry malt extracts. Stir to prevent clumping/scorching on the bottom of the pot. Return the pot to the heat.
8. Bring to a boil. If using a defoaming agent to help prevent

boilovers, add per package instructions as the foam rises from the boil.

9. Boil for 5 minutes, then add the hop pellets.
10. Boil for 15 minutes. While boiling, purée the figs and raisins with a cup of water from the kettle.
11. Add the Irish moss, figs, and raisins. Boil for 5 minutes. While boiling, put the gentian root in a blender and run until the pieces are small.
12. Add the honey. Stir well.
13. After 5 minutes, remove from the heat.
14. Add the myrrh and ground gentian root.
15. Swirl the contents of the kettle to create a whirlpool, and allow to rest for 15 minutes.
16. Cool the wort to 70°F and move to a fermenter, leaving as many solids behind in the kettle as possible. Top up to the 5-gallon mark in the fermenter.
17. Pitch the cooled wort with the yeast and ferment at 70°F.
18. On Day 2 of fermentation, add the pomegranate concentrate.
19. When fermentation has completed (about 7 days), rack to a secondary fermenter for 1 to 2 weeks or until desired clarity.
20. Before bottling, clean and sanitize the bottles and caps.
21. Create a priming solution of 1 cup boiling water and the priming sugar.
22. Siphon the beer into a sanitized bottling bucket.
23. Add the water-diluted priming solution, and gently stir.
24. Bottle and cap the beer.
25. The beer will be ready to drink in about 2 weeks.

ᴍEAL ᴘᴀɪʀɪɴɢ ꜰᴏʀ *Etrusca*

Grilled and Braised Pork Neck

by Christopher Ottosen

Serves 6

Iɴɢʀᴇᴅɪᴇɴᴛꜱ

1 pork neck, about 5½ pounds
Salt and pepper
7 garlic cloves
1 handful wild rosemary, preferably fresh
1 handful fresh thyme with stems
2 cups *Etrusca* or homebrew interpretation
½ cup pomegranate juice, freshly squeezed
2 tablespoons honey

Pʀᴇᴘᴀʀᴀᴛɪᴏɴ

ꜱᴛᴀʀᴛ ᴛʜᴇ ɢʀɪʟʟ, using only charcoal or wood, not gas, since the meat is to be smoked with herbs. Salt and pepper the meat to taste. Place the meat on the grill over medium heat, sprinkling wild rosemary and thyme on both sides as it cooks.

Prepare a deep baking tray by distributing the garlic cloves, wild rosemary, and thyme on the bottom (be generous with the herbs).

5 minutes before grilling is complete, cover the fire with additional wild rosemary and thyme and close the lid of the grill. Smoke the meat for 2 to 3 minutes.

Place the grilled meat on the prepared baking tray. Cover tightly with aluminum foil. Preheat the oven to 285°F, and cook for 4 hours. During the last hour, remove the aluminum foil and pour the *Etrusca* or homebrew interpretation and pomegranate juice over the meat. Brush the honey over the meat to glaze. The pork neck is done when the meat easily pulls away from the bone. Finely sieve the cooking juices from the bottom of the baking tray, reduce to half in a small saucepan, and serve as an accompanying broth. Pour the broth over the pork.

For mood-enhancing atmospherics and more meal suggestions, go to: http://www.penn.museum/mcgovern/ancientbrews/.

Kvasir : Nordic Heat for Frigid Nights

W e have followed the Canaanites and Phoenicians as they traversed the Mediterranean Sea in their Byblos Ships to the shores of Italy. They brought their wine culture with them, which displaced the native Etruscan grog. Now it was the Etruscans' turn to begin a similar process in Europe and uproot the long-established grogs there, eventually reaching Scandinavia, about 1300 kilometers (800 miles) to the north, where a peculiarly Nordic extreme fermented beverage held sway.

Under Phoenician tutelage, the Etruscans had their own wine-making industry up and running by 600 B.C. Domesticated vines were brought in the hulls of the Byblos Ships and planted. Crosses between the newcomers and the promiscuous wild grape population of Italy led to today's 400 to 700 native cultivars, more than for any other European country. Many of these vines produce distinct, delicious fruit.

Take the premier grape varietal of Tuscany, Sangiovese (perhaps derived from Latin, *sanguis Jovis,* "Jove or Jupiter's blood") that goes into modern Chianti, Brunello di Montalcino, and the so-called "Super Tuscans." My molecular biologist colleague, José Vouillamoz, showed that it was almost certainly a spontaneous cross between Ciliegiolo, a native Tuscan cultivar, and Calabrese Montenuovo, likely from the region of Calabria as the name implies (Sam would be proud). Without convincing ancient DNA evidence, however, there is no way of knowing when and where the cross took place. The vines might have met each other in Etruscan times when the Calabrian varietal was transplanted to the north, or the mating might have occurred much more recently. The earliest certain literary reference to the grape is in a viticultural treatise of A.D. 1600, hardly the stuff of antiquity.

HEADING WESTWARD TO GAUL AND CATALONIA

WHAT WE DO know is that the Etruscans took up the banner of the wine culture and became avid viniculturalists and exporters of wine by ship, just like the Phoenicians. Their principal target at first was southern France, on the doorstep to Gaul and the entryway to Europe as a whole via the continent's rivers. A diverse group of peoples and tribes called the Celts inhabited Europe during the Iron Age of the 1st millennium B.C. They had long been wedded to their own version of an extreme fermented beverage or grog, and the Etruscans were out to change all that.

Hundreds of Etruscan ships must have plied the waters between Tuscany and southern France during the period from 600 to 400 B.C., to explain the numerous shipwrecks that have been found. *Grand Ribaud F*, which went down off the coast of the Hyères Islands, east of Marseilles, is the paradigm example. Its hold was filled with grapevines, possibly for transplantation as well as for cushioning some 700–800 Etruscan wine amphoras. The amphoras, stacked in layers, were all stoppered with cork, among the earliest evidence for this technology.

The port city of Lattara (modern Lattes) on the French coast, south of Montpellier, revealed what kind of wine was being imported from Etruria. This site, which has been intensively excavated since the early 1980s, had storerooms lining its quays for storing goods. Some were filled with amphoras identical to those aboard *Grand Ribaud F*.

We went to work, using our battery of analytical tools, especially LC-MS-MS, GC-MS, and SPME (Preface), to test the Lattara amphoras for wine. We found that the tartaric acid content of the amphora pottery fabrics was significantly above that of the background soil, so they must have originally contained a grape product, most likely wine. We also identified the marker compounds for pine resin, showing that the wine had been resinated. There was more: the wine was laced with botanicals, probably rosemary, basil, and/or thyme. These herbs, which are native to Italy, are extremely flavorful. Moreover, ample analytical and literary evidence exists that they played a major medicinal role as herbal wines in pharmacopeias around the Mediterranean basin, including those of Egypt, Greece, and Rome. Presumably, the same was true of the Etruscans.

Although we are yet to identify the constituents of a native grog lurking in the local pottery at Lattara, which would have been supplanted by the imported Etruscan wine, we have some clues from surrounding areas. A malting floor from a 5th-century B.C. house at Roquepertuse, about 150 kilometers (93 miles) east of Lattara on the northern outskirts of Marseilles, was littered with sprouted 6-row barley grains. This malt would have provided the starting material for a good beer. A specialized oven, probably for drying and roasting it, was nearby. The excavators and scientists speculate that wheat and millet were used separately or mixed together into one brew. Celtic beers were commented on by later Roman writers, not always favorably; Pliny the Elder, however, kindly wrote of the longevity of Gallic and Spanish brews.

Grape seeds were also found scattered on the floor of the Roquepertuse house, suggesting that wine was produced locally or possibly added to the barley beer to make an extreme fermented beverage. Until a biomolecular archaeological study of the pottery vessels from the site is done, we will remain in the dark about any other ingredients to a grog, such as honey. Possible herbal additives, except bitter vetch, are also missing thus far from the archaeobotanical corpus at Roquepertuse.

To better pick up the trail of Celtic grog, we need to travel westward from Roquepertuse and Lattara, over the coastal Pyrenee Mountains to Catalonia. At Genó, near Barcelona, as early as 3000 B.C., and nearby at later sites, Spanish researchers put different-sized pottery vessels through their scientific paces using starch, phytolith, and chemical analyses. They discovered that the vessels contained fermented emmer wheat and barley beers, which were sometimes flavored with mugwort (*Artemisia vulgaris*), rosemary, mint, and/or thyme. At times, the cereals were supplemented with honey or acorn flour to make an extreme fermented beverage worthy of the name.

We've already seen that rosemary and thyme were added to the early Etruscan and Scorpion I drinks (Chapters 4 and 5). The menthol in mint oil, besides being very tasty, soothes the body and helps fight off disease. Mugwort, which contains the psychoactive compound thujone, is perhaps the most curious additive. But we shouldn't be surprised by its presence, since, as we saw for China (Chapter 3), wormwood relatives there were added to fermented beverages.

The Barcelona researchers weren't satisfied with just reconstructing the ancient beverage recipe; they wanted to find out what it might have tasted like. They enlisted the help of the Spanish-based San Miguel brewery. Taking emmer wheat from the last remaining field in Asturias in northern Spain, barley, and pure water from the Pyrenees, they carried out fermentation in a handmade pottery vessel, similar to the very large ancient jar from Genó whose residue they had analyzed. They didn't go as far as adding mugwort, but native rosemary, thyme, and mint enhanced the flavor and served as preservatives. Production was limited to 400 bottles of the thick, dark gruelly liquid with an 8% alcohol content.

TURNING NORTHWARD

ON CURRENT EVIDENCE, grogs similar to those around Barcelona were all the rage up into central and northern Europe. They were often panned by later Roman writers, who clung to the wine culture and viewed the northerners as uncouth, beer- and mead-swilling barbarians. Dionysius of Halicarnassus famously said that Celtic beer's disgusting smell came from "barley rotted in water," and Diodorus Siculus called it "the washings of honeycombs."

Fortunately, archaeologists, scientists, and brewers have come to the rescue to reinstate the reputation of the Celts and their fermented beverages. The 6th-century B.C. tomb at Hochdorf, southeast of Stuttgart, Germany, and its adjacent settlement are the premier instances of Celtic prowess in this consequential area of human endeavor. I had the occasion to visit the site with my archaeobotanical colleague, Hans-Peter Stika, in November 2010. Despite a few snow flurries, we climbed to the top of the mound, a smaller version of the Midas

Tumulus in Turkey, and surveyed the rolling countryside south to the Danube River where similar burials and sites have been excavated.

The Celtic Museum next to the Hochdorf burial mound has a reconstruction of what lay within. Like the Midas Tumulus, the burial chamber was made from a double wall of logs. More logs and soil were piled on top to a height of about 10 meters (33 feet), a quarter the size of the Turkish mound. Inside, a 40-year-old male was laid out in state on a bronze couch, adorned with a sword-dancing scene. He wore a peaked birchbark cap and pointed-toe leather shoes with intricately incised gold coverings, which were uncannily similar to those of the Phrygians.

A funerary feast, like that for Midas or Gordias, was the center-piece of the Hochdorf tomb. Place settings of bronze vessels for nine people were arranged neatly on a full-scale wagon in front of the man. The funerary meal itself was not preserved. But clearly it had been washed down with a special fermented beverage, since nine enor-mous drinking-horns had hung from a wall. Eight were aurochs (oxen) horns, accented by gold and bronze fittings; the last was made of iron over a meter (3.3 feet) long and with a 5.5-liter (1.5-gallon) capacity.

The drink that once filled the horns came from a large bronze caul-dron, like those in the Midas Tumulus. The 500-liter vat, with three recumbent lions attached to its shoulder, had been imported from Greece. But it was not filled with wine. Rather, according to the pal-ynological study of the residue inside, it contained a luscious honey mead made from the nectar of some 60 different local plants, includ-ing wild thyme and linden and willow trees.

The chieftain and his cohorts might have drunk mead, the elixir of the Nordic gods, but their subjects drank a cereal-based beer, albeit similarly refined and delicious according to the study carried out by Hans-Peter. Eight ditches measuring 6 meters (20 feet) long of the late 5th to early 4th centuries B.C. were excavated at the fortified settle-ment next to the Hochdorf mound. They contained thick layers of a dark malt, covered with charcoal. Hans-Peter argues that the unusual ditches were used to sprout the barley and then dry and toast it with an open fire lit from one end to yield a smoky-tasting malt. Today, sev-eral breweries in Bamberg, a short distance from Stuttgart, maintain the Iron Age tradition of a smoked beer (German, *Rauchbier*). They do use a somewhat more advanced technology of drying the malt over a beechwood fire.

The Iron Age brewers were a step ahead of their modern German counterparts in other respects. They were not averse to adding some wheat to the grain bill. Since hops were still a rarity as a bittering agent, they turned to mugwort and carrot as additives. Moreover, since no brewing vats were found, Hans-Peter suggests that the wort was boiled by submerging red-hot stones into wooden vessels, now disintegrated, as Sam did when he made his idiosyncratic version of a Finnish *sahti* ("homemade beer"). Small breweries in Austria and Bavaria (such as at Marktoberdorf) still make their beer (German, *Steinbier*) this way. We can imagine the first humanly contrived Palaeo-Brew, even our *Ta Henket*, being made similarly before pottery and metal vessels were invented. Hans-Peter also observed a higher than average amount of lactic acid bacteria in the malt that pointed to a more sour brew, like a Belgian lambic or red ale.

The Stuttgarter Hofbräu brewery re-created Hans-Peter's "Celtic beer." It's not clear whether they dug a ditch to sprout and roast the barley, or even whether they added some mugwort and/or carrot, but locals in Celtic attire quickly consumed the experimental batch of beer.

TO THE ENDS OF THE EARTH

LET US NOW travel by land—perhaps on an oxen cart laden down with wine barrels—and riverboat to the most northerly part of the European continent: Scotland and Scandinavia, or what the Greeks, Romans, and later medieval writers knew as Ultima Thule, the northernmost land in the then-known world.

Scotland's thirst-quencher and claim to fame in the fermented beverage world today might be Scotch, but in ages past, before the arrival of distillation sometime in the 1st millennium A.D., a "Nordic grog," an extreme hybrid alcoholic beverage rich in local ingredients, held court. As far back as 3500 B.C. during the Neolithic period and likely much earlier, archaeologists with the help of palynologists have pieced together the makings of such a beverage in the Orkney Islands, off the far northern tip of Scotland, itself an island.

Investigators observed that large vats, whose 100-liter (26-gallon) volumes would have been ideal for brewing on a large scale, were lined with blackish deposits. Since no lids were found in the excavation, the mouths of the vessels were probably covered with wood, since disintegrated, to set up the anaerobic conditions needed for fermentation. The residues were shown to contain the telltale pollen of a wildflower honey, principally of the small-leaved lime tree (*Tilia cordata*), meadowsweet (*Filipendula vulgaris*), and heather (*Calluna vulgaris*). Cereal pollen was also imbedded in the deposits, but fruit pollen was absent, possibly because fruit retains little pollen.

Later finds, until 1500 B.C., in the Orkneys and on the Scottish mainland had the same story to tell. The Nordic "grog," like those at the Spanish sites and Hochdorf in southern and central Europe, were sometimes a pure mead, at other times a combination of mead and beer, perhaps with some fruit thrown in for good measure. The meadowsweet and heather pollen might also be interpreted as deliberate additions of those herbs.

The preferred way to quaff the northern European beverage, especially at the later Scottish sites, was with a large mug or "beaker" in archaeological parlance. For example, at Ashgrove in Fife, north of Edinburgh, a male warrior was buried around 1700 B.C. with only his well-fashioned dagger and pottery beaker, whose contents provided courage and consolation in battle. The beaker was so full at the time of burial that the beverage, most likely a mead, had spilled out over the moss and leaves covering the man's upper body.

Spurred on by these discoveries, many modern brewers and even distillers have gotten into the act. William Grant and Sons, the Glenfiddich distillery in Speyside, the heartland of modern Scotch production, soon came out with a heather-honey mead at 8% alcohol. The company took its clues from the analysis of residues inside large ancient vats, like those from the Orkneys, that had been excavated on the island of Rhum in the Inner Hebrides along the western coast. The Glenfiddich distillers, however, might better have thrown in some additional barley mash to make a real grog, as they are accustomed to do in making their single malt Scotches. Cereal pollen was dispersed in the Rhum residues, showing that the vats had been used to make a combination mead and beer.

SCANDINAVIAN SPIRITS RAN HIGH

MY OWN INTEREST and research on Nordic grog is another serendipitous story. I was invited by a group of Scandinavians from Norway, Sweden, and Denmark to be their pottery and excavation specialist for a new Bronze–Iron Age project in Jordan. I had long worked in this country's Baqʿah Valley investigating the same periods, so I was only too happy to accept. The site, Tell el-Fukhar (Arabic, "mound of pottery"), lived up to its name in the four summers of excavation (1990–1993) to follow.

It's one thing to peel away the layers of a tell, one by one over thousands of years, and uncover its pottery and other artifacts. It's another thing to process all the information—defining the building trenches and pits cutting through occupational remains and sorting out the heaps of pottery. It soon became apparent that I would need to spend time in Scandinavia to complete the project because all the pottery and artifacts were being shipped there from Jordan. That wasn't a problem, especially since we could explore the countries and our ancestral roots—Doris's in Sweden and mine in Norway—at the same time.

Our first stop in Scandinavia was Uppsala in Sweden where Magnus Ottosson, a longtime colleague and co-director of the Fukhar excavation, invited me to be a visiting professor and hosted us in the fall of 1991. In between my studying the Jordanian pottery at the university, we reconnoitered the surrounding countryside by bicycle. I could not pass up the opportunity to find out more about Nordic archaeology, and we were right in the middle of it. Gamla Uppsala (Swedish, "Old Uppsala")—home to the first Swedish kings, its parliament, and main pagan cult center during medieval times—was a short ride away. We walked its burial mounds and drank the heavily spiced mead, which strangely enough for a country of Viking origins could only be made here and nowhere else in Sweden by law.

The forests, which were believed to be inhabited by trolls, elves, and other mischievous creatures in Scandinavian legends, were equally idyllic, even magical. We went hunting for aromatic chanterelle mushrooms, which we later dehydrated by sautéing them in a pan. We took those dried mushrooms back with us to the States where they kept their wonderful fragrancy for years to come. All it took was a single chanterelle in a dish to carry us back to Uppsala and Sweden.

You might think that such experiences were enough to last us a lifetime. But we were back again in the spring of 1994. This time, I was a Fulbright scholar at the Archaeological Research Laboratory of the University of Stockholm researching the Nordic grog of Scandinavia. I sifted through the fermented beverage–related artifacts in the Nordic Museum with the help of curators, archaeologists, and other scientists.

As is often the case in archaeology, I had to change my focus from the museum to the field to discover something truly exciting. This came about when I was invited to visit the island of Gotland in the Baltic Sea by its chief archaeologist, Erik Nylén. He settled us into an apartment on the wall of Visby, the best preserved medieval town in Sweden. We then set forth on a rapid but in-depth tour of the 130-kilometer (80-mile)-long island. We met with the farmers, who had re-created Viking boats, and taken them, like their ancestors, by river and overland to Constantinople (modern Istanbul). Beer was naturally the first order of the day on their journeys, especially in eastern Europe where liquor stores closed early. We had our own liquid refreshment when we stopped at farmhouses along the way to taste the traditional Gotlandsdryka (literally, "Gotland's drink"), a spiced barley beer with juniper and sometimes honey added. The locals also make a delicious birch sap ale, often flavored with bog myrtle and bog cranberry, very ancient ingredients as I was to discover.

Our final destination was the site of Havor on the southern part of the island. Here, Erik recounted how he had excavated a remarkable cache of artifacts buried under a floor beside the outer wall of a 1st-century A.D. ring fort. The hoard was contained inside a Roman wine bucket or cauldron, in keeping with the tradition of importing fancy containers from the "wine country" of southern Europe, as we have already seen at Hochdorf. The bucket was full of rare treasures: a unique gold filigreed and granulated torque (a large neck ring of Nordic design), a pair of bronze bells, and most significantly for me, three single-handled "saucepans" or drinking cups of Roman type, together with a long-handled strainer-cup and ladle nestled inside one another. I asked where the bucket, saucepans, strainer-cup, and ladle were now. Erik said they were in the Visby museum, and we could make a firsthand examination for residues tomorrow.

Erik and I sat at a table in the museum the next day with the Havor artifacts before us. I became intrigued by the reddish-brown deposit around and filling the holes of the strainer-cup. Erik agreed to part with a piece of the residue, which was about a centimeter (half an inch) square and 3 millimeters (tenth of an inch) thick. I hand-carried the valuable sample back to the lab in Stockholm and began the analysis.

Some preliminary tests of the strainer-cup residue appeared promising, but the resources at the Stockholm lab (e.g., a new X-ray diffraction instrument and standard GC-MS) were too limited. These techniques could not detect tartaric acid, the fingerprint compound of grape and wine, and some long-chain compounds that might or might not derive from beeswax, an indicator for honey mead.

Consequently, I carried the sample back to Philadelphia, where our tests by FT-IR and a wet chemical spot test showed that tartaric acid was present. But it would be another 13 years, in 2007, before we re-examined the sample with more sensitive instruments, namely LC-MS-MS and SPME (Preface). It took another six years to complete our research and publish the scientific article (McGovern, Hall, and Mirzoian 2013). Patience and persistence are often the hallmarks of a successful biomolecular archaeological investigation—that coupled with the best scientific instrumentation and just plain luck. If we hadn't made the trip to Gotland and if Erik had not excavated at Havor, we would still be searching for the Nordic grog in Sweden.

The chemical data for the Havor residue are laid out in detail in our article. It shows that the Havor bucket contained imported resinated wine from the south. Additionally, birch tree sap, but not honey, had been mixed in. Herbs were strangely absent. Still, we had the makings of yet another version of the Nordic grog, perhaps limited to Gotland.

Birch sap in a fermented beverage is not as unusual as you might think. Maple syrup is regularly used to make beers in the United States and Canada. Birch trees abound in the forests of Scandinavia, and birch sap had been used since at least Neolithic times for many other purposes—a mastic to hold weapon haftings, a sealant, and perhaps even a medicinal chewing gum as suggested by impressed tooth marks in an ancient wad. The sap has its own peculiar and enticing sensory properties. Its relatively high sugar content of up to 2.5% can be further concentrated by heating. You can still get a taste of the ingredient in *kvass* (Russian, "leaven"), whose alcohol percentage is elevated by adding leavened dark rye, wheat, or barley bread and sometimes fruit. The use of bread in beer recalls my discussions with Michael Jackson (Chapter 2) and in the making of *Ta Henket* (Chapter 4).

DANISH REVERIES

THE NEXT STOP on our journey through Scandinavia was Copenhagen where another member of the Jordanian team, John Strange, invited me as a visiting professor at the university for the spring of 1995. We were ensconced on perhaps the most sought-after (and touristic) canal street in the Danish capital, Nyhavn. The Danish National Bank provided us with an apartment with two enormous living rooms, decked out with Danish Modern furniture and a service for 12 of Royal Copenhagen porcelain.

Long windows faced on to the canal where we could watch the boats coming in from the North and Baltic seas. Swedish boats came loaded down with empty Carlsberg beer cases, which were rolled down the gangplank on handcarts, soon to be replaced with full cases for the return trip. At the time, Danish beer was a good deal less expensive and more tasty than Swedish beer. Students lolled in the outdoor cafes lining the street, beer bottles in hand.

We soon had bought used bikes and were exploring the many cas-

tles, parks, and open-air museums, such as Skansen, in the environs. It
was a short ride from our apartment to John's department at the university, where I put the finishing touches to a study of the Fukhar pottery for the excavation report.

Denmark's national museum was a five-minute bike ride away. It
turned out to be even richer in Nordic archaeological remains, especially for extreme fermented beverages, than Stockholm's museum.
The curators, archaeologists, and other scientists again took me into
their confidence and opened their storerooms to search for residues to
analyze. One of the reasons for their largesse is the Danish fondness
for alcoholic beverages of all kinds. Many an afternoon was whiled
away feasting on marinated herring on smørrebrød (dark rye bread)
and skaaling (literally, "raising the bowl to") each other with ice-cold
aquavit. Both food and drink are often flavored with herbs. Caraway
is good, but my favorite is *pors*, Danish for bog myrtle or sweet gale—
Myrica gale botanically. It has long flavored Scandinavian drinks, as I
was to learn.

Eva Koch in the prehistory department of the museum, who made
extremely important contributions to our knowledge of ancient fermented beverages (and now sadly is no longer with us), took me under
her wing. She directed me to a tumulus burial of a male warrior in
northwest Denmark at Nandrup on the island of Mors in Jutland,
dated 1500–1300 B.C. Like the warrior in the tomb at Ashgrove in
Scotland, this soldier was suitably outfitted with a bronze sword and
dagger, both intricately decorated with interlocked spirals and other
geometric designs of Celtic inspiration, and the requisite large jar for a
bracing drink in the afterlife. A dark brownish residue lined the lower
two-thirds of the vessel's interior. I was accorded two small pieces of
the residue for analysis, weighing a quarter gram (less than a hun-
dredth of an ounce).

Other samples followed. They included a massive bronze strainer
with residue filling its holes from a hoard of gold and bronze artifacts
from a pit at Kostræde in southern Zealand, not far from Copenhagen,
dated 1100–500 B.C. It was reminiscent of the much smaller strainer-
cup from Havor and its residue. But the Kostræde strainer was the earliest such implement ever found in Scandinavia. It had probably been

imported from eastern Europe. I went away with another quarter-gram sample.

A relatively late sample of Early Roman date, around 200 B.C., from Juellinge on the island of Lolland, south of Zealand, rounded out the Danish sample group. A 30-year-old female, adorned with silver fibulas (clothing fasteners), hair clips, and a necklace of glass beads, had been buried in a wooden coffin with drinking paraphernalia. She held a long-handled bronze strainer-cup, similar to the one from Havor, in her right hand. Other vessels, belonging to a canonical Roman wine set, were a large bronze bucket and incised glass beakers. A long-handled ladle was found inside the bucket. I was again granted a quarter-gram sample from the bucket's interior.

THE EGTVED PRIESTESS-DANCER AND DRINKER

ANOTHER KEY PIECE of evidence in rediscovering the ancient Nordic grog was a sample, which has been promised me but still needs to clear some bureaucratic hoops before it can be chemically analyzed. Its importance lies in its association with the extraordinary burial of a woman of about 16 to 18 years old in an oak coffin under a tumulus at Egtved in Jutland. The burial, dated to 1390–1370 B.C. by the tree ring sequence of the oak, lies about 100 kilometers (62 miles) south of the Nandrup warrior tomb.

The woman and her burial goods were excellently preserved, including intact clothing and fragments of her brain, teeth, skin, and hair (she was a Nordic blonde). She wore a short-bodiced blouse and a woolen skirt with long tassels dangling from her hips. Comparing her attire to that of contemporaneous figurine and rock art marked her as being a priestess and/or ceremonial dancer. A large bronze belt disk at her midriff displayed interlocking spirals, a well-known symbol of the Nordic sun-god. She was wrapped in a thick woolen blanket and cowhide. Intriguingly, a flowering yarrow, a favorite medieval beer spice, had been placed between the upper and lower halves of her coffin. It was also a sign that she had been buried during the summer.

Most importantly for our purposes, a birch bark container, whose interior was lined with a dark residue, had been placed at the foot of the Egtved woman inside the coffin. If that weren't inducement enough for a chemical study, the palynological and archaeobotanical findings were unequivocal that the bucket had once been filled with a version of the Nordic grog. Remains of bog cranberries and cowberries, wheat grains, bog myrtle filaments, and lime tree, meadowsweet, and white clover pollen, derived from honey, implied that the vessel once contained a spiced beer-wine-and-mead combination. This powerful extreme fermented beverage might well have inspired the woman's dancing in life.

Our chemical studies from other Danish sites, combined with the Egtved archaeobotanical findings, paint a picture of the popularity of Nordic grogs, as well as pure meads, for thousands of years in Scandinavia. The analysis of the Nandrup bucket residue provided our earliest evidence. It produced only biomarkers for beeswax of a honey mead, borne out by the same pollen spectrum as that for the Egtved bucket residue. Whereas the Egtved bucket contained a very complex fermented beverage, its older Bronze Age counterpart from Nandrup was a pure mead.

An archaeobotanical study of the much later residue from the Juellinge bucket had already shown it to be yet another version of the Nordic grog. Remnants of barley grains, a fruit that was most likely bog cranberry, lesser amounts of lingonberry or cowberry, filaments of bog myrtle, and yeast cells were dispersed throughout its residue. Our biomolecular archaeological investigation confirmed the bog cranberry and lingonberry. It also provided new information, including biomarkers for beeswax from honey, tartaric acid most likely from imported resinated wine, and bog myrtle and juniper as spices. The composite evidence was clear-cut: this bucket was once filled with an extreme fermented beverage of barley beer, fruit wine, and honey mead.

We had no archaeobotanical evidence to go on when we analyzed the residue from the Kostræde strainer, which straddled the time period between our earlier and later samples. Our chemical findings, however, gave a very detailed picture of the beverage that was filtered through the strainer. Honey, birch tree sap, and, once again, imported resinated grape wine were its principal ingredients, which were probably mixed and fermented together as a single batch. We had very elusive chemical signs of a cereal beer being part of this hybrid beverage; an archaeobotanical study is needed before we can be sure. Herbal additives of bog myrtle and juniper rounded out its flavor profile.

Juniper was an exciting find, since it is the earliest occurrence of this conifer extract in a Nordic grog. Until our discovery, the earliest mention of its use in native fermented beverages was in a handwritten recipe book from the late eighteenth century A.D. Today, it is a frequent drink additive, especially in Poland and Finland. For the ancient preparation, we might envision the juniper cones (in fact, a pseudofruit) being pounded by wooden mortar and pestle, soaked in water overnight, and boiled and strained to separate seeds and resins, following traditional practice. The Kostræde strainer might have been used for the final separation. Another possibility is that the juniper extract was leached out of branches at the bottom of a log or plank vat for filtering the wort, as is customary in making Finnish *sahti*.

As a side note on juniper as an additive to *sahti*, Sam claims that his version of the beverage (*Sah'tea*), which he did in collaboration with the Finnish brewer Juha Ikonen, is based on a 9th-century recipe. His story is unlikely, since the earliest text of any kind in the Finnic language is a 13th-century birch bark letter. Moreover, the black chai tea, flavored with ginger, cardamom, cinnamon, cloves, and black pepper in *Sah'tea*, are more appropriate additives for a drink from India than Finland, which had limited access to tea and these exotic spices. Juniper as an additive and Sam's hot-rock boiling of the wort, however, are in keeping with ancient precedents.

WINE: FIRST A TRICKLE, THEN A FLOOD

PRIDE OF PLACE for the earliest occurrence of birch tree sap in a Nordic grog, to date, likewise goes to the Kostræde beverage. But even more mind-boggling is the earliest occurrence of imported resinated wine from the south, well attested to by our chemical data. It had long been hypothesized that the amber trade routes, which followed the major rivers (e.g., the Rhine and Rhone rivers) from the

Baltic to southern Europe had been in operation by the late 2nd millennium B.C. But what did the northerners receive in return for their
beautiful and costly gemstone? They clearly appreciated the ostenta-
tious wine serving and drinking vessels of Greece and Italy. Indeed, at
Vix in Burgundy, archaeologists uncovered the largest Greek mixing
krater (cauldron) ever found. It was from a tumulus burial of a "barbarian woman," dating approximately to the same time as the princely
one at Hochdorf. It was 1.6 meters (over 5 feet) tall and had a capacity
of 1200 liters (317 gallons).

The large bronze strainers from central Europe might well have
caught the eye of a merchant following a trade route along a river, such
as the Elbe leading to the Danube. Wine, to go with the vessels for
making and enjoying the drink, was a natural accompaniment. As an
organic good, however, it was virtually undetectable in the archaeological record. With more sensitive chemical tools, we can now begin
to map out wine's initial trickle into Scandinavia and other northern realms. It had arrived at Kostræde as early as 1100 B.C. Its importation gradually picked up momentum, as shown by the wine mixed
into Havor and Juellinge grogs at the turn of the millennia. Once the
Nordic people began converting to Christianity, more and more litur-
gical wine poured in. Some of it came from the Rhineland, as shown
by our analyses of special, imported vessels excavated at the "first city
in Sweden," the 9th-century A.D. town of Birka. To reach this "inland"
port, traders navigated a long estuary of the Baltic Sea, west of Stockholm. We followed the same route by boat during our time in Sweden.

The southerners might not have appreciated the richly variegated
Nordic grog. They preferred their wine neat, except for the occasional
tree resin, seawater, or herb as needed. Their snobbishness, however,
did not blind them to innovation. The Celtic flair for making objects
from whole logs and staves is a case in point. Preeminently, the Celts
fashioned the oak barrel, which became the container of choice for
transporting wine overland and by river. They also improvised all
manner of vats, filters, and specialized tools for making fermented
beverages, as well as beehives for honey and ultimately mead production. Scandinavians continue to excel in these crafts today, using only
the best wood for the job.

The pottery amphora might have been ideal for shipping wine in the hulls of ships. A wood barrel, whose staves expanded when wet to seal the barrel from losing precious liquid or being exposed to the outside air, worked extremely well for the scows that plied the European rivers. The barrel was larger than the amphora but weighed relatively less for the greater volume of beer, wine, or extreme fermented beverage that it held. Southern winemakers took the innovation a step further when they began ageing their wines in barrels. Possibly, they discovered that oak sap was a less intrusive preservative than pine sap for the long journey north, or they were won over by the less tannic edges of a wine that had spent some time in oak.

Still, the Nordic grog held its own against the inroads of grape wine for millennia, and for good reason. Its many ingredients guaranteed a nutritious, medicinal, and flavorful drink in a difficult environment with few sugar resources. Once the birch and other trees began oozing their plentiful saps at the start of spring, it was no wonder that Nordic peoples avidly collected the sap and made it into a fermented beverage. Honey, grains, tart fruits, herbs, and fragrant flowers soon followed. Combined in the Nordic grog, they made for a high-alcohol beverage guaranteed to last through the warmer months and on into the cold winter.

The ancient Nordic assemblage of bitter herbs—most commonly, bog myrtle, yarrow, meadowsweet, and wild rosemary—continued on as the so-called gruit of medieval beers. But gruit began to lose its luster during the later Middle Ages. Its death knell came when hops were declared the only legitimate bittering agent for beer by the *Reinheitsgebot* (Chapter 1).

The Nordic herbs struggled on in the many bitters and digestives made throughout Europe, especially in the monasteries. They continued to be appreciated in distilled beverages, whether the bog myrtle of aquavit, the juniper of gin, or the infusions of vodka. They have recently become darlings of the resurgent cocktail movement and still have a prominent place in folk medicine. Their future in developing new medicines (Chapters 3 and 4) and drinks never looked brighter.

A BEVERAGE BEYOND COMPARE

I HAVE ALREADY intimated that mead, made only from honey, was at the top of the Nordic fermented beverage pyramid. It bears repeating that there were good reasons for honey mead's ascendancy. As honey is the most concentrated source of sugar in nature (over 70% by weight), its fermentation into mead yielded the highest-alcohol beverage known to humankind until distillation was invented (Chapter 9). The preservative properties of both sugar and alcohol assure that mead will last for years, even centuries, and always be at the ready for raising one's core body temperature during the darkest, coldest Nordic nights.

Moreover, mead had profound psychotropic effects due to alcohol, which assured its priority in a Nordic warrior's arsenal. The Viking berserks, who the Norse sagas describe as having gone naked into battle or wearing only a wolfskin or bearskin, were probably spurred on by mead. If they proved successful in battle, as we read in the Anglo-Saxon poem *Beowulf*, they downed cup after cup at the victory celebrations in longhouses ("mead halls"). One large swill, as it were, for incitement to battle, and a second to succor the spirits.

Spirits indeed. The Nordic world, before the arrival of Christianity, was full of gods, giants, elves, dwarfs, and beings of every kind that indwelled wild animals, trees, and prominent natural landmarks. The deep, dark waters of bogs, which dot the Scandinavian landscape, were thought to be mysterious abodes of the nether-dwellers. They could be appeased by ceremoniously throwing valuable drinking-sets into them, presumably wih the mead and Nordic grog that they contained. Odin himself, the high god of Norse mythology, is said to have died by throwing himself into the well or bog at the foot of the eternally green ash tree (Yggdrasil), whose branches and roots encompass the nine realms of creation. He sought the wisdom endowed by mead.

In some respects, the making and rediscovery of mead by Odin follows a similar story line as our resuscitation of the Nordic grog as *Kvasir*. I won't claim any supernatural powers or the same degree of poetic creation and license as Odin. The gist of the Odin story is that two opposing bands of gods settled their differences by spitting chewed-up fruit into a large cauldron. In my opinion, chewing and spitting were the initial "entrée" to making a fermented beverage, as I have touched upon throughout the book, so it was no wonder that the gods should begin this way and seal their truce by mixing their salivas together. The result was a particularly wise, poetic, and musical creature named Kvasir, who was part human and part god. Two conniving dwarfs then murdered Kvasir. They took his blood, another universal symbol for reconciliation, and mixed it with honey, the magical elixir, to make a kind of grog in three large cauldrons.

The dwarfs managed to hold onto the precious liquid until they came up against the giants. Like a scene out of *Gulliver's Travels*, they were forced onto a small deserted island and threatened by drowning if they did not surrender the magical and poetic grog. They finally relented, and the three cauldrons were handed over to the giants. They were stashed away inside a deep, dark cavern, where they were guarded by the most imposing giant's beautiful daughter, transformed into a gnarly witch to scare off any intruding imbibers.

Odin found a way into the cave by first disguising himself as the one-eyed wandering stranger, a motif also used by Wagner for Wotan in his Ring Cycle operas. Odin had sacrificed his eye to gain a draught of the water (and wisdom) from the pool of the World Tree. When his offer to work the fields of the giants in return for a drink of the grog failed, Odin magically transformed himself into a snake and gained entry to the cave. Three nights of lovemaking with the giant's daughter did the trick. His attentions were rewarded each day with some of the grog. After consuming all the beverage from the three cauldrons, Odin flew back to Valhalla, home of the gods, as an eagle. He regurgitated the magical potion into three new cauldrons, which had been set out by the gods on command at his homecoming.

RESUSCITATING OUR VERSION OF THE NORDIC GROG

WE HAD A lot to live up to in re-creating what came to be known as *Kvasir* after the wise, artistic being whose blood went into the paradaisical grog. Yet, truth be told, we had a lot of chemical and archaeobotanical information to go on. My analytical chemical associate in our Penn Museum lab, Gretchen Hall, marveled at how detailed a picture of the Nordic grog we had gleaned from our highly sensitive methods. She still says that our Scandinavian analyses are her favorite example of the enormous potential of biomolecular archaeology, besides being a lot of fun to do.

The biggest challenge of making a Nordic grog is its many ingredients. What yeast could ferment such a seeming hodgepodge? Should we stick to making a relatively pure mead, perhaps with some added gruit, or go all out and include lots of cereals and native fruits? If the former, a mead yeast might be sufficient; if the latter, we might need a jack-of-all-trades yeast.

Sam proposed that we travel to Scandinavia to find out more and do some experimentation on the ground. I was, of course, game to return to the lands of so many happy memories and adventures. So, in April 2013, we flew into Arlanda Airport, and soon we were traversing the familiar forests and terrain leading south to Stockholm and its Old Town (Gamla Stan). That evening, we were feted by an old friend from our days at Teo's Casa Baladin, Jörgen Hasselqvist, at his Oliver Twist Pub and Restaurant. After a tasting flight of *Ancient Ales*, we descended into his beer cellar deep in the bowels of the medieval capital, no doubt previously inhabited by gnomes and dragons, and tasted aged Belgian lambics and gueuzes (blended young and old lambics).

Next day, it was off through the Swedish countryside, still covered in snow, to Nynäshamn, coincidentally the same town on the coast from which we had taken the ferry to Gotland so many years before. This time, I stayed ashore to help make a truly Scandinavian version of the Nordic grog in the town. The resident brewer of Nynäshamns Ångbryggeri was Lasse Ericsson. He and Tim Hawn and Sam at Dogfish Head put their heads together and came up with a recipe, true to the biomolecular archaeological data, which would be tried first in Sweden and later be the basis for *Kvasir* in the States.

They decided on a hardy red wheat and special roasted 2-row barley for the grain bill, which was then supplemented with Swedish bog cranberry and lingonberry, which are worlds apart from their blander

American cousins. Fragrant wildflower honey from northern Sweden came next, topped off by unctuous and delicious birch tree sap. A healthy dose of the main bittering agent—bog myrtle—went into the wort boil for the last half hour, followed up during the final 10 minutes with the more aromatic yarrow. Meadowsweet was added after the heat was turned off to conserve as much of its delicacy and distinctiveness as possible. The assembled team of brewers, beer writers, scientists (include me in this number), and other hangers-on sat around a table, as we often do before a final vote on the ingredients, smelling the various herbs, one at a time and in combination, in glasses of warm water.

I reluctantly agreed to include some hops, even if they were absent from our archaeochemical formulation; we didn't want to run afoul of the all-powerful Systembolaget, the Swedish state liquor store. The somewhat spicy Tettnang noble hop, which probably originated in the same region of southern Germany where the Hochdorf prince was buried (Baden-Württemberg), was our choice.

The brewing process itself was done in modern stainless steel kettles, tuns, vats, and ageing tanks. I lent the process some historical authenticity by donning a Viking horned helmet when I poured in the birch sap. Lacking a suitable wild yeast from Scandinavia, we turned to a Scottish ale yeast—Scottish because our earliest evidence thus far for the Nordic grog dates back to 3500 B.C. there and because it is hardy enough to carry out the difficult fermentation. It handled the varied ingredients just fine—up to 10% alcohol. Besides changing out the modern brewing apparatus for more authentic cauldrons and strainers, we might also have considered spitting on the yeast, as Odin is said to do in the 14th-century A.D. Hálfs saga to assure a "good ale" for one of King Alrek's wives in a brewing competition.

Coming up with a suitable name that hasn't been already registered or patented, is always a challenge. The Swedes chose *Arketyp* ("Archetype"), which recognized the long, native tradition of the beverage. A pottery sherd of a drinking cup from Havor, with an interlocking spiral design, provided a touch of authenticity to the label. Bottles of *Arketyp* soon lined the shelves of the Systembolaget stores, and the intensely fruity and herbal concoction was given high marks by beer tasters.

Our trip to Scandinavia wouldn't have been complete without finishing up in Copenhagen, whose National Museum had provided us with so many excellent samples and also housed the Egtved dancer and priestess. We took the six-hour train ride through the snowy fields of southern Sweden and across the bridge to the Danish capital. Within an hour, we were met by the curator of the prehistoric collection, Poul Otto Nielsen, at the door to the National Museum. He provided commentary as we examined the Egtved and Juellinge women brewers and celebrants up close. All of this was captured on film by Christopher Ottosen, our Norwegian foodie and fellow traveler, who has provided some of the meal pairings for this book. He has scoured Norway for every kind of fruit, honey, birch tree sap, and herb to use in brewing. To ferment his vinegary applejack, he suspended a sack of apples in a tree where it could gather up the native yeast.

Back in the United States, Tim, Sam, and I faced our own challenges with the FDA and TTB. Meadowsweet was ruled out as an ingredient, since it contains salicylate, aspirin-like compounds considered too "medicinal" for beer. We pointed out that meadowsweet has long been an additive in fermented beverages. It is referred to as medesweete or medewurte (literally, "a pleasing agent or root for mead") in herbalist literature since the 16th century. Uninspiring clover was substituted instead.

We faced additional problems in securing all the ingredients that were called for. The most difficult (and most expensive) was birch tree sap from Alaska. We imported Swedish honey, but we weren't able to obtain fresh Swedish cranberries. The piquancy of our Nordic grog suffered somewhat, but the final complex beverage had just enough sourness and herbal bite to satisfy the most avid Belgian lambic devotee.

Now that we had the beverage to go in the bottle, how should we announce its extreme, revolutionary taste of the Scandinavian past? "Thor's Hammer," "Odin's Mindbender," and "Well of Wisdom" were already taken. Just plain "Nordic Grog" might work. Ben Potts, who was the Rehoboth brewpub's experimental brewer at the time, suggested "Bog Grog."

I especially liked the name "Ultima Thule," as pointing to a really extreme beverage at the ends of the Earth. This was ruled out by the Swedes, who said that 30 percent of their population would think it was the beer of a popular "Nazi-punkband" and the rest wouldn't have a clue in the world what it meant.

Sam's lawyers ran the various possibilities by the trademark office in Washington, D.C., and by a process of elimination and weighing the gravitas of each name (which might also be taken to mean the starting "original gravity" of the sugars in the wort or the "final gravity," a measure of the alcohol percentage), we settled on *Kvasir*. It might have been hard to say; Sam still says that the "k" is silent, while I believe that the proper Swedish pronunciation sounds out the "k." And it might be confused with the Russian *kvass*, with which it might share some etymological relationship. Nevertheless, *Kvasir* captured the wild, poetic spirit of the Nordic grog and its mythological origins.

Sam then turned to devising a stunning, eye-catching label to match the name and the bottle's contents. Since he has musical roots in the "recent" past, he dug back into the psychedelic movement of the 1960s in San Franscisco. Maybe he was dreaming of Grace Slick singing "White Rabbit." He recalled the mesmerizing artwork of the posters announcing the next concert at Filmore East. Whatever the reasons, he turned to Jim Mazza, one of San Francisco's rock-and-roll artists, and commissioned him to do an updated re-creation of the Egtved woman. On the label, she is seen arising from her oak coffin, beguilingly dressed and holding her birch bark bucket with the Nordic grog. Wisps of the beverage's aroma swirl around her and congeal under a blood-red sky. They form the name *Kvasir*, which rises up toward Valhalla.

ON THE TRAIL OF AN EVEN SOURER *KVASIR*

WE WEREN'T FINISHED with *Kvasir*. The sour hounds of the beer world cried out for more. Ben Potts and Sam wanted to satisfy their every wish at the World Science Festival in late May 2014.

Sam set Ben to work on a sourer version of the Nordic grog. Ben had long been harboring a host of Belgian microorganisms in his apartment. He had the dregs of bottles of Belgian lambics and oak chips taken from oak barrels that had been soaked in unfiltered brews. They included a *Brettanomyces* "wild" species from Fantôme and a *Pediococcus* strain from a Rodenbach Foederbier (Dutch, "cask beer"). A Flanders Red Ale had been sucked up by a chemist's pipette from a glass in one of the only two bars in the world serving the unpasteurized version. Ben had much more besides to bring him up to the scientifically cataloged quota of two thousand or so microorganisms in a lambic or gueuze. Hopefully, the good bacteria were keeping the more virulent and pathological ones in check. You didn't want enterobacterial species, which can cause food poisoning and disease, running rampant. What Ben didn't have, unfortunately, were genuine "wild" yeasts and bacteria from Scandinavia; that is a project for the future.

Ben did go a bit too far in ageing his sour brew in an oak barrel, which had been used for a Hudson Valley rye whiskey. Distillation was only a glimmer in the eye of a Bronze or Iron Age fermented beverage-maker. We don't know whether the original Nordic grog was stored and shipped in barrels, but as I have alluded to, it's a possibility. The oak introduced some vanilla, coconut, and cotton candy notes, which might be expected in a modern lambic but were not necessarily part of the ancient taste profile. Sam was satisfied with the end product and proposed to call our festival program "Nordic Grog: Yeasts Gone Wild," a kind of tribute to the Egtved dancer-priestess who started it all.

A "Viking" version of *Kvasir* was recently made in Newfoundland by the gypsy (itinerant) brewer, Stephen Canning. The occasion was the annual Canadian Archaeological Association conference, held in early May 2015 in the capital of St. Johns. The local homebrewers of the island, including Stephen, signed on to provide their versions of several *Ancient Ales*, since Dogfish Head did not have an export license for Canada. Steven's version of the Nordic grog, now transferred to the New World, was full of delicious Canadian equivalents of cranberries, lingonberries, birch tree sap, honey, and the gruit herbs, native to the circumpolar regions of the globe.

The setting in Newfoundland for a *Kvasir* clone made sense. Snow was, of course, falling when I landed at St. John's desolate-looking airport. We were nearly knocked down by howling winds the next day at Cape Spear, a ragged granite peninsula jutting out into the north

Atlantic that is the most easterly point of North America. We saw an iceberg calf making its way from Greenland down the coast. We tried to imagine what the Viking adventurers and pillagers must have thought when they first landed and built a longhouse around A.D. 1000 at L'Anse aux Meadows, farther north and buried under 3 feet of snow during my stay. They must have brought some of the Nordic grog with them, as well as the tradition of how to make it. Replica drinking horns strung to the walls of the reconstructed mead hall at L'Anse aux Meadows at least suggested as much, although none were found in the excavation. So far, we have no definitive chemical and/or archaeobotanical evidence for a New World Viking drink. We might have expected that they would have fermented one of the many North American grapes (after all, this was Vinland), or some lingonberries, cloudberries (called bakeapple by the Newfies), or birch sap.

We are at a loss to explain how the Vikings could have foregone the comforts and delights of their Nordic grog. Could it be that they were won over by the Native Americans, who had no documented fermented beverage? I prefer to believe that the most reasonable explanation is the obvious one: the Vikings did not dispense with their beloved extreme fermented beverage; rather its apparent absence is due to the vagaries of archaeological discovery.

RECIPES

Homebrew Interpretation of
Kvasir

by Doug Griffith (based on McGovern, 2009/2010)

INGREDIENTS

5 gallons	Cool water	Pre-boil
1	Grain bag	Pre-boil
¾ pound	Briess Special Roast Malt, crushed	Pre-boil
6 pounds	Bavarian wheat dry malt extract	65 minutes
1 ounce	Tettnang hop pellets	60 minutes
1 level tablespoon	Meadowsweet	During boil
1 level tablespoon	Yarrow	During boil
½ pound	Corn sugar (option 1)	During boil
1 level tablespoon	Birch bark, ground (option 1)	During boil
8 ounces	Birch syrup (option 2)	During boil
3 pounds	Honey	End of boil
8 ounces	Cranberry concentrate	End of boil
1 packet	Fermentis S-04 English Ale, White Labs WLP028 Scottish Ale, or Wyeast 1728	Fermentation
½ pound	Dried lingonberry	Day 2 of fermentation

1 teaspoon	Pectic enzyme	Day 2 of fermentation
1 cup	Priming sugar	Bottling
	Bottles and caps	Bottling

Starting gravity: 1.088
Final gravity: 1.015
Final target alcohol by volume: 8.5%
International Bittering Units: 10
Finished volume: 5 gallons

PROCESS

N.B.: IF USING the liquid yeast, we recommend making a starter 24 hours before brewing to maximize yeast cell counts.

1. Fill a brewpot with 5 gallons of cool water.
2. Fill the grain bag with the Briess malt. Tie off the top and place the bag in the brewpot.
3. Heat the pot and stir the water and grain bag every 5 minutes.
4. As the water reaches 170°F, pull out the grain bag using a large stirring spoon. Hold the bag above the brewpot for a minute, allowing most of the liquid to drain into the pot. Do not squeeze the grain bag. Continue heating the water.
5. As the water is beginning to boil, remove the pot from the heat.
6. Add the dry malt extract. Stir to prevent clumping and scorching on the bottom of the pot. Return the pot to the heat.
7. Allow the wort to come to a boil.
8. After boiling for 5 minutes, add the Tettnang hop pellets and stir.
9. Start timing a 1-hour boil at the point of the hops addition. If using a defoamer to help prevent boilovers, add per instructions.

10. Put the lingonberries in a blender, cover with liquid from the brewpot, purée, cool, and add the pectic enzyme. Refrigerate for 1 day.

11. At 30 minutes before the end of the 1-hour boil, in a separate small pot, remove 2 cups of the wort from the brewpot. Heat to just keep hot, not boiling. Add the meadowsweet, yarrow, and one of the birch options:

    OPTION 1: Add the corn sugar and birch bark.
    OPTION 2: Add the birch syrup.

    Stir well to make sure all is wet. Steep until the end of the boil.

12. At the 60-minute mark, turn off the heat. Add the honey, cranberry concentrate, and strained liquid from the steeping pot. Stir the wort for 2 minutes to build up a whirlpool effect and dissolve the honey. Stop stirring and allow the wort to sit for 10 minutes.

13. Chill the wort with a wort chiller or in a cold-water bath until it is under 75°F.

14. Transfer the wort into a fermenter; aerate (rock the baby) for 1 minute.

15. Pitch the yeast into the fermenter.

16. Top up the fermenter to the 5-gallon mark with cool water.

17. On the second day of fermentation, add the puréed lingonberries.

18. In about 14 days, the beer should be ready to bottle. The beer can be siphoned to a carboy for further clearing, if desired, for about 7 days.

19. Before bottling, clean and sanitize the bottles and caps and create a priming solution of 1 cup boiling water and the priming sugar.

20. Siphon the beer into a sterilized bottling bucket, add the water-diluted priming solution, and gently stir. Bottle and cap the beer.

21. Allow the beer to bottle-condition for another 10 days at 70–75°F. It should then be ready to drink.

ᴹEAL PAIRING FOR *Kvasir*

24-hour Gravlax

by Christopher Ottosen

Serves 4

INGREDIENTS

1½ pounds salmon fillet
⅔ cup coarse sea salt
⅔ cup fine salt
⅓ cup sugar
2 tablespoons black pepper, coarsely ground
Handful lingonberries,[*] preferably fresh, thawed if frozen,
    dried and ground
Handful cranberries, preferably fresh, dried and ground
Handful meadowsweet,[†] preferably fresh, dried and ground
1 tablespoon birch syrup[‡]

PREPARATION

CLEAN THE SALMON and remove all the bones; retain the skin. Mix
the additional ingredients together well in a bowl. Use a large plate
that accommodates the fish. Sprinkle a third of the herbal mix on the
bottom of the plate. Place the fillet, skin side down, on the herbal mix.
Sprinkle the rest of the mix over the entire fish. Cover the fish in plas-

---

[*] Online resources: http://tinyurl.com/hwd5ghf and http://tinyurl.com/jcbwllv
[†] Online resources: http://tinyurl.com/j2pzpga and http://tinyurl.com/hoc8vmy
[‡] Online resource: http://www.alaskabirchsyrup.com/albipr.html

tic wrap and refrigerate for 24 hours. Then wash the fish in cold water to remove the spices, and dry it between two paper towels. Cut the fish into desired slices, and serve with any of the side dishes posted at http://www.penn.museum/mcgovern/ancientbrews/, where mood-enhancing atmospherics can also be found.

7

Theobroma: A Sweet Concoction to Stir Romance

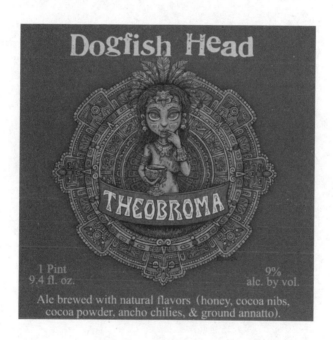

Dogfish Head

THEOBROMA

1 Pint
9.4 fl. oz.

9%
alc. by vol.

Ale brewed with natural flavors (honey, cocoa nibs, cocoa powder, ancho chilies, & ground annatto).

T he last chapter left us on the doorstep of the Americas with the Vikings' arrival in their "new found land." To Europeans, it might have been new. Taking a much longer, global perspective, the Vikings were relative latecomers on the scene, as were Columbus and the succession of Spanish, French, and English explorers to follow.

ICE AGE ADVENTURERS

NEAR THE END of the last glacial period, some 15,000 to 20,000 years ago, as the ice pack of the northern hemisphere began to break up and melt, some of our enterprising ancestors saw an opening to a new land from east Asia across a land-bridge (Beringia), now the Bering Sea and Strait, to North America. The speed at which they moved from north to south along the western shores of the Americas, reaching Patagonia at the tip of South America in short order, implies that they traveled, at least part of the way, by some kind of watercraft, perhaps log rafts or leather kayaks.

The first "Americans" followed the Inside Passage along the Pacific Northwest Coast by boat, leapfrogging from one inlet to the next, much as our ancestors had traversed central Asia oasis by oasis and the Mediterranean Sea island by island. They were driven on by the lushness of their new environment, worlds apart from landlocked, frigid Siberia.

The estuaries of the bays and fjords, which were gradually freed up from ice, were refuges for new life. They would have been a fisherman's and a fruit lover's delight. The many wild berries—strawberries, elderberries, *manzanita* (Spanish, "little apple") soapberries, thimbleberries, salmonberries—gave them the sugar they needed, not just for an energy boost but also for a delicious, refreshing drink. When the bounty of one bay was depleted, the enticements of the next beckoned. They traveled ever southward in search of the next culinary discovery and to stay alive.

My wife and I experienced some of the bounty of this new land when I taught at the University of Victoria, British Columbia, in the fall of 2011. We were treated to what the Inside Passage had to offer at its most southerly extent. Our home base was a bungalow tucked away behind the first microbrewery on Vancouver Island, Spinnakers. Locally produced apple butters, black currant compotes, barley wine vinaigrettes, and raspberry ice cream were just some of the delectables we enjoyed, along with wild salmon, duck, and mushrooms. The last class of my course was naturally a field trip to a meadery, cidery, and winery/vinegar factory, starting from our home brewery. A wildflower honey mead (or melomel), whose rich flavor was rounded out by raspberries, was especially memorable. At 13.4% alcohol, such a beverage would have been a powerful inducement for early Americans to settle down.

But did our native American ancestors take a refreshing fruit drink one step further and make a fermented beverage? Did they bring the necessary traditions with them? Did they have the requisite containers and leisure time to gather up masses of fruit, successfully ferment it, and keep it for future quaffing?

We know little of what Siberian fermented beverage-makers were capable of 20,000 years ago. Shamans today and in the recent past, who likely practice millennia-old traditions, prepare their drug of choice— the hallucinogenic fly-agaric mushroom (*Amanita muscaria*)—by decocting and mixing it with berry juice. In season, the tundra is rife with flowers and berries of all kinds, including lingonberry and cloudberry that also grow in Scandinavia, and other rarities, such as the groundberry, honeyberry, and kiwiberry.

Early Native Americans would undoubtedly have spotted *A. muscaria* and related American species growing in the dense forests along the inland bays. The mushroom is readily distinguished by its crimson red umbrella-like cap, speckled in white spots or warts. Any shamans along for the prehistoric ride and worth their salt must have been tempted to mix together some berries and mushrooms, much like what is still done by Athabascan and Ojibwa shamans farther inland in the Mackenzie Mountains of northwestern Canada and along the shores of Lake Superior in Michigan. As our ancestors moved farther south, warming temperatures and more sugar resources, including honey, would almost certainly guarantee that our ancestors would have begun to enjoy a fermented beverage of one kind or another—in short, an extreme beverage.

Women, as the consummate fermented beverage-makers around the world, both work alongside male Siberian shamans today and serve in this role. They not only collect and prepare the mushrooms and berries. They also chew pieces of the mushroom to make quids, which are presented to the shaman. As I stress throughout this book, making a chewed mouth-sized mass of a natural product—whether a fungus, fruit, grain, or tuber—is likely the earliest means by which our species "extracted" the necessary sugars and other substances for fermentation. Moreover, women might well have been instrumental in experimenting with new plants and concocting fermented beverages on the journey south.

The persistence of the chewing tradition for making an extreme fermented beverage shows up at the Patagonian site of Monte Verde, Chile, dated to about 15,000 years ago, soon after our ancestors crossed over to North America. They must have progressed quickly southward into uncharted territory, because Monte Verde was some 8000 kilometers (5000 miles) distant. Because the site lay for thousands of years under a peat bog, the preservation of organic materials was extraordinary.

The newcomers came prepared to build a permanent village of sorts in stark contrast to the usual ephemeral hunter-gatherer camp of Palaeolithic times. One building, probably the living quarters of the community, was 6 meters (20 feet) long. It had been constructed of logs and planks with a covering of animal skins tied down by reed ropes. The interior was divided up into rooms, each with a small fire pit, around which were the remains of meals. Besides mastodon, palaeo-llama, and freshwater mollusks, the cravings of any vegetarian in the group would have been well satisfied by the variety and abundance of seeds, nuts, tubers, mushrooms, and berries that were scattered about. Congealed animal fat on the floor of a second tent building implied that mastodons were butchered and their hides prepared there.

Chewed remains of plants as quids were also recovered from the buildings. They showed that the Monte Verde community—still an itinerant and inquisitive lot—were willing to travel far afield to collect the best botanicals. *Boldo* tree fruit and leaves came from over 200 kilometers (125 miles) to the north, and seven species of seaweed were collected on the Pacific coast, 58 kilometers (36 miles) away. These healthful and savory ingredients were combined with local carbohydrate-rich *junco* reeds and chewed together. We will also see in the next chapter how avidly the early arrivals to the western coast of Mexico chewed newly discovered plants there.

Remnants of *junco* embedded in the pores of wooden mortars, along with sweet bulrush and wild potato—all of which would make fine fermented beverages—add another dimension to the Monte Verde story. They tell us that the Monte Verdeans might well have taken their chewing method to a higher level. Rather than simply taking a plant—fibrous stalks, leaves, rhizomes, and all—popping it in your mouth, and trying to chew it, a sensible human would first "preprocess" it by grinding it up into smaller bits and pieces.

The technological advance of pulverizing the starting material might have been a boon to the fermented beverage-maker, but it also meant that many quids, which might otherwise have been excavated at the site, more easily broke up and were destroyed.

This hypothetical scenario of first grinding up the plants and then masticating them as quids to make a fermented beverage is still practiced today in Patagonia. The Mapuche and Huilliche peoples of Chile, who have inhabited Patagonia since time immemorial, make fragrant and delicious *chichas* from the same fruits found at Monte Verde, and they exploit wild potato tubers for a very potent potato *chicha*. They also produce a mushroom *chicha* from the fruit-like clusters of fungus (*Cyttaria* sp.) that grow on beech trees.

Despite these tantalizing possibilities for the first American fermented beverages, they remain just that: plausible stories, still to be substantiated by archaeological evidence from the earliest encampments and human habitations along the coasts. Unfortunately, many of these sites, unlike Monte Verde, are now submerged underwater and difficult to find and excavate. But a spate of inland sites of similar date or even earlier than Monte Verde, showing ties to the coasts of both North and South America, have been located and excavated in recent years. They may provide more answers.

SERENDIPITY AT PLAY

LIKE THE TRAVELS of our ancient ancestors, our *Ancient Ales and Spirits* have not followed a single pathway to their discovery and re-creation. It could be a casual comment about some 40-year-old residues sitting in museum storage (*Midas Touch*), an invitation to take part in a new excavation in China (*Chateau Jiahu*), or a Fulbright to Scandinavia (*Kvasir*) that was the catalyst for rediscovering and re-creating the ancient fermented beverage. The only generalization you can make is that you had to be at the right place at the right time with the right people to guide and assist you.

The initial impetus for *Theobroma* also came out of the blue. I grew up in Ithaca in upstate New York and went to Cornell. When its *Arts & Sciences Newsletter* arrived in fall 2001, I was struck by the headline on the front page. Beside an ancient incised jar that might well have been a drinking-cup, it read: "The Birth of Chocolate or, The Tree of the Food of the Gods." I turned to the story inside, which had been written by John Henderson, a professor of anthropology, and read that chocolate was much more than a sweet condiment. It had a storied history, from the days of the Aztec Montezuma (more correctly, Motecuhzoma), who had 50 large jars of different kinds of chocolate drink served to him in gold cups as standard dinner fare, to the European fascination with it as a mark of social status, cure-all, and aphrodisiac.

Cacao beans were also the currency of the Aztec realm, and Montezuma was said to have had a billion of them stashed away at his capital of Tenochtitlán, near Mexico City. His money literally grew on trees. Like something out of a scene from the sci-fi movie *Invasion of the Body*

Snatchers, the large fruit pods of the aromatic *criollo* variety seemed almost extraterrestrial, at least to European eyes: the warty-looking masses grew directly out from the main trunk and lined it and the larger branches of the tree (a cauliflorous habit in botanical terminology). No wonder the great Swedish botanist and taxonomist, Carl Linnaeus, named it *Theobroma cacao*, "chocolate food of the gods" in Latin.

There was more. John headed up an excavation, together with Rosemary Joyce of Berkeley, at the site of Puerto Escondido in northern Honduras, on the lower reaches of the Ulùa River, close to the Gulf of Mexico. They claimed to have found one of the earliest settled villages in the Americas, dating back to before 1600 B.C., much more recent than Monte Verde and developments elsewhere in the world but very significant for Mesoamerica. The excavators were particularly struck by the beautifully decorated pottery vessels, some of the earliest yet found in Mesoamerica, which included thin, high-temperature-fired bowls that would have been ideal for drinking a beverage. The pottery types were nearly identical to those of sites of the same period on the Pacific side of the Central American isthmus in the region of Soconusco, a strip of very fertile coastal land straddling Mexico and Guatemala. The two regions, separated by about 800 kilometers (500 miles), could well have been in communication with each other by routes that followed east-west rivers through mountain passes and skirted active volcanos.

Together, Puerto Escondido and the Soconusco sites appear to have laid the foundation for the first urban society of the Americas, the Olmecs of Mexico's Veracruz and Tabasco provinces on the Gulf coast. These peoples, besides their fame in sculpting gigantic stone heads and building cities, were also avid consumers of a chocolate beverage on celebratory and ritual occasions. Their drinking-vessels for the beverage were clearly derived from those of the more southerly, earlier sites. The Olmecs spread the heavenly drink far and wide. It was to become the elite beverage of the later Maya and Aztecs.

Scientific support, however, for any chocolate at Puerto Escondido, at the Soconusco sites, or in the Olmec region was limited. The wet tropical climate had conspired to destroy any archaeobotanical evidence for cacao. The article finished on a note that was music to a biomolecular archaeologist's ear: the only hope was to test some of the pottery for "chemical fingerprints of cacao."

How could I resist the call to scientific arms from a fellow classmate in Arts and Sciences? It turned out that John and I had attended Cornell at the same time during the mid-1960s. Our paths never crossed, perhaps because John was already immersed in ancient studies and I was still undecided about my future. I majored in chemistry and minored in English literature, which eventually led me to the bridging of the humanities and sciences at Penn via biomolecular archaeology.

I decided it was high time to meet John and sent him an email, introducing myself, offering my services, and proposing that we catch up on the intervening years. John's answer came back immediately: a resounding "yes." We were slowed down by negotiations with the antiquities authorities, who took nearly a year to grant permission for exporting and analyzing the pottery sherds. When they arrived, we had our game plan in place.

SWEET DISCOVERIES

WE DECIDED TO take a two-pronged approach to our analyses. The Penn lab would extract the sherds and carry out an initial probe for ancient organics by FT-IR (Preface). We would follow up with GC-MS analysis in search of adjunct ingredients, including maize or corn that was regularly added to *chichas* (Chapter 8), other indigenous plants first domesticated in Mesoamerica such as agave and prickly pear (Chapter 9), native herbs recorded in the Spanish chronicles, and perhaps a mushroom or two.

We also enlisted another laboratory and scientist, who had already carried out numerous cacao analyses of ancient Mesoamerican pottery vessels using HPLC-MS. Jeff Hurst was the new member of our team, located close by in Hershey, Pennsylvania. His lab was tucked away in the research complex of The Hershey Company, the largest producers of chocolate in the world. Milton Hershey, its founder, had built a town, theme park, and museum on the rolling countryside. The factory was at the center, a testimony to chocolate, much like breweries all over Africa are placed in the middle of villages to announce and easily distribute their principal fermented beverage for every occasion.

At the time, Jeff had the distinction of having discovered the earliest chocolate vessel. It was a highly unusual pottery jar from a late Maya tomb at the site of Río Azul in northern Guatemala, dated to around A.D. 500. What set the jar apart from others was its screw-on lid—perhaps the first of its kind in the world and as effective as any modern lid in protecting the contents inside. The jar was beautifully decorated with a pattern of leopard-like spots that covered the lid's massive handle. Mayan hieroglyphs, highlighted in Maya Blue pigment, ran around the body of the vessel. They showed the head of a fish and a fin, which was later deciphered to read *ka-ka-w* ("cacao") in ancient Mayan. The full inscription was read as "a drinking-vessel for *witik* cacao, for *kox* cacao." The words in italics are yet to be translated, but they might refer to additives to the drink. The hieroglyphs proclaimed to all that the jar once contained the precious liquid.

From all appearances, tomb 19 at Río Azul, in which the inscribed jar had been found, had not been disturbed or robbed in antiquity. The inscribed jar with its screw-top lid was unique, arguing for its genuineness. Another six cylindrical jars with tripod bases lay nearby; they were covered with simpler lids topped with small effigy figures. Residue tide-lines of an evaporated liquid on their interiors, like those inside the Scorpion I jars, pointed to their once having been filled with a beverage. The affiliations of the single male in the tomb, whether a local or foreigner, are yet to be determined. Surrounded by mysterious, large-scale hieroglyphic frescoes, he was wrapped in a textile shroud.

Just to be sure that the jars did contain chocolate, residue samples from the inscribed jar and four cylindrical jars were sent to Jeff for analysis. He confirmed that the inscribed jar and two of the cylindrical jars were positive for the fingerprint compound of cacao: theobromine. The presence of caffeine in the inscribed jar, another biomarker for cacao but present at a tenth of the amount of theobromine, sealed the case that the unknown occupant, perhaps a trader in the precious fruit or a purveyor of the drink, carried a chocolate beverage with him to his grave.

Theobromine and caffeine occur in other American plants, especially members of the *Ilex* (holly) family in South America. The stimulatory properties of these xanthine compounds, together with a range of mildly psychoactive compounds, create a similar buzz as that from coffee. For example, maté or yerba-maté, still a very popular drink in South America, is made from *I. paraguariensis*; it is traditionally drunk through a silver drinking-tube from a gourd. Even in North America where fermented beverages were unknown on current evidence, a so-called "black drink," made from *I. vomitoria* was drunk by midwestern and southeastern peoples. The Latin species name says it all: besides being a stimulant, this plant induces vomiting, an important part of rituals to cleanse and purge the body. Yet, these plants and drinks were unknown to the Mesoamericans. The cacao tree and its fruit were the only sources for theobromine and caffeine there. If they were identified in an ancient pottery vessel used for preparing, serving, or drinking a beverage, it was virtually certain that the drink was wholly or partly made from cacao.

PUERTO ESCONDIDO TAKES CENTER STAGE

THE POTTERY SHERDS from Puerto Escondido, which John sent us, might not have looked as spectacular as the complete Río Azul jar. They carried no inscriptions and were unpainted. Glossy reds, browns, and grays in patterns, with the occasional molded or incised design, were about as fancy as they got. What they lacked in stylistic flare, however, they made up for in the technological proficiency of their manufacture and their very early dates, ranging from 1400 B.C. to 200 B.C. The corpus included bowls, jars, and bottles, all quite suitable for serving and drinking a beverage.

Two vessel shapes stood out in our assemblage of 13 sherds. The earliest came from the 1400–1100 B.C. phase of the site. It was a spout fragment from an extremely tall and narrow-necked jar or bottle, with pronounced ridges and grooves running the length of its body from top to bottom. As a complete vessel, it would have fitted comfortably into your hand, ready to take a sip from. The second vessel was also a spout fragment, but of later date (900–200 B.C.). It belonged to a "teapot," more specifically what archaeologists called a "chocolate pot," presumably because of its similarity to European hot chocolate decanters that became popular after the Spanish brought the exotic foodstuff back from the New World and it took the continent by storm. It was yet to be proven whether the ancient jar lived up to its archaeological designation.

Jeff was already on the trail of the "chocolate" teapot. He analyzed samples from 14 intact jars from the Maya site of Colha in northern Belize. Three of the samples were positive for theobromine. The archaeological surmise had been correct, and his finding pushed the earliest date for the ancient chocolate beverage back to 600 B.C., over a millennium earlier than the Río Azul jars.

We now had the opportunity with the earlier of the two Puerto Escondido jars to push the earliest date for making a cacao beverage back another 800 years. We were particularly intrigued by the shape and decoration of the long-necked bottle. Its protuberances, indentations, and neck appeared to match those of the cacao pod itself, hanging down by its stem from the trunk of the tree. In a preliterate period, could this design have served as a visual advertisement, instead of an inscription, for what lay inside? True to form, Jeff's analysis with HPLC-MS came back positive for theobromine, as did ours using GC-MS.

Our excitement grew when we obtained similar results from the spouted teapot. Altogether, 11 out of the 13 sherds tested positive for theobromine. Caffeine, which would have provided added confirmation, was lacking, but that was likely because it was below our detection level. More importantly, we now had the chemical evidence for drawing out other cultural and technological inferences for this early period in Mesoamerica.

DID THE EARLIEST CACAO DRINK
CONTAIN SOMETHING MORE?

WE KNEW FROM the later Mayan inscriptions and murals that the peoples of Mesoamerica both literally consumed and, in return, were consumed figuratively by a chocolate drink. Detailed, even exuberant, descriptions and illustrations of Aztec customs in the chronicles of the Spanish travelers told the same story. It had been the elite drink for millennia, like grape wine and barley beer were in the Middle East and rice and millet beers in China. The tree itself was one of the four "world trees," supporting the universe on the south from where the best Aztec chocolate came. The drink from the tree was equated with blood, whose symbolism ran through the mythology, human sacrifices, celebrations, dances, and music of royals and commoners alike.

The burial of a Maya "shaman" around A.D. 400 in the Bats'ub Cave in a remote part of Belize captures some of the preternatural allure of cacao and its beverage. The male's head had been removed after death and placed beside his hips. A bowl-shaped pottery fragment, containing a jade bead, was put in its place. Another bowl with water-worn pebbles and five cacao beans, confirmed by Jeff's analyses, lay upside down over the man's pubic area.

This strange mortuary ritual, not seen anywhere else, strikes some chords if we think back to the much earlier custom at Jiahu in China of placing jars for drinking an extreme beverage in the afterlife close to the heads and mouths of the departed. Masses of pebbles there were also placed inside containers (tortoise shells), likely used in divination. The depiction of turtle carapaces (the upper sides of their shells) on an anthropomorphic jar from the cave burial, perhaps intended for a chocolate beverage, strengthens the comparison. In both China and the New World, the turtle and tortoise were closely tied to the creation of the Earth and universe and were associated with strength and fertility.

Similarly, jade carried deep religious significance of the universe and eternity in ancient China and among the Maya. In Han Dynasty China, only several centuries earlier than the Bats'ub burial, the custom reached its apex when bodies were clothed from head to toe in "burial suits" of the stone. The jade bead near where the mouth of the decapitated male had been might then represent jade pervading his body. Thirteen additional large jade beads, together with two shells and four black beads, formed a necklace or belt, in the chest area.

Is it possible that the Bats'ub Cave burial carried on traditions from the time the first Americans crossed over from Asia? They could no longer make a fermented beverage of rice. Chocolate, as symbolized by the beans in the bowl, would be a wonderful substitute. Another burial item, a maize cob, told the story of another fermented beverage (Chapter 8).

If we are to believe the post-conquest Spanish historical and ethnographic chronicles (and it's difficult not to, given their exquisite detail and that they are often by eyewitnesses), the Mesoamerican elite drink was more than just chocolate. Friar Bernardino de Sahagún, for example, in his 16th-century masterpiece, *General History of the Things of New Spain*, wrote of "green cacao-pods, honeyed chocolate, flowered chocolate, flavored with green vanilla, bright red chocolate, *huitztecolli*-flower chocolate, flower-colored chocolate, black chocolate, white chocolate" being served to the Aztec ruler. Such additives—and there were many, many more—gave different flavors, aromas, and colors to the chocolate. Native American chiles added fiery properties to the beverage, nicely counterbalancing any sweetness. One spice, achiote or annatto from the pulp and seeds of a small evergreen, gave an intense reddish color to the drink in keeping with blood symbolism. Other Spanish historians report that when a beautiful young Maya man was to be sacrificed atop a pyramid, he might be granted a sip of chocolate drink to steady and ready him for a ritual dance before his death. Sometimes, real blood from the obsidian blade of a previous sacrifice was dripped into the beverage; annatto, as a substitute, was also allowed. If a young woman were chosen instead, she might be spared if she made good chocolate.

We had hoped that our chemical investigation would shed light on when such additives began to be used in the chocolate drink. We ran the GC-MS analyses and combed through the data: there was no sign of an additive. Maize might have been expected, since the domestication area in southern Mexico is close to Honduras and the cereal was commonly added to beverages (Chapter 8). For example, thousands of years later, Spanish chroniclers describe how the Yucatán Indians, descendants of the Maya, made a "foaming drink [from cacao and maize] which is very savory, and with which they celebrate their feasts." But no evidence of maize showed up in the prehistoric beverage.

We were left with the working hypothesis—long argued by John and Rosemary—that the more complex chocolate drink, which was focused on the cacao bean and numerous additives, was a much later development. When our ancestors first encountered the cacao tree, they were not drawn to it by the seeds, hidden away and embedded in the warty fruit's thick whitish pulp. If they did taste the beans, they would have found them to be extremely bitter because of their high concentration of theobromine. The pulp, on the other hand, was very sweet—up to 15% sugar—and contained smaller amounts of theobromine. It could be eaten straight from the pod, spitting out the seeds as you went. If you were more patient, you might squash the fruit and leave the pulp to ferment in the sun. The Spanish observed large-scale production of a drink made this way in canoes when they arrived much later. The result would have been an alcoholic beverage with 5–7% alcohol, more than enough to alter one's consciousness and enter the realm of the gods and ancestors.

Our chemical data fit with John and Rosemary's hypothesis that the original cacao drink was simply made from the unadulterated pulp. You could go a step further and argue that the driving force for domesticating the tree, like for so many other plants around the world, might well have been the relatively high alcoholic content of such a beverage. Refreshing, delicious versions of both the fermented and nonfermented drink, made only from the pulp, are still served up in traditional Mesoamerican and South American societies.

I am yet to taste and compare these modern drinks. The closest I've come was on a brief trip into Amazonia from the Peruvian highlands (Chapter 8). I picked a pod directly from a tree growing behind a hut in a remote village and opened it up. The unfermented cacao pulp was sweet with a mild chocolatey flavor.

A BEVERAGE FOR THE TRUE
CHOCOLATE AFICIONADO

AS ROSEMARY CONTENDS, if you wanted the bitter bite of dark chocolate from the beans, you probably had to wait at least another 500 years until the Maya made their appearance. South American peoples appear never to have progressed beyond the pulp drink. The less aromatic properties of the numerous subspecies and cultivars of cacao there, generally of the *forastero* variety, perhaps discouraged further experimentation.

The Maya astutely observed that the beans developed fine nuances of flavor and aroma when they came in contact with fermentating pulp, the first stage in making dark chocolate. After the beans have been dried, roasted, and ground, the chocolate takes on the characteristics of an aged red wine. You can pick out hints of tobacco and leather, dark berry fruits, and flowery essences. During the several years of our Puerto Escondido analyses and the run-up to publication, my wife and I spent many pleasant hours comparing different dark chocolates. Our favorite was a *criollo*-variety from the valleys of Ocumare, near the Gulf coast of Venezuela. Mexican Soconuscan chocolate was a close second.

Even before we analyzed the spouted teapot from Puerto Escondido, we might have guessed that it had once held the "new" chocolate beverage made from fermented beans. The vessel dated to the period when the Maya first introduced this shape, and, thanks to Jeff's analyses, it was apparent that many teapots contained a chocolate drink. Possibly, the new pottery type marked new technological advances in how the beverage was made. The teapot quickly spread from the main areas of chocolate production in southern Mexico southward to El Salvador along the Pacific coast, and from Belize to Honduras along the Gulf of Mexico. By A.D. 200, it was a common find at important inland sites, including Monte Albán in Oaxaca, Mexico, where nearly half the vessels were teapots. If the Maya teapot were any measure, the popularity of the chocolate bean beverage had crescendoed. Then it mysteriously disappeared from the archaeological record.

The apparent demise of the teapot was not the death knell of the chocolate drink. Tall cylindrical jars, sometimes with tripod bases like those at Río Azul, continued to be made until Maya civilization itself collapsed and inexplicably vanished around A.D. 900. The chocolate drink carried on, and came roaring back by A.D. 1300 when the Aztecs wholeheartedly embraced the drink at Tenochtitlán.

Was the shift from the teapot to the cylindrical jar a change only in fashion or did it have a deeper significance? Jeff and his colleagues made a novel proposal. They closely examined the available corpus of teapots from across Maya Mesoamerica. They noted that the teapots' spouts were most often bent strangely backward or extended vertically upward well above the mouths of the vessels. Such spouts were hardly suited for easy pouring.

Something more than serving the beverage must have been involved. Jeff and his colleagues hint at a possible solution when they describe how important frothing or making a "head" on the drink was to the Maya. Unfortunately, we do not have any direct pictorial evidence for how the teapots were used. We do have such, however, for the cylindrical jars, which probably took their place. Illustrations from both Maya and Aztec times show women and goddesses alike frothing the beverage by raising one cylindrical jar on high, sometimes as much as 5 feet into the air, and pouring its liquid into a second vessel below. The result was a magnificent foam. In other Mayan paintings, the ruler sits comfortably on his throne while he lifts high a cup of the frothy beverage.

The starting liquid in all the pouring scenes, over a period of about two millennia, is believed to have been a chocolate "liquor," the technical term for the semisolid mass made by pulverizing chocolate nibs (shelled beans) rather than a distilled beverage. Some water was probably added to the liquor. At this stage, ground maize and/or other native plants and herbs were possibly mixed in, as is done today throughout Mesoamerica to make breakfast gruels (Spanish, *atoles*), breads, sauces such as mole, and drinks of all kinds (Chapters 8 and 9). The additives might also have come later in the process.

A composite image in the Florentine Codex of Sahagún's *General History of the Things of New Spain* drives home the point that grinding the beans into a liquor and frothing it were essential. There we see, beneath a cylindrical jar frothing scene, an Aztec woman laboring over her grinding stones (Spanish, *mano* and *metate*). Sahagún's accompanying text reads like a sidebar. He writes that the woman beverage-maker "grinds cacao [beans], she crushes, breaks, pulverizes them . . . She adds water sparingly, conservatively; aerates it, filters it, strains it, pours it back and forth, aerates it; she makes it form a head."

Without such evidence, you might have been tempted to interpret the pouring-and-frothing scenes as so much legerdemain, like what a bartender might do when presenting a special cocktail. But frothing the beverage had a more practical and ultimately a more symbolic purpose than providing a good show.

The method of pouring and frothing worked by applying simple physics. The ancient Americans did not understand the force of gravity, but they had an empirical appreciation for what it could do. If the distance between the two cylindrical jars was large, then the chocolate beverage struck the lower jar more violently and dispersed its liquid and solid particles into the air, making an aerated foam. Pouring a bottle of beer with abandon into a glass is comparable.

The goal of frothing the new Mayan version of the chocolate drink might also explain the awkward-looking teapots. Although not depicted artistically, one might envision blowing vigorously through the long spout, perhaps stirring the liquid in the jar or shaking it at the same time, maybe even adding a foaming agent (such as the yet to be identified vine mentioned in the Spanish chronicles) to create a foam.

As the foam rose up inside the teapot, it might eventually come shooting out through the narrow spout as if by magic. One could then either inhale the foam, similar to how the smoke of tobacco and other psychoactive plants were ingested in ancient America, or decide to carefully tilt the vessel and drink and snort simultaneously. Air-in, foam-out might also have been an apt metaphor for the mysterious life-force in humans and throughout nature. According to a central religious tenet of the Zapotecs of Oaxaca, chocolate foam, in particular, was animated by this force. These are the same people who had their capital at Monte Albán, where the highest concentration of teapots in the Mayan world was excavated. Most likely, that finding was not coincidental but a result of the high ceremonial regard in which the teapots and their foam were held.

As we await more definitive evidence for the role(s) of the teapot in ancient Mesoamerica, one crucial point bears repeating. Once the Maya had adopted the all-bean drink, they could no longer make a foam by natural fermentation from the pulp. They had to find another way forward, since the bean itself does not ferment. New pottery types such as the teapot and cylindrical jar, coupled with new mechanical methods, might well have been their response.

We might further conjecture that the inspiration for the high spouts of the teapots was the unusually tall neck of the Puerto Escondido cacao pod-shaped bottle. The pods on the tree are attached by much less-pronounced stems, and if the bottle were mainly intended for pouring, there was no need to make such a tall neck. However, if an actively fermenting cacao pulp beverage was poured into the bottle through the spout, then foam would come spewing back up. One would be tempted to first breathe it in, and then to blow back down into the spout, either to stop the flow or stir it up more.

The Maya probably grew to appreciate the unique sensory and mind-altering effects of dark chocolate, which comes as no surprise to a modern chocolate lover. They could make other alcoholic beverages from the riches that the New World had to offer—maize, agave, squashes, prickly pear, and much more (Chapters 8 and 9)—so why not go full-bore with dark chocolate? That's not to say that they didn't appreciate a small dose of the fermented pulp in their chocolate drink from time to time.

WE ARE BEAT OUT

OUR 15 MINUTES of fame of having discovered the earliest chocolate did not last long. Only a month had passed when Jeff and his other collaborators published new analytical results for chocolate residues, dated to about 1500 B.C. at the latest and in advance of the Puerto Escondido pod-shaped bottle. The pottery came from sites in the famous chocolate region of Soconusco and in the pre-Olmec "heartland" area along the Gulf of Mexico. Only one sherd from each site tested positive for theobromine and caffeine, but that was enough to swing attention to the other key areas in the quest for better understanding the cultural and technological dynamics behind the chocolate drink and its rise to prominence in Mesoamerica.

The newly analyzed sherds did not come from pod-shaped bottles. However, the one from Soconusco, likely from an open-mouth jar or bowl (Spanish, *tecomate*), was decorated with vertical fluting and ridges similar to those on the Puerto Escondido bottle. Could it be that the Soconusco jar was also providing a visual clue, albeit more veiled than the Puerto Escondido bottle, to its contents? The Gulf sherd was from a deep cylindrical bowl, and we know how important an expanded version of that pottery shape—the tall cylindrical jar—was to become later for frothing and consuming a chocolate drink.

Rosemary and John soon responded to the new findings. They rightly pointed out that chronological priority was not the real issue. Once pottery from even earlier phases at Puerto Escondido were excavated and analyzed, the pendulum might swing back in that direction. They stressed that we still do not have enough data—a constant refrain of archaeologists—to connect the dots and say which of the three areas—or perhaps another one lurking in the jungles—was the heartland of the chocolate drink. Instead, they wanted to know what drove humans to domesticate the tree and improvise pottery for making, serving, and drinking beverages made from its fruit or beans. And why had chocolate beverages—whether fermented or nonfermented—played such a central role in the social life, ceremonies, and religion of ancient Mesoamerica?

CRAFTING OUR INTERPRETATION OF THE ANCIENT CHOCOLATE BEVERAGE

WHEN SAM AND I set out on our quest to make an authentic (and flavorsome) rendition of the chocolate beverage in November 2007, it would appear that we had two possibilities: to make a fermented version purely from the cacao pod fruit or to whip up a more foamy version, with additives, from the chocolate beans. But there was a third possibility: Why not take the most well-attested to (and interesting) ingredients for both the fermented and nonfermented interpretations and make a truly extreme fermented beverage? For all we knew, there might have been a transitional phase between the pulp and bean drinks when the two approaches overlapped and were combined. Later, the all-bean beverage took off on its own. We had lots of evidence from around the world that our ancestors often preferred mixing ingredients together, whether to increase the alcohol content or give new taste and aroma sensations. We also wanted to make a beverage worthy of both the townspeople of Puerto Escondido and still appeal to the later royal taste buds of the Maya and Aztecs.

Our first let-down in our new venture into the wilds of ancient America was finding out that we couldn't obtain fresh cacao pulp from Honduras or anywhere else in Mesoamerica, for that matter. If it were transported to the United States, it would spoil, and no one was ready to invest in sending it in bulk, under refrigeration, to a small population here who might still appreciate its culinary value. It made more sense to leave the stuff to "rot" and enhance the flavor of the beans on their home ground, the cacao plantations of Central America. Sam and I considered traveling there, as we had done in making so many of our other *Ancient Ales*, and carrying out the fermentation on site—perhaps even at Puerto Escondido in Honduras, or barring that, in one of the other major areas of chocolate production.

Since linking up with a local brewer in the vicinity of a cacao plantation was a difficult proposition, we did the next best thing. We culled through online supply houses and found what we were looking for: chocolate nibs and powder from the premier area of Aztec chocolate production, Soconusco. It might not be the pulp per se, but the nibs carried the sensory imprint of its fermentation. At the time, only one boutique chocolate house in the States—Askinosie Chocolate of Springfield, Missouri—sold this dark chocolate. Soconusco chocolate probably hadn't been imported to this county in over a century, and it certainly hadn't been made into specialty chocolate here until Askinosie came along. We went for the best and paid accordingly.

We then considered how to obtain and handle the other main ingredients. Maize was the cereal of the Americas, so it should be front row and center. We might chew it, as our ancestors probably first did, to extract the sugars. Alternatively, we could grow our own Mexican variety, preferably with an ancient pedigree, out behind the Dogfish Head brewery in the small town of Milton, Delaware, which is surrounded by fields of corn and soy. This approach would entail gathering and processing the maize kernels, perhaps with replica ancient tools, and then sprouting seeds and making a malt.

We decided to take a shortcut and buy already prepared flaked corn from a large American distributor. The cereal was of a standard variety, which had gone through many genetic permutations and crosses since the days of Montezuma, but you can't do everything when you make a re-created beverage. Compromises are sometimes necessary, and we will have opportunities to try out other approaches in the future.

Honey was the next most important fermentable, which was added to Mayan and Aztec chocolate drinks, as well as many other ancient beverages throughout the Americas. We used a luscious wildflower honey from Delaware. Although it had not been made by the stingless American bee (*Melipona* sp.) but rather its European cousin (*Apis mellifera*), at least it was derived from native American plants. We then tossed in a minimal amount of barley to round out the grain bill and some hops to satisfy the TTB.

We had a wide choice of other possible additives for our extreme beverage. All kinds of exotic ingredients might be used, from the "black flower" orchid (our vanilla) to seeds and herbs with special flavors (e.g., pumpkiny allspice or bitter almond-flavored *sapote* seeds). The possibilities were endless for our ancient American ancestors, who must have been entranced by the vast botanical largesse of the New World. In the end, we settled on the raisin- and paprika-tasting ancho chile, which is the dried version of the poblano pepper, since its astringency nicely counterbalanced the sweetness from the honey and cereals without completely overwhelming our taste buds.

Modern chocolatiers in the United States have taken up where the ancient Maya and Aztecs left off, especially in combining dark chocolate with chiles across the full spectrum of pungency and heat. You never know when the next chocolate haven will show up. When I was exploring downtown Sante Fe, New Mexico, I came across Kakawa Chocolate House, suitably named after the Mayan word for chocolate. You could sit down at the store's counter and try one delicious hot chocolate after another, the same way the Aztecs enjoyed it—with a prized honey or agave nectar, an ancho or rare Oaxacan chile, or some sapote seeds and rose-scented popcorn flower.

Sam and I were also after the right color for the beverage. Red, because of its association with blood in Maya and Aztec religious ceremonies and sacrifices, naturally suggested itself. It could easily be obtained from annatto/achiote, which Native Americans added to the drink for the same purpose. We decided that the drinking public was not ready for real blood. For the same reason, we stayed away from hallucinogenic mushrooms for the time being, although psychoactive plants were much appreciated in ancient America.

Our drink was fermented with a German ale yeast. We probably should have chosen an American one. We have yet to obtain a "wild" yeast from the cacao plantations of Central America, like we did for *Ta Henket* in the date groves near the pyramids.

We quickly agreed on the name of the beverage: *Theobroma* ("food of the gods") said it all. Fortunately, it had not been copyrighted, so we could avoid some more far-fetched alternatives, like Montezuma's Revenge (the malady tourists often suffer through on their first trip to Latin America). For those old enough to remember, our preferred name had one drawback. It might be associated with Bromo-Seltzer, which was once an antacid for upset stomachs, again an allusion we wanted to avoid.

Sam's label, perhaps inspired by another dream, shows an Aztec maiden, no doubt a superb maker of the beverage whose life was spared for this reason rather than being sacrificed. She is surrounded by the gods of the four quarters of the universe. She dips her finger into a golden chalice, inlaid with turquoise, raises the chocolate beverage to her lips, and tastes. Excess chocolate flows over her body. Her large, languorous eyes may tell the rest of the story. . . .

We went through several experimental iterations before deciding that we had the right balance of ingredients for the re-created liquid inside the bottle. It still lacked one essential element: it was not frothy enough. The homebrew interpretation provides a very partial solution by including a barley malt (Carapils) with a higher protein content to promote foam formation. However, barley, an Old World cereal, should not be the solution for a New World fermented beverage. Other "heading agents," as they are known in the brewing community, are similarly suspect for ancient America, whether the enzyme pepsin from animal stomachs or alginates from seaweed. Pumping in nitrogen or carbon dioxide is definitely not appropriate.

More in keeping with ancient precedent, we might have tried frothing *Theobroma* by replicating ancient teapots and cylindrical jars, and experimenting with some of the physical approaches I proposed above—blowing into the spout, shaking, stirring, and/or pouring from on high from one vessel into another. Or we might have gone in search of the mysterious ancient vine and tried that approach.

Once you've produced the foam, however, it would be nearly impossible to bottle it up for future quaffing. We might try the approach of the Real Ale movement that advocates a return to traditional British cask-conditioned beer. The ale goes into a reused wooden barrel where yeasts have taken up residence. Some residual fermentable sugars will then secondarily ferment to produce a fresh, natural head of carbon dioxide when the beer is served. The same effect can be achieved in a glass bottle. Still, the amount of foam would not be enough to meet ancient Mesoamerican standards.

Meanwhile, we did bring one version of *Theobroma* back to life, a truly innovative beverage that captures the spirit of the New World. At 9% alcohol, one first detects the distinct aroma of dark chocolate. The aromatic accents of the honey and the smokiness and earthiness from the annatto follow. It finishes off with the light heat of the ancho chile.

I was not privy to the final formulation of the amount of each ingredient that went into the re-created *Theobroma*. When I first tasted it, I thought that the dark chocolate was too understated. I pleaded at length with Sam to throttle up the chocolate. After all, in making a re-created fermented beverage worthy of the name *Theobroma*, you want to make sure everyone smells and tastes the chocolate. Finally, Sam complied and made a very intense version in 2014, which left me choking. I was won over to a milder interpretation.

Arguments can be made on both sides for how much dark chocolate is needed. A subtler interpretation of the beverage better accords with the mysterious and ineffable nature of love, symbolically represented by chocolate in our culture. Yet our ancient American ancestors did not shy away from a more intense chocolate beverage, which embodied the wilder aspects of love and the uncontrolled forces at work in the universe.

RECIPES

Homebrew Interpretation of *Theobroma*

by Doug Griffith (based on McGovern, 2009/2010)

INGREDIENTS

2 quarts	Water	Pre-boil
1 pound	Pre-gelatinized flaked maize (corn)	Pre-boil
1 tablespoon	Gypsum	Pre-boil
16 ounces (1 pint)	Cold water	Pre-boil
2 ounces	Coffee malt	Pre-boil
½ pound	Carapils malt	Pre-boil
8 ounces	Cocoa nibs	Pre-boil
1 pound	Brewers malt	Pre-boil
4 gallons	Water	Pre-boil
1	Grain bag	Pre-boil
5 pounds	Light dry malt extract	65 minutes

½ ounce	Simcoe hops	60 minutes
1 teaspoon	Irish moss	15 minutes
1 ounce	Chopped ancho chile pepper (dried)	15 minutes
½ ounce	Crushed annatto seeds	15 minutes
3 pounds	Honey	5 minutes
1 ounce	Cocoa powder	5 minutes
1 packet	Fermentis US-05, White Labs WLP001, Wyeast 1056 or 4134 (Sake #9)	Fermentation
1 cup	Priming sugar	Bottling
	Bottles and caps	Bottling

Starting gravity: 1.082
Final gravity: 1.015
Final target alcohol by volume: 8.5%
International Bittering Units: 10
Finished volume: 5 gallons

PROCESS

1. In a 1-gallon or larger pot, bring the 2 quarts water to a boil. Add the flaked maize (corn) and gypsum, reduce the heat, and simmer for 20 minutes, stirring frequently to keep corn from sticking to or scorching the bottom of the pot. Remove from the heat. The mixture will be very thick.

2. Add the 1 pint cold water; stir well. Add the malts and cocoa nibs; stir well. Check the temperature and adjust to 122°F by adding cold water to cool or heating to raise. Rest for 10 minutes at 122°F.

3. After the rest, raise the temperature to 140–145°F and hold for 30 minutes. While the corn and malt are resting, put the 4 gallons water in a brewpot and heat to 170°F.

4. After the 30-minute rest, spread a grain bag over something that will contain the liquid and grains to be transferred from the pot. Carefully pour the hot contents of the pot into the grain bag. Move the grain bag to the brewpot

and bounce the bag like a tea bag for 5 minutes to dissolve the sugars out of the grains. Lift the bag to drain, do not squeeze. Discard the grains and bag.

5. Add the remaining liquid from the grain transfer to the brewpot. Bring the brewpot to a boil.

6. As the water is beginning to boil, remove the pot from the heat.

7. Add the dry malt extract. Stir to prevent clumping and scorching on the bottom of the pot. Return the pot to the heat.

8. Once boiling, boil for 5 minutes before adding the Simcoe bittering hops.

9. Start timing a 1-hour boil at the point of making this hops addition. If using a defoaming agent to help prevent boilovers, add per package instructions as the foam rises from the boil. Boil for 45 minutes.

10. Add the Irish moss, chopped ancho chile, and crushed annatto seeds. Boil for 10 minutes.

11. Add the honey and cocoa powder. Stir well.

12. After 5 minutes, remove from the heat.

13. Swirl the contents of the kettle to create a whirlpool, and allow to rest for 15 minutes.

14. Cool the wort to 70°F and move to a fermenter, leaving as many solids behind in the kettle as possible. Top up to the 5-gallon mark in the fermenter.

15. Pitch the cooled wort with the yeast and ferment at 70°F until fermentation is complete, 7 to 10 days.

16. Rack to a secondary fermenter for 1 to 2 weeks or until desired clarity.

17. Before bottling, clean and sanitize the bottles and caps.

18. Create a priming solution of 1 cup boiling water and the priming sugar.

19. Siphon the beer into a sanitized bottling bucket.

20. Add the water-diluted priming solution and gently stir.

21. Bottle and cap the beer.

22. The beer will be ready to drink in about 2 weeks.

Meal pairing for *Theobroma*

Duck Mole

by Kevin Downing and Zach Dick

Serves 6

Ingredients

3 tablespoons (or more as needed) peanut oil (preferably
  unrefined), divided
5 pounds duck thighs, skinless and boneless
Salt and pepper
2 cups *Theobroma* or homebrew interpretation
4 prickly pears, freshly juiced
½ cup peanuts, sliced
1¼ pounds tomatillos, sliced
4 ounces dried pasilla chiles, stemmed, seeded, torn into 1-inch
  pieces, and rinsed
1 ounce dried mulato chiles, stemmed, seeded, torn into 1-inch
  pieces, and rinsed
4 teaspoons allspice, ground
5 teaspoons Mexican oregano
¼ cup dried elderberries[*]
3 ounces Mexican chocolate,[†] chopped
6 flour or corn tortillas
Fresh cilantro, chopped

---

[*] Online resource: http://tinyurl.com/jb959ka
[†] Online resource: http://tinyurl.com/h3thol4

PREPARATION

HEAT 1 TABLESPOON of the oil in a heavy large pot over medium-high heat. Sprinkle the duck thighs on both sides with salt and pepper. Working in batches, add the duck to the pot; sauté until lightly browned, about 3 minutes per side, adding more oil in tablespoonfuls as needed. Transfer the duck to a large bowl. Deglaze the pan with the *Theobroma* or homebrew interpretation and prickly pear juice. Add water and bring to a boil to make a "duck stock." Add the duck back to the pan. Reduce the heat to medium low, cover, and simmer until the duck is tender and cooked through, about 25 minutes.

Meanwhile, heat the remaining 2 tablespoons oil in a heavy, large saucepan over medium-high heat. Add the peanuts and toast until they begin to color, about 2 minutes. Add the tomatillos and chiles and cook, stirring occasionally, until darkened and thick, about 10 minutes. Add the allspice and oregano.

Using tongs, transfer the duck to large bowl. Pour the duck stock into the saucepan with the tomatillo mixture (reserve the pot). Add the elderberries to saucepan. Cover and simmer until the chiles are very soft, stirring occasionally, about 30 minutes. Remove from the heat; add the chocolate. Let stand until the chocolate melts and the sauce mixture cools slightly, about 15 minutes.

Working in small batches, transfer the sauce mixture to a blender and purée until smooth; return to the reserved pot. Season the sauce to taste with salt and pepper. Coarsely shred the duck and return it to the sauce; stir to coat.

This meal can be made up to 3 days ahead. Chill until cold, then cover and keep chilled. Rewarm over low heat before serving. Serve on warm tortillas with chopped fresh cilantro.

For mood-enhancing atmospherics and more meal suggestions, go to: http://www.penn.museum/mcgovern/ancientbrews/.

8

Chicha:
Chewing Our Way to Corn Beer

W hen the umbilical cord is cut and we exit the womb into this life, our mammalian sucking instinct kicks in, assuring us that we will not go without sustenance. That first nourishment is in liquid form: our mother's milk. Lactase deficiency for most human populations—decrease in the enzyme for processing the sugar lactose, the main energy source in milk—then sets in, as we are weaned onto liquidy cereal pablums. At the same time, our "milk" or primary teeth begin to erupt from our jaws, and our chewing instinct becomes active. The message is clear: we should begin to eat solid foods, but this does not exclude some liquid refreshment to wash down our meals.

Given these biological imperatives, we might ask what drew our ancestors to the New World. Archaeologists have long held that it was meat provided by gargantuan Ice Age creatures, including woolly mammoths and mastodons, which could have fed an army and gotten them through the cold winters. They pointed to numerous kill-sites such as the one at Jake Bluff in Oklahoma where, almost 11,000 years ago, humans corralled a herd of bison into a dead-end canyon and killed them with knives and spears from above. The intermingling of animal bones and stone weapons told the story. They provided the basis for what came to be known as the "Clovis First" theory, after the name of the site in New Mexico where the distinctive, beautifully contoured stone blades ("Clovis points") of these newcomers were first found.

But, as we have seen when our species emerged in Africa (Chapter 1), our ancestors were probably after much more than meat. They were lured on by the luxurious and varied botanical resources of the New World. Bones and stones had been found, because they were inorganic and virtually indestructible. What about more fragile organic remains, which readily degrade to nothing? When the methods of archaeobotany became available (Preface), a new light was shed on the first Americans. Very well-preserved botanical remains from sites such as Monte Verde, sometimes predating the Clovis sites by thousands of years, could not be explained away. Humans, it seemed, sometimes had a gentler side to them.

We should have been wary of the Clovis First theory to start with, because our permanent (adult) teeth of small molars and canines are ideally suited to processing plants, especially fruits. Grasses and cereals are tougher for us to handle. We also don't have the four-compartment stomach of a ruminant, such as a cow, goat or sheep, for gleaning the maximum amount of nutrition from these natural products. Nevertheless, since we initially roamed the savannahs of Africa where grasses abounded, some accommodation to this "roughage" was needed.

A partial answer came by way of diastase enzyme (ptyalin) in our saliva, which breaks down carbohydrates into sugars. Microorganisms in our gut follow up with more processing, and our cells then receive the right combination of compounds for keeping us alive and reconstituting our bodies over and over again until we die. Ruminants take this approach several steps further. They first chomp up the vegetation and mix it with a similarly constituted saliva in their mouths, which then keeps working in the first two compartments of their stomachs. The cud is formed there, regurgitated for additional chewing in saliva, and finally swallowed.

We can't extract a fibrous plant's full nutritional value like ruminants can. But this physiological limitation might well have had an unintended and potentially very significant side benefit for our early ancestors. Their objective in chewing a plant was to get as much sugary liquid from it as possible. Eventually, they had to spit out the indigestible mass of coarse vegetal matter. In doing so, they would realize that some sweet liquid, which saturated the wad, was lost. They would be tempted to squeeze the mass and collect this remaining liquid somehow. If they were to collect enough liquid and leave it for several days, it might have been inoculated with yeast by a passing insect and converted into a fermented beverage. One sip, and our ancestors would be hooked. They would surely repeat the experiment, this time trying not to swallow any liquid while chewing and spitting out as much as possible.

CAVES FULL OF QUIDS

IT WAS ONLY a matter of time before other very early sites besides Monte Verde, brimming over with organic remains, were discovered in the Americas. Caves, which were protected from rain, wind, and temperature fluctuations so detrimental to organic preservation, were the most productive. Over the past half century or more, archaeologists have located and excavated numerous caves over the length and breadth of the Mexican highlands and up into the Sonoran and Chihuahuan deserts of southern New Mexico, Arizona, and western Texas, even as far north as the Great Salt Lake. The caves sometimes go by quixotic names: Danger and Jukebox Caves in Utah, Granado Cave in the Rustler Hills of Texas, and Frightful Cave in the Mexican state of Cohuila near the U.S. border. Farther south, in the Sierra de Tamaulipas mountains along the Gulf coast, there is Diablo Cave and those of the Infiernillo (Spanish, "Little Hell"). The caves had been occupied for millennia by hunter-gatherers as far back as 10,000 B.P. and up until the Spaniards arrived in the 15th century A.D.

The organic remains, concealed within the caves until the archaeologists and scientists came along and excavated them, read like a compendium of the New World's botanical riches, which our ancestors went on to exploit and domesticate. Squashes, pumpkins, and gourds, chile peppers, guava, prickly pear, yucca, bulrush, hog plum, agave, mesquite, and many other plants were all there. Last, but not least, came the primary powerhouse of the Americas, the cereal maize (*Zea mays*), which was to go on to become the basis of its most celebrated fermented beverage, corn beer or *chicha*.

Nearly every part of the maize plant was represented in the caves, including cobs, ears, husks, tassels, stalks, and leaves. The corn remains from Tamaulipas and other caves in the Tehuacán Valley of Puebla state, southeast of Mexico City, numbered in the thousands. Some appeared to be "unprocessed," just so much debris from conveniently gathering up the entire plant from nearby fields. The main objective might have been to glean the highly prized sugary kernels by shucking the ears and letting the debris fall where it might.

But perhaps our ancestors had a more far-reaching goal in their sights. Many of the maize remains were congealed together, apparently as the result of assiduous chewing. Quids (chewed wads) of husks, leaves, or stalks were even separated out from one another. It was as if the early Americans were whiling away the hours, perhaps to calm themselves in the face of ever-present danger and deprivation, like a modern human might do with a stick of gum or a chaw of tobacco. But why deal with each part of the maize plant separately? Was there a logic in their seeming madness?

It turns out that sugar is found not only in the maize kernels. As the plant matures, a lusciously sweet sap flows up through the main stalk and is concentrated in the kernels over time. This liquid can be sucked out of the stem like a mother's milk from her breast. To get even more sugar, you can follow up your sucking by chewing the stem and other parts of the plant. Thanks to the enzymes in our saliva, some of the tough carbohydrates will be converted to the sweet stuff in liquid form, ready to be fermented. From this perspective, the "unprocessed" maize remains were so much food for fodder, awaiting their turn for sucking, chewing, expectorating, and being made into corn beer.

OUR PRIMAL INSTINCTS HAVE REVOLUTIONARY CONSEQUENCES

WE DO NOT have the definitive biomolecular evidence to prove that the cave peoples were making a *chicha* from their maize sap and quids. Pottery was not invented until around 4500 B.P. in Mesoamerica, so that vessels of that versatile and durable material are not available for testing. Gourds were recovered from the caves, and these served as all-purpose vessels for making, storing, and drinking a fermented beverage in antiquity, as they continue to do so today. They are yet to be tested for fingerprint compounds of maize and any associated botanicals.

Nevertheless, there's good reason to think that our ancestors' biological drives would have led them to discover and enjoy a corn *chicha*, or any prehistoric fermented beverage for that matter (Chapter 1). As starters, we are preprogrammed to smell, chew, taste, and spit out, as needed, the raw materials that go into a fermented beverage. We naturally test our foods and drinks for palatability and nourishment as infants and later in life.

We avoid poisonous and spoiled products, for example, by their bitter tastes and putrid smells. Instead of the FDA, ancient rulers often had a steward or cupbearer (a modern-day sommelier of sorts) at their sides to take the first sip or bite. Before that, reaching back to the beginning of our species, everybody was on their own. Oral traditions passed on by a shaman, parent, elder, or storyteller were your only recourse apart from tasting for yourself. Yet a wonderful world of possibilities lay before our ancestors as they tested one plant and animal after another and decided whether it was edible and delicious.

Careful discrimination is needed to sort out the good from the bad. Fortunately, the hormetic effect—the key concept of the "Drunken Monkey Hypothesis"—kicks in to guide our pragmatic experimentation. Our bodies can actually benefit from a moderate amount of a bitter substance that might otherwise be unsafe, even deadly. The harsh alkaloid, theobromine, in chocolate is a good example (Chapter 7). We gradually work our way up to higher and higher doses, until a violent reaction, like dyspepsia or something worse, tells us to cut back so that we achieve the right balance. Our taste buds and olfactory receptors can even begin to enjoy what was once an off-taste or offensive aroma, and if the substance affects our neural circuits, we may eventually begin to crave it. In Western culture, fermented beverages, stinky cheeses, chocolate, and coffee set the standards.

Modern medicine has gone on to fashion its most effective and best-selling palliatives and remedies by building upon these natural physiological propensities of our species. I've already mentioned the universal pain reliever aspirin, which comes from birch bark. ACE (angiotensin-converting enzyme) inhibitors for lowering blood pressure, derived from a Brazilian viper venom, is an example of how a good thing in moderation can be lethal if taken in excess. From the world of microorganisms, we have penicillin to fight off bacterial infections and statins to reduce our bad cholesterol.

I can personally attest to the beneficial medicinal effect of at least one South American plant. While preparing a book on ancient Egyptian pottery in Austria, I was laid low by an excruciating toothache. The University of Vienna's dental institute was unable to provide relief after a week of suffering, so I turned to a private dentist. He prescribed a Peruvian tree sap of uncertain species, which had me up and smiling within an hour.

Combining our natural desire to taste and test with the phantasmagoric realm of New World plants, we have the formula for discovering not only new medicines but also fermented beverages of all kinds. One of those was probably made from the sugary sap inside the stalk of an inconspicuous mountain grass, which was the wild ancestor of maize: teosinte (genus *Tripsacum*). Comprehensive DNA investigations have shown that this precursor to the most widely planted cereal in the Americas today came from the central Balsas River basin of southwestern Mexico, not far from many of the earliest caves with corn quids.

Even from the vantage point of a lifetime spent studying human cultures, I continue to marvel at how early Americans latched onto such an unassuming, diminutive plant, which blended into its environment. With only 5 to 12 small kernels sealed up inside a 3-centimeter (1-inch)-long "ear," teosinte was but a shadow of what it was to become. A single kernel of the 500 or more kernels inside a 20-centimeter (8-inch)-long husk of sweet corn today has as much sugar as an entire teosinte ear.

I would never have guessed that maize had such humble beginnings in my youth, when I spent many summers on our family farm in South Dakota. To my uninformed mind, the cornfields, which spread out as far as the eye could see across the heartland of North America, must have dominated the landscape for millennia. Today, more corn is produced than any other cereal in the world—nearly a trillion metric tons per year, compared to about 600 billion tons for wheat and rice. How did this come about?

Some enterprising human with a sweet tooth must have taken that first taste of the sap inside teosinte's many thin, billowing branches. He or she might have carried some stalks with their small ears back to camp or cave and invited others to chew on them. It was tough going because of the plant's fibrous exterior. They swallowed the juice with difficulty at first, but surely some of it was spit out along with the indigestible chaff and perhaps pressed or filtered into a gourd container. After a time, a fermented beverage—a combination "beer-and-wine" from the sweet sap and the starchy exterior of the teosinte—was born. More tastings might then have ensued, with the final verdict of the community being that here was a plant worth cultivating or, in less scientific parlance, making a lot more of.

Like all the other major cereals of the world (barley, wheat, millet, sorghum, and rice), the demand for more and more of the alcoholic beverage must have been a powerful incentive to fashion teosinte into a new plant, so as to produce as much sugar as possible for fermentation. It was yet another take on the long-standing question in anthropology: Which came first, bread or beer? For most humans, the immediate and nearly irrefutable answer now and likely in the past has been: if you had your choice, it would be beer, of course!

Unlike bread, fermented beverages have mysterious, mind-altering effects, which made them central to societies and religions, first in Africa and then nearly everywhere that our species traveled. Moreover, beer didn't require as much processing as bread. You didn't need to grind the cereal into a fine powder, sift out chaff and other debris, knead the dough, and bake the loaf in an oven. You just needed to salivate the stalk and ear in the case of corn, gather up the expectorated quids and liquid in a container, set it outside, and presto, you had your elixir.

You also didn't need genetic biotechnology to accomplish the task of domesticating the plant, although that can speed things up. Rather, on current DNA and archaeobotanical evidence (seeds and other macroremains, phytoliths, pollen, and starch grains), our ancestors patiently crossed one desirable plant with another, collected the seeds, and replanted them, over and over again from about 7000 B.P. to 3000 B.P. Large ears with very large kernels, without the extremely tough exteriors of teosinte, were the end result. A single strong stalk made certain that the sugary sap was directed to and concentrated in the kernels. Now, you had a corn ear that had some heft to it. You could take it in both your hands and work your teeth across it row by row, like playing a harmonica. In the process, maize became totally dependent on humans to plant its seed and to propagate it elsewhere in the Americas, including South Dakota.

You also had an ear that was eminently chewable for extracting the maximum amount of sugar for *chicha*. In contrast to their "pushing the envelope" in plant breeding, our ancestors were not ready to abandon their proven method for making a tantalizing, nutritious fermented beverage, which was undergirded by strong social and religious tradition. They continued to chew over thousands of years, as the cave remains eloquently testify. By the time the Spanish chroniclers arrived with pen and paper in hand, they were still at it.

Throughout the Americas, the Spanish writers observed that, almost without exception, the preferred method of making corn *chicha* was to "chew and spit," or more politely, to "masticate and salivate." This predilection persisted, despite the fact that our ancestors had likely observed that corn kernels readily sprouted and could be made into a "more hygienic" malt with much less effort.

By the 15th century A.D., corn *chicha* had long secured its place as the premier fermented beverage of both Central and South America, only surpassed by cacao among the elite of Mesoamerica. The beverage permeated every aspect of social, political, and religious life. Like the pyramids in Egypt or the other massive stone structures of the Old World, whose construction was spurred on by large quantities of the fermented beverages made from cereals native to those regions, corn beer fueled the building of the extensive water and irrigation works and monumental buildings of the New World.

Indeed, the maize god was essential to the stability of the universe. It was a sad day when he died. In one rendition of the Maya story, recorded in the *Popol Vuh* ("Book of Counsel") as reconstructed by the Spanish chroniclers from now lost, millennia-old hieroglyphic originals, he was brought back to life by displaying his head to a ruler's daughter. She was inspired to then give birth to the Hero Twins, who reconstituted the god. Further on in the epic, humans are created from maize, sweet fruits, and cacao, all essential ingredients of a good fermented beverage.

UP TO MACHU PICCHU . . .

ALMOST AS SOON as maize had been transformed and jump-started its own version of a Neolithic farming revolution in southern Mexico, it began to be transplanted to Central and South America. As a result, corn *chicha* had become firmly entrenched in the cultures and religions there by around 3000 B.P.

No better example of *chicha*'s hold on the Americas can be given than the Incan empire of Peru. From small beginnings in the 12th century A.D., an ostensibly insignificant, Quechuan-speaking people on the Andean plateau or Altiplano (Spanish, "high plain") began a series of conquests in A.D. 1438. They went in every direction from their home base at Cuzco at 3400 meters (more than 11,000 feet) above sea level: west to the Pacific coast, north and south into the seemingly endless mountains and deserts, and east to lowland Amazonia. At the height of its power, the empire stretched nearly 5000 kilometers (3000 miles) from Columbia to Chile and Bolivia, about two-thirds the length of South America.

Inca dominance was short-lived. In 1533, just over a century later, the Spanish conquistador Francisco Pizarro and his cavalry marched into Cuzco and plundered the city. The Inca had already been weakened by smallpox, introduced from Europe, and by a civil war.

Only impregnable fortresses, like Machu Picchu (Quechuan, "old peak"), might have escaped the predations, but the Inca saved the Spanish the trouble by abandoning it for unknown reasons. The site "resurfaced" in the 19th and 20th centuries when foreign adventurers and archaeologists like Hiram Bingham were led to it by native guides. The dramatic setting, with the precipitous peaks of the encircling snowy Andes, reaching up into the azure Peruvian sky, is a sight to behold. It's no wonder that Machu Picchu has become a beckoning icon for the romance of archaeology.

On my exploratory trip to Peru in February 2009 in search of fermented beverages, I first saw Machu Picchu out of my airplane window, with its granite buildings set off by manicured, lush green grass. A week later, after taking the train through the Sacred Valley along the wild, picturesque Urubamba River, I was there in person to greet the sun rising over the emblematic pinnacle of Huayna Picchu. I had nearly the whole site to myself, having come in the off-season.

The main goal of my trip, however, was not to swoon in archaeological delight over the impressive monuments of Incan ingenuity, although I saw my fair share of those before boarding the train in the middle of the valley. Under the guidance of my passionate and very knowledgeable guide, Juan Cardenas, we viewed the stonework at Pisaq, whose citadel was constructed of huge, undulating boulders fit together like an intricate jigsaw puzzle. We followed the maze of passages cut into the hill at Q'enko, with its *chicha* cave and "cups" hewn into the rock for offering the precious beverage, llama's blood, and spring water to the gods. We climbed the steeply terraced fortress at Ollantaytambo, said to be laid out in the shape of a corn cob. I spotted a black-and-red painted sherd, likely from an *aribalos*, the highly decorated Incan decanter for *chicha*, and left it in place for future archaeologists. We stopped at small Incan way stations, like Puka Pukara, along the ancient road through the valley. We could have walked the whole way to Machu Picchu, but we had more pressing matters to attend to: What beverages sustained the ancient Inca in their journeys and how were they made?

To start answering these questions, we stopped at one *chicheria* (tavern for drinking *chicha*) after another along the route. The *chicherias*, both commercial and family enterprises, were easy to spot: they sported colorful flags, festoons of flowers, or even plastic bags, most often in vibrant reds or greens, over their front doors. Bunches of twigs or a broom were used, too, as has long been the tradition for announcing a freshly prepared fermented beverage in central and northern Europe. Here, it was freshly made corn *chicha* to be tasted. We were more than happy to oblige, especially when we were welcomed into a private home where it seemed as if the whole village had turned out to gossip and enjoy themselves. Like so many other places on this planet, taverns are the consummate meeting places.

In between glasses of the yellowish, somewhat sour, and faintly bubbly brew, we plied their makers with questions. The brewers were almost exclusively female, lest the Incan *apus* (Quechuan, "spirits of the mountain") or the corn goddess, *Mama Zara* (Quechuan, "maize mother") be offended. We learned that chewing was now out of fashion. Sprouting the grain to make a malt is now considered less "dirty." Some women, however, confided that they still did their masticatory "rites" in secret, carefully concealed from their husbands and other men.

In making a malt, kernels of the predominant yellow maize variety of the Cuzco region (Quechuan, *chamingo*; Spanish, *maiz amarillo*) are first soaked in gunny sacks for a day, followed by constant moistening under plastic sheets (testimony to the inroads of the modern world) over the next week until the sprouts grow to about 12 centimeters (4 inches) long. They are then deemed to be most succulent for making *chicha de jora* (Spanish, "sprouted"). After drying and crushing the resulting malt, it goes into a pottery jar (Quechuan, *raqui*) filled with warm water and is boiled from 30 minutes to several hours to make the mash (Quechuan, *upi*). The grain bill is usually on the order of 6 kilograms (13 pounds) of malt to 4 liters (quarts) of water. A second boiling may follow to assure full mashing.

After a day of cooling the *upi*, there are several options to separate the liquid from the dregs (Spanish, *borra*). Some settling out occurs naturally by gravity, so all you need to do is carefully pour off the supernatant liquid. You can go a step further and pour the liquid through a filter. In one establishment, we saw a woman using a plastic sieve; in another, the woman used the traditional Quechuan basket (*isanq'a*) made from straw and lined with Andean grass.

The last step is to transfer the *upi* to large pottery fermentation jars (Quechuan, *maq'as*). They are often set into recesses in the earthen floors overnight or for several days. The mouth of the vessel is covered with a wooden board. When ready to drink, the woman of the house traditionally scoops out the newly fermented *chicha* to her assembled guests or patrons with a squash ladle (Quechuan, *wango*). She may pour out some of the beverage on the ground and recite the traditional phrase, *Pachamama* (Quechuan, "earth mother"), *santa tierra* (Spanish, "sacred ground"), in homage to the gods and ancestors, after which she partakes of the first glass herself. She adds the sediment at the bottom of the glass to that from the *maq'as*.

The dregs from both the *raqui* and *maq'as* jars are important. The *raqui* dregs are often fed to the animals, but they are also thought to guard against coughing, pneumonia, and even prostate cancer. They can also be put through the mashing process a second time and the liquid used to dilute the *upi*. The *maq'as* dregs, to which solid residues from old *chichas* are added, serve as a yeast starter. The best yeasts are shared by the women of a village. By fermenting in the same *maq'as* jars over and over again, you could also keep the same yeast humming along.

BACK TO CUZCO . . .

BUOYED BY COPIOUS amounts of nonaddictive coca tea back at my home base of Cuzco, I had acclimated to the high altitude. The occasional pisco sour also helped me along. Its main ingredient, pisco, is a grape brandy (Spanish, *aguardiente*), so called because the Spanish brought in domesticated vines through the port of Pisco soon after their invasion and laid out vineyards, first in Cuzco and later in the Ica valley, near Pisco. It was the first time, as well, that native South Americans made their acquaintance with a high-octane distilled beverage. We will see in the next chapter that their cousins to the north in Mexico were possibly one step ahead of the Spanish.

Juan and I also took up our hunt for *chicherias* in the streets of the Incan capital, tasting and probing the locals for more information. We were fortunate in that most of the *chicherias* are concentrated along one thoroughfare, aptly named Cultural Street, perhaps because a lot of yeast cultures were at work there and many different human cultures were intermingling for a drink. Large jugs and glasses of *chicha* were served up from wooden planks, as guinea pigs scooted between our legs and slightly tipsy patrons tried to land bottle caps in a frog or turtle carapace, perhaps a throwback to earlier times when the animals were symbolically important in both the Old World and New World (Chapters 3 and 7). We feasted on *seco de cordero* (Spanish "lamb stew") in which tender chunks of lamb had been boiled in spiced *chicha*, and I thought of Midas (Chapter 2).

To our knowledge, only the malted *chicha de jora* is now made in Cuzco. A little wheat might be tossed in to make it bubble up more. Longer fermentation times produce more alcohol, as much as 5%.

We tried our luck at brewing up a good batch of the malt *chicha* at a small restaurant, Picanteria "La Wally." We took over the kitchen during the off-hours, while the brewers, mainly women, instructed us. Later, we visited a workshop where the malt was crushed in the old-fashioned way with two grinding stones (Spanish, *batan*) by hand. Six kilograms could be done in about a half hour. An electric grinder stood by for when you tired.

The best *chicha* we tasted in Cuzco was fruit based (Spanish, *frutillado*), most often with wild strawberries or berries of the pepper tree (*Schinus molle*). The fresh fruit helps to offset any staleness of an older *chicha*. The reddish color of *frutillado* is sometimes accentuated with the "prickly pear" cactus (*Opuntia soehrensii*) fruit of South America. Whether or not the goal is to make a beverage with symbolic overtones of blood, like the annatto seeds in the chocolate drink, is uncertain. The strawberry drink today is topped off with a whole berry and some Old World cilantro leaves.

We received special instruction in making the pepper berry *chicha de molle* from a husband and wife team, Nilo Mendoza and Anacleta Avilés, in the town of Cotabamba, south of Cuzco. The Cuzco area was ablaze with the intensely red drupes of the ripe fruit in February, which are gathered up and sun-dried for two to three weeks. The thin bitter skins are easily removed by hand. The fruit is then soaked in cold water overnight or, ideally, for a full day. The sweetness of the fruit gradually intensifies and picks up a peppery aroma. More water is added, up to 10 liters (quarts) for 1.5 kilograms (3.3 pounds) of the berries. Fermentation will not occur naturally unless you add some *chicha de jora*; 2 kilograms (4.5 pounds) is usual. Within a day and a half, you are rewarded with a refreshing, mildly alcoholic drink, which even the Spanish chroniclers enjoyed, despite their warning against native beverages being the "work of the devil."

Nilo and Anacleta shared other tidbits of Peruvian fermented beverage-making with us as well. To the northwest of Cuzco, cornstalks were still chewed for the sweet juice and made into a corn stalk "beer-and-wine" called *chicha huyro* (Quechuan, "stalk"). Anacleta confided that she still did the same, and, without adding any *jora*, the "chew" fermented to about 1–2% alcohol in several days. Her husband emphasized that the liquid still needed to be boiled.

Juan and I dipped into much more of the Peruvian fermented beverage lore in our highland peregrinations. Every kind of natural product had been domesticated and made into alcoholic drinks. Many had ancient precedents. Take the humble potato (*Solanum tuberosum*), for example, which was ground up, chewed, and converted into drink since our species first arrived in South America. It was likely domesticated in the southern Andes by 7000 B.P. Peru has thousands of varieties, more than anywhere else in the world. In high mountain villages, it is freeze-dried in straw at –20°C. It develops a black coloration on the skins, which is easily rinsed off in a fast-running Andean river before making *chicha chuño*.

Dark purple, almost blood-like, *chichas* have often been preferred. Salivated from purple potatoes or corn (*chicha morada*), they are frequently served today as a nonalcoholic drink mixed with pineapple, cloves, and cinnamon (the latter two having been introduced from the Old World). The purple potato has been called the "gem of the Andes" and was reserved for the emperor. *Chicha de año* is made from sweet potato—either the common *Ipomoea batatas* or the rarer *Oxalis tuberosa*—following an age-old formula. The tubers are dried in the sun to concentrate their sweetness, and the beverage is uniquely fermented underground.

. . . AND DOWN INTO THE AMAZONIAN JUNGLE

THE LIST OF fermentables in highland Peru went on and on. As we went from one busy market to another, we tried *chichas* made from squash, quinoa, peanuts, palm tree sap, mesquite pods, plantains, bananas, and nonnative sugarcane, a plant in the teosinte/maize family whose stalk also oozes with sugar juice.

We had one last stop to make: the jungle. Traveling over treacherous, muddy mountain roads by public bus (prone to breaking down) and taxis, we descended deep into the rainforest. We visited native peoples still living in thatched huts, surrounded by a profusion of exotic fruiting trees and flowers, which I had never seen before. Cacao trees flourished there, of course, and we saw pods being squashed and filtered to make a refreshing, nonalcoholic soft drink. After several days of fermentation, it becomes alcoholic. A bitter chocolate was made by frying the beans, adding hot water to make a paste, and drying it in a mold. The premeasured capsule could then be dissolved in boiling milk and water to make hot chocolate.

Manioc or cassava (*Manihot esculenta*, also known as yuca and arrowroot) and other root vegetables, some still unnamed by Western science, were growing around the hut of a woman beverage-maker, Susana Piñarreal, whom we visited in Otishi National Park. This jungle paradise is not far from the Manu National Park where bird-watchers delight in observing flocks of multicolored macaws and parrots. This region is home to more than 1000 species of the 1900 found in Peru. Juan had a keen ability for spotting birds, as well as archaeological remains and fermented beverages, and I regularly reported back to my wife, a bird-bander and compiler for Philadelphia, on what I had seen.

Susana and her female associates handled most of their botanical resources alike. They were dried, crushed, and grated, sometimes boiled, and usually chewed to make a plethora of *chichas*. Purplish *chicha morada*, without additives and decidedly alcoholic, was their favorite corn *chicha*.

The most popular jungle drink, however, was made from manioc. Since its raw roots contain cyanogenic glycoside compounds, which break down and are converted to deadly cyanide in the human stomach, the plant needs to be specially prepared. The skin of the tubers must first be removed, then cut up and boiled, so that the glycosides are instead converted to gaseous hydrogen cyanide, which escapes into the air. (Don't stick your head in the vapors or do the boiling in a tight space!) You test how far along you are in the process by probing the pulp with a finger. When the pulp is soft enough, it's ready to be chewed and expectorated into a waiting vessel. Some *jora* is then added to get the fermentation going. Soon, you will have your manioc *chicha* or *masato*, with a sweet, tapioca-like taste.

I tried many other jungle drinks. Another potato-flavored "root beer" (*macato*) is made from *uncucha*, the arrowleaf elephant ear plant. Thankfully, it lacks cyanide compounds. The jungle sweet potato (Quechuan, *machotio*) also gives a purple drink like the upland purple potato. It is so alcoholic that three to four glasses will have you groveling on the hut floor.

I could regale you with many more stories of fermented beverages, especially of the herbal or hallucinogenic type in which the San Pedro cactus and cocaine play a role. Let me just say that if you travel to Peru, be assured that you will be treated to experiences—culinary, archaeological, ornithological, and bibulous—beyond compare. You need to go to Peru soon, before the mighty international brewing companies— the Anheuser-Busch, InBevs, and SABMillers of this world—have taken over and all vestiges of the native drinks disappear.

CORN *CHICHA* AS THE QUINTESSENTIAL INCAN FERMENTED BEVERAGE

EVEN A SHORT visit to Cuzco will dispel any doubts that corn *chicha* is at the very heart of ancient and modern Peruvian life. The supreme temple of the Incan empire, the Qurikancha (Quechuan, "gold enclosure"), was located at the center of the Incan capital. Dedicated to the sun god, Inti, its walls were of solid gold, which shone brightly in the clear, mountain sunlight. The silver and gold statues, offering vessels, and other items within were "fabulous beyond belief," according to the Spanish.

Not much remains of the temple today, except for a few stretches of intricate stonework of the outer walls. The Spanish carried away all the gold and silver, razed the temple, and replaced it with the church and convent of Santo Domingo. The centerpiece of the temple was an enormous gold bowl, representing the navel of the universe and "gullet of Inti." The bowl—a gold-plated replica now stands in the central plaza—was where the emperor poured copious amounts of corn *chicha* offerings to quench Inti's overwhelming thirst. If that weren't enough, human sacrifices, royal mummies, and ancestors were "bathed" in *chicha* dregs at major festivals, where the populace in their flamboyant attire joined in with music and dancing, spurred on by the prodigious drinking of *chicha*. The many festivals and religious celebrations of today—taking up a full month of the year—recall the past, except that you needn't worry about being sacrificed to the sun god.

The emperor and his court spared no expense in assuring that the best corn *chicha* came their way. Palaces were built and set aside for the most beautiful women in the realm (the *mamakona*), where they chewed and salivated their chaste lives away to supply the demand for *chicha*, according to the chroniclers. It is uncertain, but not unlikely, that their balls of salivated maize flour went only into vessels made of precious metals, thus assuring the most refined end product. We do know that the king drank his *chicha* from a gold or silver cup or a drinking-tube.

Archaeological excavations throughout Peru have yielded masses of pottery, dating back to about 5000 B.P. and preceding the earliest pottery of Mesoamerica. Most specialists in the field, including my Penn Museum colleague, Clark Erickson, who serves as the associate curator of the South American collection, assure me that many of the pottery shapes were intended for making, storing, serving, and drinking corn *chicha*.

The only problem with the *chicha* hypothesis for explaining the pottery forms is that it has not been proven chemically. I put one of my students, Josh Henkin, to the job of searching through and identifying likely candidates for analysis in storage. Unfortunately, only hints of residues were detected, and because many of the vessels come from old excavations, we had doubts about their proveniences, subsequent handling, and possible contamination in the storeroom over the years. Recently, the identification of chocolate in vessels kept in storerooms has been questioned, since they might have been exposed to modern caffeine and theobromine when museum staff and volunteers— sometimes called "mummy keepers"—prepared their morning coffee or tea or indulged in some chocolate. Another problem is that gloves were rarely worn until recently. Before investing time and money in analyses, you must be sure that you have the best samples as possible for testing.

As we keep our eyes out for better samples, Clark, also an avid homebrewer, remains convinced of the corn *chicha* hypothesis. I am inclined in the same direction, partly because it fits with my underlying conviction that fermented beverages explain much about human biological and cultural development. Once an alcoholic beverage has been firmly integrated into a society's culture, especially its religion, it can be perpetuated for millennia. Our species has often been innovative in discovering a drink, domesticating the plant from which it is made, even if seemingly impossible (teosinte being a case in point), and devising ways of making, drinking, and celebrating with it. We can also be quite stubborn about giving up our "tried-and-true" traditions of how it should be made, drunk, and offered up to the gods and ancestors.

For whatever reasons (religious injunction, special flavors, etc.), female chewing and salivating likely became entrenched in societies in Peru and throughout South America. How else do you explain the perpetuation of such a labor-intensive, secretive method among women *chicha*-makers today? Moreover, much of the pottery in use today for corn *chicha* is nearly identical to the shapes and decorations of their ancient counterparts, which must have been passed on from generation to generation. You cannot rule out the occasional vessel being used for a manioc, sweet potato, pepper berry, or San Pedro cactus *chicha*. Only time and analyses will tell.

A RETURN TO OUR BIOLOGICAL,
CULTURAL, AND DENTAL ROOTS

I HAD LONG argued that our species was primed to make the first alcoholic drink by chewing and salivating. Sam had been ready to go with that approach when we made our earliest chemically attested re-creation, *Chateau Jiahu*, in 2006. I had dissuaded him then. Now the time had come to bite the bullet and take a chance with *Chicha* in 2009.

The scientific proof for corn *chicha* in the ancient vessels might still be out, but we did know that if you were to make *chicha* the old-fashioned way, you had to apply some serious mouth action. You couldn't cheat by sprouting maize and making it into a malt. Sam and I had the masticatory resources—rapid-talking jaws and decent salivary glands—to handle that. We could at least see how the method worked and what the final product tasted like.

To get us started, I drew on the experiences from my Peruvian trip. I garnered all the advice I could from Clark and other cognescenti on how best to proceed. Archaeobotanist David Goldstein, whom I first met in a Lima restaurant for *chicha* fondue on my return trip from Cuzco, had much to offer. He had been part of the team who had excavated the mountaintop fortress site of Cerro Baúl, dubbed the "Masada of the Andes," in the south of the country. When the ancient inhabitants, the Wari, could no longer hold back their adversaries, the Tiwanaku, they served a final farewell feast, burned down their citadel—temple, palace, and most importantly, their brewery—and abandoned the site about A.D. 1000. *Chicha* cups and serving jugs were scattered in every direction.

The "brewery" at Cerro Baúl was not focused on a corn *chicha* but rather a wine believed to have been made largely from pepper tree berries (*chicha de molle*). Hardly any maize was excavated, but tens of thousands of seeds and stems from pepper berry drupes were found. Many of them came from a multiroom complex for preparing, heating, and fermenting some 1800 liters (450 gallons) of the drink at a time. Forerunners of the *mamakona* women appear to have been in charge of the operation, since they left behind many of their distinctive shawl pins.

With advice from a local *chicha*-maker, David carried out his own experiments in re-creating the beverage in Peru, using freshly picked fruit. He boiled the liquid, as implied by fire pits and ash layers found in the excavation. He also took some liberties: on the advice of his informant, he added cinnamon and cloves to the boil and then two tablespoons of cane sugar to assure fermentation, all Old World plants unavailable to the Wari. It is also difficult to imagine how he got his fermentation going, because boiling will destroy any yeast associated with the fruit. His fermentation vessels were also tightly sealed, so that after the boil, yeasts could not have adventitiously dropped down into the liquid wort from rafters in the ceilings above or been brought in by insects. If the ancient *chicha*-maker had insisted on boiling the mash, rather than just heating it up, she probably would have added *chicha de jora*, as Nilo and Anacleta did, or even more likely would have salivated some corn and left it out to be inoculated by yeast and then added to the liquid.

Sam, Bryan Selders, his brewmaster at the time, Clark, David, and I weighed our options in coming up with another formulation for a re-created ancient *chicha*, in keeping with the available archaeobotanical evidence and traditional practice in the Cuzco area. In the end, we settled on imported purple corn and pepper berries (pink peppercorns) from South America combined with "wild" strawberries from the United States. We planned to salivate about 5 pounds (2.3 kilograms) of the purple corn. The grain bill would be filled out with gelatinized yellow corn flakes and, to satisfy government authorities, barley malt. A token amount of hops was also added. Some rice hulls would help in filtering the mash.

The date for our experimental brew at the Rehoboth Beach brewpub, using the antiquated 6-barrel (186-gallon or 705-liter) system, was set for September 9, 2009, in time for the launching of my new book, *Uncorking the Past*, on October 8 at the Penn Museum. There was *Chicha* to be made, and in Sam's inimitable style, he called up a *New York Times* reporter to record the happening. Clark and David were also invited to attend. The more chewers, the better. Clark jumped at the opportunity but, unfortunately, David was away in Peru.

Sitting on overturned pickle cans, each of us took up our first "chaw" and experimented moving it around in our mouths, lubricating it, and finally popping it out to be dried overnight, when the enzymes in our saliva would do their work. If you want more of the gory details, the *Times* article captures the challenges and raptures of the moment. In short, we spent eight hours chewing red Peruvian corn until our gums were chafed and our jaws ached. About midway through, we decided that it might help to grind up the corn first, like the ancient Inca did. We didn't have a stone *batan* handy, so we sent someone out to a nearby store to get an electric grinder. A female waitress from the pub also stepped in when we were fading to finish up the salivation.

The next day, we made a show of dropping our salivated red corn quids into puréed pepper berries and wild strawberries in the mash tun. We made sure to boil the mixture, so we would not be accused of poisoning the populace. A standard American ale yeast carried out the fermentation. After some conditioning, it was ready to be served at the book launching.

Despite the saliva, our *Chicha* was enthusiastically received by the public at the 2009 Great American Beer Festival, so much so that the Anheuser-Busch and Miller breweries complained that long lines of people, waiting to get a taste of *Chicha* and other *Ancient Ales*, blocked access to their booths. Those who dared drink it enjoyed the deep crimson color of the piquant beverage. Later versions of the drink were made with soursop, which originates in Central America; the prickly, avocado-shaped fruit has a pineapple-strawberry taste in keeping with modern South American interpretations of *chicha morada*.

Sam wondered: Why should he and some academics have all the fun? He put his Dogfish employees to salivating at their desks in between other responsibilities. It turned out that the Inca had it right: women have better enzymes for breaking down the carbohydrates. The cloudy, unfiltered liquid made by their combined efforts was served at an *Ancient Ale* dinner at the Rehoboth pub on November 9, 2014. Tasting like a Belgian white beer or pilsner, it paired nicely with a Peruvian-style ceviche of ahi tuna, corvina, and chile pepper. At 5.5% alcohol, our *Chicha* was not only safe to drink, but also it epitomized the way a real American corn beer should taste and make you feel. It was a far cry from the adjunct-laden corn beer of the behomoth beer companies, so despised by homebrewers.

RECIPES

Homebrew Interpretation of *Chicha*

by Doug Griffith (based on McGovern, 2009/2010)

INGREDIENTS

1 pound	Purple corn	See processes, below
1 pound	Fresh or frozen strawberries (option 1)	Brew Day
1 teaspoon	Pectic enzyme	Brew Day
1 pound	Pre-gelatinized flaked corn	Pre-boil
1 gallon	Water	Pre-boil
1 pint	Cold water	Pre-boil mash
2 tablespoons	Gypsum	Pre-boil mash
1 pound	Brewers malt, crushed	Pre-boil mash
½ pound	Carapils malt, crushed	Pre-boil mash
1	Grain bag	Pre-boil mash
3 pounds	Light dry malt extract	60 minutes
1 teaspoon	Irish moss	10 minutes
3 pounds	Blue corn syrup	10 minutes

¼ teaspoon	Pepper berries (allspice)	End of boil
1 packet	Lallemand Belle Saison,	Fermentation
	White Labs WLP566 Belgian Saison	
	or Wyeast 3711 French Saison	
1 cup	Priming sugar	Bottling
4 ounces	Strawberry concentrate (option 2)	Bottling
	Bottles and caps	Bottling

Starting gravity: 1.069
Final gravity: 1.012
Final target alcohol by volume: 6.5%
International Bittering Units: 0
Finished volume: 5 gallons

PROCESS

Method 1: Traditional Process

1. Three days before Brew Day, cover the whole corn with water in a bowl and soak overnight to soften.
2. Two days before Brew Day, grab some friends and some beer and chew the purple corn. Spit and store for 48 hours.
3. If using fresh or frozen strawberries (option 1), purée the strawberries on Brew Day. Add the pectic enzyme and allow to sit for 24 hours. Add to the fermenter the next day (see step 15 of method 2).
4. Add the 1 gallon water to a brewpot, add the gypsum, and bring to a boil.
5. Add the flaked corn to the brewpot, stirring well, and bring back to a boil. After the boil starts, reduce the heat to a simmer. Stir to keep the corn from sticking to the bottom and burning. Rest for 30 minutes. The mixture will get very thick.
6. Remove from the heat, and add the chewed corn.
7. Go to step 5 of Method 2.

Method 2: Modified Process

1. Brew Day: purée the fresh or frozen strawberries, if using. Add the pectic enzyme and allow to sit for 24 hours. Add to the fermenter the next day (see step 15).

2. Add the 1 gallon of water to a pot, add the gypsum, and bring to a boil.

3. Add the flaked corn and unchewed, crushed purple corn to a brewpot, stirring well, and bring back to a boil. After the boil starts, reduce the heat to a simmer. Simmer for 30 minutes. Stir to keep corn from sticking to the bottom and burning.

4. Remove from the heat. Add the 1 pint of cold water and stir well.

5. Add the crushed malts and stir well. Check the temperature. Adjust it to 122°F by adding cold water to cool or heating to raise. Rest (protein rest) for 10 minutes at 122°F.

6. After the protein rest, raise the temperature to 140 to 145°F and hold for 30 minutes (starch conversion). While the corn and malt mixture is resting, heat 3 gallons of water in the brewpot to 170°F.

7. After the 30-minute rest, spread a grain bag over a container that is large enough to contain the hot liquid and grains from the pot. Carefully pour the hot contents of the pot into the grain bag. Add the grain bag with the grains and the strained hot liquid to the 3 gallons water in the brewpot. Bounce the bag like a tea bag for 5 minutes to dissolve the sugars out of the grains. Hold above the brewpot to drain; do not squeeze. Discard the grain and bag.

8. Turn up the heat on the brewpot, and bring to a boil.

9. Remove the pot from the heat and add the dry malt extract. Stir well until dissolved.

10. Return the pot to the heat and bring to a boil again. Boil for 60 minutes. During the boil, crush the pepper berries.

11. 10 minutes from the end of the boil, add the Irish moss, and slowly add the blue corn syrup while stirring.

12. Remove from the heat after the 60-minute boil and add the crushed pepper berries. Stir well. Let sit for 15 minutes.

13. Cool the wort to 70°F and move to a fermenter, leaving as many solids behind in the kettle as possible. Top up to the 5-gallon mark in the fermenter.

14. Pitch the cooled wort with the yeast, ferment at 70–75°F until fermentation is complete, about 7 to 10 days.

15. Add the puréed strawberries the next day, after fermentation has started (foam will form over the top of the beer). If the strawberries are sweetened, add them slowly to avoid excessive foaming (from the response of the yeast to the extra sugar).

16. Rack to a secondary fermenter for 1 to 2 weeks or until desired clarity.

17. Before bottling, clean and sanitize the bottles and caps.

18. Create a priming solution of 1 cup boiling water and the priming sugar.

19. Siphon the beer into a sanitized bottling bucket.

20. Add the hot priming solution. If using the strawberry concentrate (option 2), add to taste. Gently stir.

21. Bottle and cap the beer.

22. The beer will be ready to drink in about 2 weeks.

ℳEAL PAIRING FOR *Chicha*

Peruvian Ceviche

by Kevin Downing and Zach Dick

Serves 6

INGREDIENTS

1½ pounds white-fleshed ocean fish (such as corvina or white
   sea bass, very fresh)
4 garlic cloves, crushed
½ cup lime juice, freshly squeezed
½ cup *Chicha* or homebrew interpretation (alternatively, add
   another ½ cup lime juice or bitter orange juice)
2 fresh serrano peppers, finely diced
1 red bell pepper, seeded, small dice
1 red onion, thinly sliced
2 tablespoons cilantro, chopped
1 avocado, small dice
1 tablespoon extra virgin olive oil
½ teaspoon salt

Garnishes
Lettuce leaves
Cancha, tostado, or chulpe corn nuts
Microwaved or boiled fresh corn
Sweet potato: thinly fried or baked chips, or boiled thick slices
Chifles or fried green plantain chips
Slices of hot peppers

PREPARATION

CUT THE FISH into ½-inch squares and place into a nonreactive bowl. Add the crushed garlic, and cover with the lime juice and *Chicha* or homebrew interpretation. Cover and refrigerate for 3 to 4 hours. Add the peppers, onion and cilantro to the fish and marinate for another 30 minutes in the refrigerator. Add the avocado, oil, and salt and adjust to taste. Serve with some of the garnishes.

For mood-enhancing atmospherics and more meal suggestions, go to: http://www.penn.museum/mcgovern/ancientbrews/.

9

What Next?
A Cocktail from
the New World, Anyone?

It has been over 15 years since Sam and I began our adventure of re-creating ancient fermented beverages with *Midas Touch*. Since then, we have traveled to many parts of the world in our time machine. But we still have a long way to go: India, Australia, Indonesia, sub-Saharan Africa, the Arctic, and Antarctica beckon. For example, it's said that you can make a fermented beverage from polar bear fat; whether it is alcoholic is another matter. What our ancestors took with them to the bottom of the sea, representing over 70 percent of Earth's surface, is another frontier, which we've only begun to explore (Chapter 5). I described the wine cargo in the earliest Mediterranean shipwreck at Uluburun and hypothesized how humans spread around the world by land and sea—whether to Australia many thousands of years ago or more recently along the west coast of the Americas. My European colleagues have shown what is possible when they analyzed and reconstructed a 19th-century champagne from bottles in the hull of a Baltic Sea shipwreck (Chapter 1).

You never know when a new discovery will be made. Without notice, an archaeologist or homebrewer with beaming face may pop through my office door, or an unexpected email may arrive in my inbox. Just when you thought you knew everything, you're shaken from your slumber by a fortuitous event.

A MEETING OF MINDS AND EXPERTISES

I COULD NOT have asked for a better partner than Sam in the exploration of humankind's love affair with fermented beverages, likely from our beginnings and over millions of years. He was definitely not wedded to the *Reinheitsgebot*, the Bavarian law of the 15th and 16th centuries that demanded that only hops, barley malt, and water be used to make beer. Sam was much more off-centered than this from the start when he decided to throw some maple syrup from his family's farm into the wort in his New York City apartment. We all know what happened next—the founding of Dogfish Head and one crazy creation after another.

There was method in Sam's wild brewing experimentation. He was exploring the boundaries, pushing the envelope, and trying to figure out what brewing beer was all about. He expected a similar attitude from the "tasters" of his finished products. He writes in one place that they should "be promiscuous" in their beer choices and not confine themselves to the *Reinheitsgebot* of the big beer companies. They should "cheat on their go-to beer—their same old, same old" and should explore the full spectrum of what the beer world has to offer. I would add that hops have their place, but they were a relative latecomer. Their soporific properties, which dull the senses, might have appealed to the Protestant reformers, but the aphrodisiac, even hallucinogenic, qualities of good, old-fashioned medieval "gruit" herbs still had a lot going for them (Chapter 6).

The beer world, seen from this vantage point, took a powerful leap forward when Sam (and now many other craft brewers) began to realize what ancient brewers had long known: there was scarcely a limit to the ingredients you could gather up from your environment—which constantly varied from place to place around the globe—and make into delicious, often medicinal, and certainly mind-altering beers. Call them what you might—extreme, hybrid, or mixed-breed fermented beverages—these brews had stood the test of time wherever you looked on Earth.

At the same time that Sam was exploring the full dimensions of his craft, biomolecular archaeology had come of age. Highly sensitive chemical instruments had become available to separate out and identify the ancient molecules from organic residues left behind inside vessels of all kinds (made from metals, glass, woven barks, grasses and textiles, and, above all, pottery). The evaporated remains of liquids, which had spilled on the floors of ancient houses, palaces, and temples, could be gathered up and tested. Even our ancestors' bones and other tissues might contain telltale signs of what they had been drinking.

Our laboratory at the Penn Museum was at the forefront of this new interdisciplinary field, which promised to open up whole new chapters on what it means to be human. It was only a matter of time until those first ancient wine and beer samples from Iran arrived on my doorstep, and I began to realize how important fermented beverages are to the story of humankind.

Our analysis and reconstruction of *Midas Touch* in the late 1990s (Chapter 2), leading to the re-creation of the funerary feast at the Penn Museum in 2000, are what finally opened my mind to a new perspective on ancient fermented beverages. This research—the first time that an ancient meal and its beverage had been unraveled and reconstituted from only the chemical evidence—drove home the point. *Midas Touch*, as a combination beer-wine-and-mead all wrapped up in one, was unlike any that I had imagined. There was nothing like it on the market at the time. More analyses from many other sites and my relationship with Dogfish solidified the concept: most ancient fermented beverages were not simply a wine, beer, or mead; they were usually complex mixtures. They were truly "off-centered ales for off-centered people," as the Dogfish motto puts it.

Obviously, Sam and I were meant for each other when we combined forces and began producing one *Ancient Ale* after another. My job was to hunt down new samples and discover previously unattested fermented beverages in the archaeological record. Sam's job was to apply his brewing expertise and adventuresome taste buds in making as authentic a re-creation from the ancient "recipe" as possible.

WHAT'S IN THE WORKS?

A QUESTION THAT often comes up at tastings and other events is a natural one: "What are you working on now?" Sam, as the businessman, has a quick comeback: "That's secret."

An academic has a harder time answering this question. We always want to learn more, and collaboration is often the way forward. Sam understands this notion, since he benefits from jointly brewing with other craft breweries. If the questioners are experts in their own right—and not prying or merely curious—then I am all ears. They might be able to elucidate some obscure chemical or archaeological facet of our ongoing investigation. An engineer with an instrument company might know of a new, more sensitive, method to use. Homebrewers and competing craft brewers, if they know their craft well, can be a wealth of practical information. Sometimes, I need to walk a thin line in picking an expert's brain and not revealing our ongoing investigations and possible re-creations.

Without giving away too much then, I will summarize several key concepts here on how Sam and I go about re-creating an ancient fermented beverage. I will follow up by giving a concrete example of what we have in the works but are not yet ready to commit ourselves to commercially. For other possible future plans, the ardent reader must take on the role of archaeologist and start "digging" through my publications for ideas.

As you will have already gathered by now, we base our re-creations on the "available evidence." We usually do not have an airtight argument that a particular re-created beverage was made in antiquity in the same way or with all the same ingredients. We don't base our re-creation on 100 percent chemical certainty, which is unobtainable in any case (Preface). We also examine the general archaeological context for clues and corroborating archaeobotanical and other scientific evidence. Ancient textual descriptions and pictorial depictions, as well as modern ethnographic observations, of the beverage being made, stored, served, and drunk can sometimes be crucial (*Chicha* in Chapter 8 is a good example).

Our ultimate objective is to gather as many well-verified pieces of the puzzle as possible, hypothesize about what ingredients most likely went into the brew and how it was brewed, and then try to replicate it in the laboratory or at Dogfish Head. We sometimes take liberties in using modern equipment, substituting nonnative ingredients or yeasts, serving up the beverage more carbonated than might have been the case in antiquity, and presenting it to the public in anachronistic glass bottles with crown caps (corks are not much better).

In our defense, we can only do so much in each experiment. By focusing on several variables at a time rather than every conceivable one, we can carry out more controlled experiments. At the top of our list is whether the specific ingredients work well together and can produce a palatable drink, given that ancient humans probably had sensory organs similar to ours. But we can't always import what we need (one of the reasons we did other versions of most of our re-created beverages in their countries of origin), and we often do not know what the ancient yeast was or have any means to collect and guarantee the genuineness of a "wild yeast" (*Ta Henket* and *Etrusca* were partial exceptions). As for using modern brewing equipment and techniques for the most part, we did substitute ancient pottery, bronze, and oak vessels in making *Etrusca*, and we chewed our way to glory in making *Chicha*.

ANOTHER NEW WORLD ADVENTURE

AS IF THE Americas had not yielded up enough riches with their chocolate, maize, and myriad other alcoholic drinks, we once again turned to that hotbed of ancient extreme fermented beverages in our latest investigations.

Through a series of fortuitous events, I came in contact with a husband-and-wife botanical team in Mexico, Daniel Zizumbo-Villarreal and Patricia Colunga-GarcíaMarín, who had done groundbreaking research on the earliest cultivated and domesticated plants there. They had taken up the theory of Joseph Needham, the famous historian of science, that as early as 1500 B.C. during the so-called Capacha period, people in the state of Colima in the west-central highlands of Mexico were not only fermenting some of these plants to make naturally fermented beverages but also were distilling them into "spirits." This was a revolutionary idea, since it would be another 3000 years before the Spanish arrived with their European stills to make rum and other hard liquor.

Daniel and Patricia worked with local Colima archaeologists, Laura Almendros-López and Fernando González-Zozaya of the National Institute of Anthropology and History, to test their ideas by experimental archaeology. They made modern replicas from local clay of ancient Capacha double-chambered pottery jars, which Laura and Fernando had recently excavated in Colima. They then successfully distilled agave (also called maguey and the century plant), one of the early Mexican domesticates, in the replica jars to an alcohol content as high as 22.5%. That amount is less than that of modern tequila and its traditional forerunner *mezcal*, also made from agave, that are in the 45–55% range, but it exceeds that of naturally fermented agave, such as traditional *pulque* with 2–8% alcohol.

Daniel and Patricia, however, had reached an impasse that required our chemical input. Since no agave remains had been found inside the ancient jars or elsewhere in the excavation, they needed our laboratory to carry out analyses of the ancient jars in search of the biomarkers for agave. The same compounds should be present in the ancient jars as those in their replicas. We were excited by the prospects of possibly discovering the earliest distillation in the world, but since Daniel and Patricia lacked funding, our joint project lay in limbo for several years.

Then David Suro-Piñera stepped in to help. David is a local Philadelphia restaurateur and tequila-maker. As part of his Tequila Interchange Project he offered to pay my way to Mexico in December 2013, so that I could collect samples of the replicas and ancient jars and hand-carry them back to the States. I had already been bitten by the bug of ancient distillation, of which little is known, and accepted his offer. My colleagues and I were willing to donate our time, effort, and laboratory equipment and supplies to find out more.

SOME MORE EXPERIMENTAL ARCHAEOLOGY

WHILE THE ANALYSES went forward, I thought that some practical knowledge about how to ferment and distill agave and other native Mexican plants might prove useful in the long run. The apparatus for doing our own experimental archaeology was already in place, and Sam and his team were eager to play their customary role in exploring the possibilities. We also wanted to have a new re-created beverage ready for the 2015 World Science Festival, as in previous years.

In November 2014, I met with the Dogfish brewers and distillers to discuss and map out our plans. I gave them an overview of what we knew for sure. I started from the beginning with the Mesoamerican "caves full of quids" from 10,000 B.P. onward (chapter 8), which showed that early Americans were quick to exploit the botanical riches of the New World. Agave was just one of many plants—including hog plum, mesquite, maize, guava, and prickly pear—which were later domesticated and went on to become the mainstays of Mexican cuisine. Here was a well-established body of archaeobotanical evidence, which pointed toward the making of fermented beverages by the newcomers, presumably by the chew-and-spit method. I went on to speak of later developments, especially the Aztec *pulque*, and then described what could be the most dramatic discovery of all, pending the necessary chemical evidence—pre-Hispanic distillation.

As Patricia and Daniel had discovered and as Sam and I knew from our long-standing collaboration, experimental archaeology often provides a good check on unwarranted hypotheses concerning fermented beverage technology, together with a realistic assessment of a drink's palatability.

One possible experiment to test how best to make a traditional *pulque* and *mezcal* was to carry out the initial fermentation in a wood canoe. The idea was that this tradition was undoubtedly of pre-Hispanic origin, unlike the as yet unresolved issue of distillation. When the Spanish arrived, they observed many kinds of fermented beverages being made in hollowed-out logs and canoes, including the elite chocolate drink and the unusual *balché*-bark mead of the Lacandón Maya of Chiapas, who still make it this way. Such a widespread, entrenched tradition is a good sign of deep antiquity.

A canoe experiment got Sam's creative juices flowing. I dug further into the ethnographic literature and queried my colleagues. Canoes of two specific trees were still being made and used today for fermenting agave: the parota or devil's ear tree (*Enterolobium cyclocarpum*) and the oyamel or sacred fir tree (*Abies religiosa*). The latter is the preferred tree of migrating monarch butterflies on their winter hibernation grounds in Michoacán, the state to the east of Colima. Fernando tracked down several old fermentation canoes in the Colima area, but they were either too small or falling apart, and the cost of customs and shipment was exorbitant. Sam proposed obtaining the parota staves here in the States and building our own super-sized open "barrel" or canoe. Instead, we turned to other options.

Since the definitive chemical word was still out on the hypothesized prehistoric agave still, I advocated sticking with the well-attested archaeobotanical evidence from the cave quids. The question was then what combination of ingredients, equipment, and fermentative microorganisms we should use. Naturally, we turned to the small experimental brewing facility at the Rehoboth brewpub, which we had used for our other *Ancient Ales*, to do the initial fermentation of an Aztec-like *pulque*. That ferment would then be taken upstairs in the pub to the "primitive" apparatus that had been dubbed the Frankenstill and distilled into a *mezcal*, our first *Ancient Spirit*. We were on shaky scientific and historical grounds for this last step, but we wanted to see how distillation affected the flavor profile.

After debating the many possible ingredients for a "Palaeo-cocktail" and later sourcing their availability, we settled on the following: agave, of course, as a syrupy agave sap (Spanish *aguamiel*, "honeywater"), mesquite-smoked jalapeño chile or chipotle, some fresh prickly pear and guava fruit, and chocolatey mesquite pod powder for good measure. We were unable to secure a batch of *Zymomonas mobilis*, the highly selective bacterium for fermenting agave, so we went with some "wild" Delawarean yeasts. As a final touch, we would chew some purple corn and add the quids to the mix.

AN AZTEC ELIXIR: TWO-RABBIT *PULQUE*

WE MAY NOT have the chemical verdict on prehistoric *mezcal*, but we already know a lot about naturally fermented *pulque* from the Spanish chroniclers. Bernardino de Sahagún is again very informative in his *General History of the Things of New Spain*. He relates how the Aztecs made *pulque* over a four-day period in huge vats, brimming over with foam (compare the chocolate drink in Chapter 7), how they drank it with reed straws and pottery vessels of all sizes and shapes, how honey and botanicals (yet to be identified roots, herbs, and woods) were used to promote fermentation and add flavor and medicinal properties, and how they made different versions of the beverage (blue, white, and five-fold or sacred *pulque*).

With such a powerhouse of a fermented beverage, it's no wonder that the Aztecs strictly regulated its drinking among the general populace. It was even off-limits to the army, perhaps to assure their battle readiness, or for religious reasons or propaganda. Only the elderly were exempt from these rules and spent their final days in *pulque* bliss.

Other chroniclers portray a more liberal attitude to drinking *pulque* among the Aztecs (as seen in the drawing from Codex Magliabechiano at the beginning of this chapter), implying that prohibition was just as successful among this people as our own. Men and women alike are shown lapping up the foam, letting it run from their mouths, sweeping it up by hand, drinking it from bowls or through straws, sharing it with one another, and generally delighting in this "life-giving" elixir. The Aztec gods were also enchanted by the beverage; Sahagún describes Quetzalcoatl, the resplendent "feathered serpent," as drinking *pulque* through a straw.

Drinking bouts, like that in the Codex Magliabechiano, have precedents in pre-Aztec times. The most spectacular example, appropriately named "The Drunkards," is a 50-meter (165-foot)-long mural, dated to A.D. 200, inside the largest manmade pyramid in Mesoamerica at the site of Cholula, southeast of Mexico City. Young men and women, as well as the elderly and one monkey—110 strong—are shown dipping into large jars with their goblets and small bowls, similar to those in the Codex Magliabechiano and that are still used today. They avidly consume the beverage and sometimes its foam, which swells over the tops of the vessels. Many of the individuals are depicted naked, with no regard for modesty, and with bulging, otherworldly eyes suggesting inebriation. Without confirmatory chemical and archaeobotanical evidence, however, we cannot be sure whether the beverage being drunk is *pulque*. Corn *chicha*, *mezcal*, and a hallucinogenic psilocybin mushroom drink are all possibilities.

Pulque eventually assumed mythic proportions among the Aztec and became their religious beverage of choice and central to their religious lore and practice. Its patron god was Ometochtli (Náhuatl, "Two-Rabbit"), whose name refers to a complicated set of myths about the "400 Rabbits," who take on the infinite forms of inebriation. Rabbits fought rabbits, hearts were torn out and thrown into the lake, but in the end, one heart magically becomes the island on which the Aztec capital of Tenochtitlán was founded. Mayahuel, the mother of "Two-Rabbit" and the goddess of agave and *pulque*, is also significant to the cycle of myths. She is often depicted as an anthropomorphized agave plant, holding a foaming bowl of *pulque* in one hand. For the everyday Aztec, *pulque* was an aphrodisiac potion, which encouraged virility and fertility and eased menstruation.

In Mexico City today, *pulque* is fast becoming the in-beverage, as people draw on Mexico's Aztec roots and take pride in their accomplishments (excepting the human sacrifices). The drink is no longer considered lower class. Old-fashioned and boutique *pulquerias* stand cheek-by-jowl along the streets of the city and in outlying towns. Sawdust floors are intended for pouring out the first portion for the "earth mother," like the Peruvian custom with *chicha*. They offer up a wide variety of *pulques*, including *curado* (Spanish, "cured"). These are *pulques* mixed with anything and everything under the sun but especially native plants and fruits in season—including early domesticates such as hog plum, prickly pear, guava, mesquite, and chile. They are "cocktails" of an unusual kind.

GOING TO WORK

I WAS THERE at the pub for the experimental brew of our *pulque* on a Sunday in April 2015. I wouldn't have missed it for the world! While Sam and I cut up the fruit and smoked the chile on a fiery grill, Tim Hawn, the brewmaster, fired up the mash tun. The rest of the operation went smoothly, and I returned home to await word on how it had turned out.

I wasn't there for the subsequent distillation, but I have it on good word from Graham Hamblett, the head distiller, that all went as planned. The *pulque* went through a single distillation, which gave a 50% alcohol content and was later cut with water down to 32.5% for the *mezcal*. Post-distillation, a second, rougher, and more forward-tasting version of the *mezcal* was obtained by infusing the distillate with macerated fruit for three days. By contrast, modern tequila and even traditional *mezcal* are more specialized and refined spirits.

Native domesticated fruits and other natural products are to be expected in a prehistoric fermented beverage. They provided additional sugars and special tastes, offsetting any harsh flavors from a more primitive, less controlled distillation. Accentuating the finished product with fruit, perhaps even suspending an armadillo or chicken breast in the distillation gases as is done when making a *mezcal pechuga* (Spanish, "breast"), has become increasingly popular in modern Mexico and might well have been appreciated long ago.

CHRISTENING AND UNVEILING OUR RE-CREATIONS

THE PENULTIMATE STEP in making an ancient ale or spirit is to give it a name. As I have explained in other chapters, you can go around and around in trying to come up with a suitable, memorable moniker that has not already been trademarked.

I first proposed using the names for the patron god and goddess of *pulque*, Ometochtli and Mayahuel. Those names, however, might be too challenging for an English speaker. The phrase "Two-Rabbit," enigmatic in its own way, would be easier to remember, while still arousing curiosity and interest. Another possibility I dreamt up was "Ms-cal," referring to the female role of Mayahuel in discovering agave *aguamiel*, which was also equated with her blood. Sam nixed that one, because it is also his grandmother's nickname.

We decided to go with three straightforward names: *Two-Rabbit Pulque*, *Two-Rabbit Mezcal*, and *Two-Rabbit Mezcal Fruta*. Even with a limited knowledge of Spanish, *fruta* would be readily understood.

Even if we were not going commercial with these beverages—and we were not at this stage—we still wanted feedback from the general drinking public. Except for our first re-creation, *Midas Touch*, which saw the light of day at the Penn Museum, we have always launched our liquid time capsules simultaneously at a New York City venue and the brewpub in Rehoboth. *Two-Rabbit* was no different. For the last four years, we have released our new beverages in conjunction with the World Science Festival. The venue has moved from one hip location to another in Manhattan and Brooklyn, and we were always guaranteed a sell-out, exuberant, and thirsty crowd.

The 2015 venue for *Two-Rabbit* was Ace Hotel on West 29th Street. We loosened up the audience with a quick tasting tour of the Middle East, China, and Scandinavia by serving *Midas Touch*, *Chateau Jiahu*, and *Kvasir*, while we verbally sparred about how the *Ancient Ales and Spirits* lineup had come about.

We had never done an *Ancient Spirit* before, so the audience was in for a surprise. Fortunately, Graham and Tim pulled off their parts of the process magnificently. *Two-Rabbit Pulque* had a highly unusual but very appealing aroma and taste from the fruit. It had a smoky undertone, and the chile, as usual, added piquancy to the aftertaste. *Two-Rabbit Mezcal* was similar, although less aromatic, as one would expect for a distilled beverage in which volatile and dissolved compounds of the liquid can be lost. As the more expert Graham wrote in his emails: the complex, mixed ingredients are "melded together," with more "subtle" notes of smokiness and pepperiness, by distillation. *Two-Rabbit Mezcal Fruta* was less subtle but still very smooth.

A rousing round of applause went up with the taste of each agave drink cum fruit, chile, mesquite, and masticated corn in turn. As everyone enthusiastically enjoyed the beverages, the question was how they should be classified. Because of their extreme character, should we call them liqueurs, spirits, or primordial cocktails? Cocktail implies a mixture, and these drinks were certainly that. Each *Two-Rabbit* could also be used as a separate ingredient in improvising new tequila- or *mezcal*-like cocktails, already legion and not limited to margaritas and tequila sunrises.

Another gratifying result of the *Two-Rabbit* premiere was that my editor-to-be and my literary agent had front-row seats. Not only did they taste the newly re-created spirits, but they also learned how the *Ancient Ales and Spirits* series came about. They got to experience how eager old and young alike were to learn (and taste) more. This book is another step toward that end.

THE FUTURE IS THE PAST

IT GOES WITHOUT saying that Sam and I are looking forward to more adventures in extreme fermented beverage-making. A dream of mine helps to capture the "spirit" of where we're headed in our time machine. A picture of a strange and wonderful past rolls before my eyes: it's like an attic or medicine cabinet full of exotic, long-forgotten cure-alls and curios. Black-and-white movies of people long gone, but somehow vibrantly alive, flicker by as I see "as if through a glass darkly" my most cherished memories and disembodied thoughts, the accumulated debris of a lifetime. They were once physically expressed in my body's DNA, brain, and surrounding environment and culture. Yet, out of the old, new fresh ideas spring up. It could be a glimpse of a random person's face, a traumatic event, or a dramatic moment "caught on tape" in my dream that kindles the idea. I embellish on it, play with it. I try to rein it in with my conscious mind.

Archaeology is like my dream. It plays out on a much larger stage, since it is a composite of many fragmented human selves and the things they surrounded themselves with in life (including other life-forms, houses, even the clothes they wear). We pick away at the remains that are left and apply the best scientific tools to discover who they once were.

Our re-created extreme fermented beverages epitomize this process: they open up and recover the past. They also break down the boundaries of conscious thought, tap into dreams—like a cherished wine or beer cellar—and make the past live again.

Hopheads and Belgian sour heads take notice. You may think that you have hit the motherlode of all fermented beverages. But you have a long way to go. There are many more taste sensations and novel brewing techniques yet to be discovered, and many of them are lurking in the remains of our species' millennia-long sojourn on this planet. The accompanying homebrew recipes tap into that history and the wonderful future before us. Meals and mood-enhancing atmospherics for enjoying those extreme fermented beverages now and in the future are provided online at http://www.penn.museum/mcgovern/ancientbrews/.

Cheers!

RECIPES

Homebrew Interpretation of
Two-Rabbit Pulque

by Doug Griffith (based on communications from P. E. McGovern and Dogfish Head)

INGREDIENTS

1 pound	Purple corn	See processes, below
½ pound	Dried guava	Two days before Brew Day
½ pound	Fresh prickly pear (when available)	One day before Brew Day
1 teaspoon	Pectic enzyme	One day before Brew Day

3	Fresh jalapeño chiles OR ⅛ ounce dried jalapeño chile (chipotle)	Brew Day
2 tablespoons	Gypsum	Pre-boil mash
1 pound	Brewers malt, crushed	Pre-boil mash
¼ pound	Caramel malt 40 Lovibond, crushed	Pre-boil mash
¾ pound	Cherry smoked malt, crushed	Pre-boil mash
1	Grain bag	Pre-boil mash
5½ pounds	Agave syrup	30 minutes
1½ pounds	Blue corn syrup	30 minutes
1 ounce	Mesquite powder	5 minutes
1 packet	Lallemand Belle Saison, White Labs WLP566 Belgian Saison, or Wyeast 3711 French Saison	Fermentation
1 cup	Priming sugar	Bottling
	Bottles and caps	Bottling

Starting gravity: 1.080
Final gravity: 1.015
Final target alcohol by volume: 8.5%
International Bittering Units: 10
Finished volume: 5 gallons

METHOD 1: TRADITIONAL PROCESS

1. Three days before Brew Day, cover the whole corn with 1 gallon water in a bowl and soak it overnight to soften.
2. Two days before Brew Day, grab some friends and some beer and chew the purple corn. Spit and store for 48 hours. Soak the dried guava in 2 cups water.
3. One day before Brew Day, purée the prickly pear and guava. Add the pectic enzyme per directions and allow to sit for 24 hours.
4. On Brew Day, if using fresh jalapeños, grill until thoroughly charred and dice them fine.
5. Add 3.5 gallons of water to a brewpot and heat to 153°F.

6. Add the gypsum, crushed malts, and chewed corn in a grain bag to a brewpot; maintain a temperature of 153°F to mash the grains. Rest for 30 minutes.

7. Turn the heat up on the brewpot; when the temperature reaches 170°F remove the grains.

8. Continue to heat to a boil. Remove from the heat.

9. Go to step 9 of Method 2.

METHOD 2: MODIFIED PROCESS

1. Two days before Brew Day, place the dried guava in a bowl and cover with 1 gallon water to soak.

2. One day before Brew Day, purée the prickly pear and guava. Add the pectic enzyme per directions and allow to sit for 24 hours.

3. If using fresh jalapeños, before starting the brew, grill the jalapeños until thoroughly charred and dice them fine.

4. In a 1-gallon or larger pot, bring 2 quarts of water to a boil. Add unchewed, crushed purple corn and the gypsum, reduce the heat and simmer for 20 minutes, stirring frequently to keep the corn from sticking to or scorching the bottom of the pot. Remove from the heat. The mixture will be very thick.

5. Add 1 pint of cold water; stir well. Add the crushed malts and stir well. Check the temperature. Adjust it to 122°F by adding cold water to cool or heating to raise. Rest (protein rest) for 10 minutes at 122°F.

6. After the protein rest, raise the temperature to 140 to 145°F and hold for 30 minutes (starch conversion). While the corn and malt mixture is resting, put 4 gallons of water in a brewpot. Heat to 170°F and maintain the temperature.

7. After the 30-minute rest, spread a grain bag over a container that will hold the liquid and grains from the pot. Carefully pour the hot contents of the pot into the grain bag. Move the grain bag and liquid from the container to the brewpot

and bounce the bag like a tea bag for 5 minutes to dissolve the sugars out of the grains. Lift the bag to drain; do not squeeze. Discard the grain and bag.

8. Turn up the heat on the brewpot. As the water is beginning to boil, remove the pot from the heat.

9. Add the agave syrup and bring to a boil. Boil 25 minutes.

10. Add the blue corn syrup, puréed pear/guava mixture, grilled or dried chile, and mesquite powder. Stir well and bring back to a boil. Boil for 5 more minutes.

11. Cool the wort to 75°F and move to a fermenter, leaving as many solids behind in the kettle as possible. Top up to the 5-gallon mark in the fermenter.

12. Pitch the cooled wort with the yeast; ferment at 70 to 75°F until fermentation is complete, 7 to 10 days.

13. Rack to a secondary fermenter for 1 to 2 weeks or until desired clarity.

14. Before bottling, clean and sanitize the bottles and caps.

15. Create a priming solution of 1 cup boiling water and the priming sugar.

16. Siphon the beer into a sanitized bottling bucket.

17. Add the water-diluted priming solution, and gently stir.

18. Bottle and cap the beer.

19. The beer will be ready to drink in about 2 weeks.

MEAL PAIRING FOR *Two-Rabbit Pulque*

Rabbit Stew

by Kevin Downing, Zach Dick, and Christopher Ottosen

Serves 6

INGREDIENTS

3 tablespoons olive oil
One 3¼-pound frozen rabbit, thawed, cut into 8 pieces[*]
Salt and pepper to taste
5 garlic cloves, minced
1 yellow onion, small dice
One 1-pound pumpkin, cleaned and diced
½ cup *Two-Rabbit Pulque* or homebrew interpretation
½ pound tomatoes, chopped, with seeds and juice
½ pound tomatillos, husks removed, chopped
3 poblano peppers, roasted, skins and seeds removed, small
     dice
1 cup chicken or vegetable stock
1 teaspoon epazote[†] (Mexican tea/wormseed)
1 teaspoon allspice
½ teaspoon ancho chile (or other) powder
2 tablespoons fresh Mexican oregano, chopped
¼ cup prickly pear or guava juice, freshly pressed if possible
Pepitas (pumpkin seeds), toasted, for garnish
Squash blossoms[‡] for garnish

---

[*] Online resource: http://honest-food.net/2010/05/19/how-to-cut-up-a-rabbit
[†] Online resource: http://tinyurl.com/jyca4kh
[‡] Online resource: http://tinyurl.com/hjc9eko

PREPARATION

HEAT THE OIL in a heavy, large pot over high heat. Sprinkle the rabbit with salt and pepper. Add the rabbit to the pot and sauté until browned on all sides, about 10 minutes. In the same pan as the rabbit, add the garlic and onion and sauté until tender and translucent. Add the pumpkin and sauté until the pumpkin begins to caramelize. Deglaze with the *Two-Rabbit Pulque* or homebrew interpretation. Add the tomatoes, tomatillos, roasted peppers, and stock. Bring to a boil, scraping up any browned bits. Reduce the heat to medium, cover, and simmer about 30 minutes, until the rabbit is cooked through.

Using tongs, transfer the rabbit pieces to a plate. Add the herbs, spices, and prickly pear or guava juice to the sauce in the pot. Simmer until slightly reduced, about 5 minutes. Return the rabbit to the pot. Stir until heated through, about 3 minutes. Season with salt and pepper and serve. Garnish with *pepitas* and/or squash blossoms.

For mood-enhancing atmospherics and more meal suggestions, go to: http://www.penn.museum/mcgovern/ancientbrews/.

ACKNOWLEDGMENTS

This book takes off where my other books ended—principally *Ancient Wine* and *Uncorking the Past*—and is equally ambitious in trying to encompass the worldwide, millennia-long "love affair" of our species with fermented beverages.

As ever, I continue to rely on an enthusiastic cadre of analytical chemists in our home Penn Museum laboratory, currently Gretchen Hall and Ted Davidson. Most recently, we have also drawn on the scientific expertise and facilities of the Monell Chemical Senses Center (George Preti, Kate Prigge, and Fabian Toro), the Goddard Space Flight Center (Mike Callahan and Karen Smith), the U.S. Department of Agriculture's Tax and Trade Bureau laboratory (Armen Mirzoian), and the Scientific Research and Analysis Laboratory of the Winterthur Museum Conservation Laboratory (Jennifer Mass and Chris Petersen).

I cannot do justice to the numerous individuals here and abroad who have helped me by providing advice and support of every kind—archaeologists, archaeobotanists, chemists, fermented beverage-makers, historians, geneticists, physical anthropologists, ad infin.—so I won't try. You know who you are, and I hope to respond to you in kind someday.

Special thanks go to Sam Calagione and the many employees at Dogfish Head Brewery who had a hand in producing this book. I especially thank chefs Kevin Downing and Zach Dick (for their meal pairings), Wally Hines (for mood-enhancing atmospheric suggestions), and Alan Weeth (for images). Then there are the brewers and distillers without whom none of the *Ancient Brews* would exist: Bryan Selders,

Mike Gerhardt, Floris Delee, Tim Hawn, Graham Hamblett, and Ben Potts.

Other extremely important contributions to the book were made by Doug Griffith of Xtreme Brewing (for his homebrew interpretations, each carefully tested beforehand) and chef Christopher Ottosen of Norway (for his additional meal pairings).

Finally, I am greatly indebted to my literary agent, Clare Polino, and my editor, Amy Cherry, and the whole team at Norton who made this book a reality.

You all deserve an *Ancient Brew*!

SELECT BIBLIOGRAPHY

N.B. This bibliography is not intended to be all-inclusive. For those who wish to dig deeper, please consult my other books and articles. The latter are available in pdf form on my website: http://www.penn.museum/mcgovern/ancientbrews/.

One book will be particularly useful in providing maps and illustrations to go with my prose throughout this book: McGovern, P. E. 2009/2010. *Uncorking the Past: The Quest for Wine, Beer, and Other Alcoholic Beverages.* Berkeley: University of California.

GENERAL

Buhner, S. H. 1998. *Sacred and Herbal Healing Beers: The Secrets of Ancient Fermentation.* Boulder, CO: Siris.

Calagione, S. 2012a. *Extreme Brewing, A Deluxe Edition with 14 New Homebrew Recipes: An Introduction to Brewing Craft Beer at Home.* Gloucester, MA: Quarry Books.

————. 2012b. *Brewing Up a Business: Adventures in Beer from the Founder of Dogfish Head Craft Brewery.* 2nd ed. Hoboken, NJ: Wiley.

————. 2016. *Off-Centered Leadership: The Dogfish Head Guide to Motivation, Collaboration and Smart Growth.* Hoboken, NJ: Wiley.

Hornsey, I. S. 2012. *Alcohol and Its Role in the Evolution of Human Society.* London: Royal Society of Chemistry.

Katz, S. 2014. *The Art of Fermentation.* White River Junction, VT: Chelsea Green.

McGovern, P. E. 2003/2007. *Ancient Wine: The Search for the Origins of Viniculture.* Princeton: Princeton University.

McGovern, P. E., and Hall, G. R. 2015. Charting a future course for organic residue analysis in archaeology. *Journal of Archaeological Method and Theory;* doi: 10.1007/s10816-015-9253-z.

McQuaid, J. 2015. *Tasty: The Art and Science of What We Eat*. New York: Scribner.

Mosher, R. 2004. *Radical Brewing: Recipes, Tales and World-Altering Meditations in a Glass*. Boulder, CO: Brewers Publications.

Schultes, R. E., Hofmann, A., and Rätsch, C. 1992. *Plants of the Gods: Their Sacred, Healing, and Hallucinogenic Powers*. Rochester, VT: Healing Arts.

Shepherd, G. M. 2011. *Neurogastronomy: How the Brain Creates Flavor and Why It Matters*. New York: Columbia University.

Siegel, R. K. 2005. *Intoxication: The Universal Drive for Mind-altering Substances*. Rochester, VT: Park Street.

Stewart, A. 2013. *The Drunken Botanist*. Chapel Hill, NC: Algonquin Books.

Walton, S. 2003. *Out of It: A Cultural History of Intoxication*. New York: Harmony Books.

CHAPTER 1: THE HOLY GRAIL

Almeida, P., et al., 2014. A Gondwanan imprint on global diversity and domestication of wine and cider yeast *Saccharomyces uvarum*. *Nature Communications*, article no. 4044; doi: 10.1038/ncomms5044.

Arce, H. G., et al. 2008. Complex molecules in the L1157 molecular outflow. *Astrophysical Journal* 681:L21–L24.

Biver, N., et al. 2015. Ethyl alcohol and sugar in comet C/2014 Q2 (Lovejoy). *Science Advances* 1(9); doi: 10.1126/sciadv.1500863.

Bozic, J., Abramson, C. I., and Bedencic, M., 2006. Reduced ability of ethanol drinkers for social communication in honeybees (*Apis mellifera carnica* Poll.). *Alcohol* 38:179–183.

Carrigan, M. A., et al. 2014. Hominids adapted to metabolize ethanol long before human-directed fermentation. *Proceedings of the National Academy of Sciences USA* 112:458–463.

Dudley, R. 2004. Ethanol, fruit ripening, and the historical origins of human alcoholism in primate frugivory. *Integrative and Comparative Biology* 44:315–323.

———. 2014. *The Drunken Monkey: Why We Drink and Abuse Alcohol*. Berkeley: University of California.

Ghislain, W. E. E., and Yamagiwa, J. 2014. Use of tool sets by chimpanzees for multiple purposes in Moukalaba-Doudou National Park, Gabon. *Primates* 55:467–472.

Gochman, S. R., Brown, M. B., and Dominy, N. J. 2016. Alcohol discrimination and preferences in two species of nectar-feeding primate. *Royal Society Open Science* 3: 160217; doi: 10.1098/rsos.160217.

Goesmann, F., et al. 2015. Organic compounds on comet 67P/Churyumov-Gerasimenko revealed by COSAC mass spectrometry. *Science* 349(6247); doi: 10.1126/science.aab0689.

Henry, A. G. 2012. The diet of *Australopithecus sediba*. *Nature* 487:90–93.

Hockings, K. J., et al. 2015. Tools to tipple: ethanol ingestion by wild chimpanzees using leaf-sponges. *Royal Society Open Science*; doi: 10.1098/rsos.150150.

Jeandet, P., et al. 2015. Chemical messages in 170-year-old champagne bottles from the Baltic Sea: revealing tastes from the past. *Proceedings of the National Academy of Sciences USA* 112: 5893–5898; doi: 10.1073/pnas.1500783112.

Johns, T. 1990. *With Bitter Herbs They Shall Eat It: Chemical Ecology and the Origins of Human Diet and Medicine*. Tucson: University of Arizona.

Lewis-Williams, J. D. 2005. *Inside the Neolithic Mind: Consciousness, Cosmos and the Realm of the Gods*. London: Thames & Hudson.

Majno, G. 1975. *The Healing Hand: Man and Wound in the Ancient World*. Cambridge: Harvard University.

Olson, C. R., et al. 2014. Drinking songs: alcohol effects on learned song of zebra finches. *PloS One* 9(12): e115427.

Smith, K. E., et al. 2014. Investigation of pyridine carboxylic acids in CM2 carbonaceous chondrites: potential precursor molecules for ancient coenzymes. *Geochimica et Cosmochimica Acta* 136:1–12.

Spitaels, F., et al. 2014. The microbial diversity of traditional spontaneously fermented lambic beer. *PloS One* 9(4):e95384.

Tattershall, I., DeSalle, R., and Wynne, P. J. 2015. *A Natural History of Wine*. New Haven: Yale University.

Thomson, J. M., et al. 2005. Resurrecting ancestral alcohol dehydrogenases from yeast. *Nature Genetics* 6: 630–635.

Turner, B. E., and Apponi, A. J. 2001. Microwave detection of interstellar vinyl alcohol, $CH_2=CHOH$. *Astrophysical Journal* 56:L207–L210.

Wiens, F., et al. 2008. Chronic intake of fermented floral nectar by wild treeshrews. *Proceedings of the National Academy of Sciences USA* 105:10426–10431.

Wrangham, R. 2009. *Catching Fire: How Cooking Made Us Human*. New York: Basic Books.

Wright, I. P., et al. 2015. CHO-bearing organic compounds at the surface of 67P/Churyumov-Gerasimenko revealed by Ptolemy. *Science* 349 (6247); doi: 10.1126/science.aab0673.

CHAPTER 2: *MIDAS TOUCH*

Crane, E. 1999. *The World History of Beekeeping and Honey Hunting.* New York: Routledge.

Department of the Treasury, Alcohol and Tobacco Tax and Trade Bureau 2014. *The Beverage Alcohol Manual (BAM): A Practical Guide.* Vol. 2: *Basic Mandatory Labeling Information for Distilled Spirits.* N.p.: CreateSpace Independent Publishing Platform; http://www.ttb.gov/beer/bam/chapter4.pdf.

Dietler, M., and Hayden, B., eds. 2001. *Feasts: Archaeological and Ethnographic Perspectives on Food, Politics, and Power.* Washington, DC: Smithsonian.

The Golden Age of King Midas 2015. Special issue devoted to Midas and the Phrygians. *Expedition* 57(3).

Gordion 2009. Special issue devoted to the site. *Expedition* 51(2).

McGovern, P. E. 2000. The funerary banquet of "King Midas." *Expedition* 42:21–29.

————. 2001. Meal for mourners. *Archaeology* 54:28–29.

McGovern, P.E., et al. 1999. A feast fit for King Midas. *Nature* 402:863–864.

Meussdoerffer, F., and Zarnkow, M. 2014. *Das Bier: Eine Geschichte von Hopfen und Malz.* Munich: C. H. Beck.

Roller, L. 1984. The legend of Midas. *Classical Antiquity* 2:256–271.

Rose, C. B. 2013. *The Archaeology of Phrygian Gordion, Royal City of Midas.* Gordion Special Studies 7 (University Museum Monograph). Philadelphia: University of Pennsylvania Museum of Archaeology and Anthropology.

Sams, G. K. 1977. Beer in the city of Midas. *Archaeology* 30:108–115.

Simpson, E. 2011. *The Gordion Wooden Objects.* Vol. 1: *The Furniture from Tumulus MM.* Culture and History of the Ancient Near East. Leiden: Brill.

Young, R. S. 1981. *Three Great Early Tumuli.* University Museum Monograph 43. Philadelphia: University of Pennsylvania Museum.

Zarnkow, M., Otto, A., and Einwag, B. 2013. Interdisciplinary investigations into the brewing technology of the ancient Near East and the potential of the cold mashing process. In *Liquid Bread: Beer and Brewing in Cross-Cultural Perspective*, eds. W. Schiefenhövel and H. Macbeth, 47–54. Anthropology of Food and Nutrition, Book 7. Brooklyn: Berghahn Books.

CHAPTER 3: *CHATEAU JIAHU*

Bestel, S., et al. 2014. The evolution of millet domestication, Middle Yellow River Region, North China: evidence from charred seeds at the late Upper Paleolithic Shizitan Locality 9 site. *The Holocene* 24:261–265.

Dodson, J. R., et al. 2013. Origin and spread of wheat in China. *Quaternary Science Reviews* 72:108–111.

Efferth, T. 2007. Willmar Schwabe Award 2006: antiplasmodial and anti-tumor activity of artemisinin—from bench to bedside. *Planta Medica* 73:299–309.

Grosman, L., Munro, N. D., and Belfer-Cohen, A. 2008. A 12,000-year-old shaman burial from the southern Levant (Israel). *Proceedings of the National Academy of Sciences USA* 105:17665–17669; doi: 10.1073/pnas.0806030105.

Gross, B. L., and Zhao, Z. 2014. Archaeological and genetic insights into the origins of domesticated rice. *Proceedings of the National Academy of Sciences USA* 111:6190–6197; doi: 10.1073/pnas.1308942110.

Harper, D. 1998. *Early Chinese Medical Literature: The Mawangdui Medical Transcripts*. London: Kegan Paul International.

Henan Provincial Institute of Cultural Relics and Archaeology. 1999. *Wuyang Jiahu (The Site of Jiahu in Wuyang County)*. Beijing: Science Press.

————. 2000. *Luyi Taiqinggong Changzikou mu (Taiqinggong Changzikou Tomb in Luyi)*. Zhengzhou: Zhongzhou Classical Texts.

Hsu, H.-Y., and Peacher, W. G., eds. 1982. *Chinese Herb Medicine and Therapy*. New Canaan, CT: Keats.

Huang, H. T. 2000. *Biology and Biological Technology*, Part V: *Fermentation and Food Science = Science and Civilisation in China* by J. Needham, vol. 6. Cambridge: Cambridge University.

Juzhong, Z., and Kuen, L. Y. 2005. The magic flutes. *Natural History* 114:42–47.

Lee, G.-A., et al. 2011. Archaeological soybean (*Glycine max*) in East Asia: does size matter? *PLoS ONE* 6(11):e26720. doi: 10.1371/journal.pone.0026720.

Li, X., et al. 2003. The earliest writing? Sign use in the seventh millennium B.C. at Jiahu, Henan Province, China. *Antiquity* 77:31–44.

Liu, L., and Chen, X. 2012. *The Archaeology of China: From the Late Paleolithic to the Early Bronze Age*. Cambridge World Archaeology. Cambridge: Cambridge University.

Lu, H., et al. 2005. Culinary archaeology: millet noodles in late Neolithic China. *Nature* 437:967–968.

McGovern, P. E., et al. 2004. Fermented beverages of pre- and proto-historic China. *Proceedings of the National Academy of Sciences USA* 101:17593–17598.

―――――. 2005. Chemical identification and cultural implications of a mixed fermented beverage from late prehistoric China. *Asian Perspectives* 44:249–275.

―――――. 2010. Anticancer activity of botanical compounds in ancient fermented beverages (Review). *International Journal of Oncology* 37:5–14.

Michel, R. H., McGovern, P. E., and Badler, V. R. 1992. Chemical evidence for ancient beer. *Nature* 360:24.

Morwood, M., and Van Oosterzee, P. 2007. *A New Human: The Startling Discovery and Strange Story of the "Hobbits" of Flores, Indonesia.* Washington, DC: Smithsonian.

Nadel, D., et al. 2012. New evidence for the processing of wild cereal grains at Ohalo II, a 23,000-year-old campsite on the shore of the Sea of Galilee, Israel. *Antiquity* 86:990–1003.

Paper, J. D. 1995. *The Spirits Are Drunk: Comparative Approaches to Chinese Religion.* Albany, NY: State University of New York.

Piperno, D. R., et al. 2004. Starch grains on a ground stone implement document Upper Paleolithic wild cereal processing at Ohalo II, Israel. *Nature* 430:670–671.

Tadić, V. M., et al. 2008. Anti-inflammatory, gastroprotective, free-radical-scavenging, and antimicrobial activities of hawthorn berries ethanol extract. *Journal of Agricultural and Food Chemistry* 56:7700–7709; doi: 10.1021/jf801668c.

Underhill, A. P., ed. 2013. *A Companion to Chinese Archaeology.* Hoboken, NJ: Wiley-Blackwell.

Wang, J., et al. 2016. Revealing a 5,000-year-old beer recipe in China. *Proceedings of the National Academy of Sciences USA* 113 (23) 6444–6448; doi: 10.1073/pnas.1601465113.

Wu, X., et al. 2012. Early pottery at 20,000 years ago in Xianrendong Cave, China. *Science* 336:1696–1700.

Xu, Q., et al. 2013. The draft genome of sweet orange (*Citrus sinensis*). *Nature Genetics* 45:59–66; doi: 10.1038/ng.2472.

Yan, M. 1998. *Martin Yan's Feast: The Best of Yan Can Cook.* San Francisco: KQED Press.

CHAPTER 4: *TA HENKET*

Barnard, H., et al. 2011. Chemical evidence for wine production around 4000 BCE in the Late Chalcolithic Near Eastern highlands. *Journal of Archaeological Science* 38: 977–984.

Cavalieri, D., et al. 2003. Evidence for *S. cerevisiae* fermentation in ancient wine. *Journal of Molecular Evolution* 57:S226–232.

Dreyer, G. 1999. *Umm el-Qaab I. Das prädynastische Königsgrab U-j und seine frühen Schriftzeugnisse.* Deutsches Archäologisches Institut, Abteilung Kairo, Archäologische Veröffentlichungen 86. Mainz: P. von Zabern.

Hartung, U. 2001. *Importkeramik aus dem dem Friedhof U in Abydos (Umm el-Qaab) und die Beziehungen ägyptens zu Vorderasien im 4. Jahrtausend v. Chr.* Deutsches Archäologisches Institut, Abteilung Kairo, Archäologische Veröffentlichungen 92. Mainz: P. von Zabern.

Hillman, G. C. 1989. Late Palaeolithic plant foods from Wadi Kubbaniya in Upper Egypt: dietary diversity, infant weaning, and seasonality in a riverine environment. In *Foraging and Farming: The Evolution of Plant Exploitation*, eds. D. R. Harris and G. C. Hillman, 207–235. One World Archaeology 13. London: Unwin Hyman.

Malville, J. M., et al. 1998. Megaliths and Neolithic astronomy in southern Egypt. *Nature* 392:488–491; doi: 10.1038/33131.

Manniche, L. 1989. *An Ancient Egyptian Herbal.* Austin: University of Texas.

McGovern, P. E. 1997. Wine of Egypt's golden age: an archaeochemical perspective. *Journal of Egyptian Archaeology* 83:69–108.

———. 1998. Wine for eternity. *Archaeology* 5:28–34.

McGovern, P. E., Mirzoian, A., and Hall, G. R. 2009. Ancient Egyptian herbal wines. *Proceedings of the National Academy of Sciences USA* 106:7361–7366.

McGovern, P. E., et al. 1997. The beginnings of winemaking and viniculture in the ancient Near East and Egypt. *Expedition* 39/1:3–21.

Wendorf, F., and Schild, R. 1986. *The Prehistory of Wadi Kubbaniya.* Dallas: Southern Methodist University.

Wendorf, F., et al. 2001. *Holocene Settlement of the Egyptian Sahara.* New York: Kluwer Academic/Plenum.

CHAPTER 5: *ETRUSCA*

Dietler, M. 2015. *Archaeologies of Colonialism: Consumption, Entanglement, and Violence in Ancient Mediterranean France*. Berkeley: University of California.

McGovern, P. E. 2012. The archaeological and chemical hunt for the origins of viticulture in the Near East and Etruria. In *Archeologia della vite e del vino in Toscano e nel Lazio: Dalle tecniche dell'indagine archeologica alle prospettive della biologia molecolare*, eds. A. Ciacci, P. Rendini, and A. Zifferero, 141–152. Borgo San Lorenzo: All'Insegna del Giglio.

McGovern, P. E., and Hall, G. R. 2015. Charting a future course for organic residue analysis in archaeology. *Journal of Archaeological Method and Theory*; doi: 10.1007/s10816-015-9253-z.

Ridgway, D. 1997. Nestor's cup and the Etruscans. *Oxford Journal of Archaeology* 16:325–344.

Sebastiani, F., et al. 2002. Crosses between *Saccharomyces cerevisiae* and *Saccharomyces bayanus* generate fertile hybrids. *Research in Microbiology* 153:53–58.

Stern, B., et al. 2008. New investigations into the Uluburun resin cargo. *Journal of Archaeological Science* 35:2188–2203.

Turfa, J. T., ed. 2013. *The Etruscan World*. Routledge Worlds. London: Routledge.

Tzedakis, Y., and Martlew, H., eds., 1999. *Minoans and Mycenaeans: Flavours of Their Time*. Athens: Greek Ministry of Culture and National Archaeological Museum.

CHAPTER 6: *KVASIR*

Bouby, L., Boissinot, P., and Marinval, P. 2011. Never mind the bottle: archaeobotanical evidence of beer-brewing in Mediterranean France and the consumption of alcoholic beverages during the 5th century B.C. *Human Ecology* 39:351–360.

Dickson, J. H. 1978. Bronze Age mead. *Antiquity* 52:108–113.

Dineley, M. 2004. *Barley, Malt and Ale in the Neolithic*. Oxford: Archaeopress.

Koch, E. 2003. Mead, chiefs and feasts in later prehistoric Europe. In *Food, Culture and Identity in the Neolithic and Early Bronze Age*, ed. M. P. Pearson, 125–143. BAR International Series 1117. Oxford: Archaeopress.

Madej, T., et al. 2014. Juniper beer in Poland: the story of the revival of a traditional beverage. *Journal of Ethnobiology* 34:84–103.

McGovern, P. E. 1986. *The Late Bronze and Early Iron Ages of Central Trans-jordan: The Baq`ah Valley Project, 1977–1981.* University of Pennsylvania Museum Monograph 65. Philadelphia: University of Pennsylvania Museum.

McGovern, P. E., Hall, G. R., and Mirzoian, A. 2013. A biomolecular archaeological approach to "Nordic grog." *Danish Journal of Archaeology* 2112–2131.

McGovern, P. E., et al. 2013. The beginning of viniculture in France. *Proceedings of the National Academy of Sciences USA:* 110:10147–10152.

Nelson, M. 2005. *The Barbarian's Beverage: A History of Beer in Ancient Europe.* London: Routledge.

Nylén, E., Lund-Hansen, U., and Manneke, P., eds. 2005. *The Havor Hoard: The Gold, The Bronze, The Fort.* Kungliga Vitterhets, Historie och Antikvitets Akademiens Handlingar, Antikvariska 46. Stockholm: KVHAHA.

Stika, H.-P. 1996. Traces of a possible Celtic brewery in Eberdingen-Hochdorf, Kreis Ludwigsburg, southwest Germany. *Vegetation History and Archaeobotany* 5:81–88.

Strange, J., ed. 2015. *Tall al-Fukhar: Result of Excavations in 1990-93 and 2002.* Proceedings of the Danish Institute in Damascus 9. Aarhus, Denmark: Aarhus University.

Unger, R. W. 2007. *Beer in the Middle Ages and the Renaissance.* Philadelphia: University of Pennsylvania.

Zimmerman, J. 2015. *Make Mead Like a Viking: Traditional Techniques for Brewing Natural, Wild-Fermented, Honey-Based Wines and Beers.* White River Junction, VT: Chelsea Green.

CHAPTER 7: THEOBROMA

Bruman, J. H. 2000. *Alcohol in Ancient Mexico.* Salt Lake City: University of Utah.

Coe, S. D., and Coe, M. D. 1996. *The True History of Chocolate.* New York: Thames & Hudson.

Dillehay, T. D., and Rossen, J. 2002. Plant food and its implications for the peopling of the New World: a view from South America. In *The First Americans: The Pleistocene Colonization of the New World,* ed. N. G. Jablonski, 237–253. San Francisco: California Academy of Sciences.

Dillehay, T. D., et al. 2008. Monte Verde: seaweed, food, medicine, and the peopling of South America. *Science.* 320 (5877):784–786.

Erlandson, J. M. 2002. Anatomically modern humans, maritime voyaging, and the Pleistocene colonization of the Americas. In *The First Americans:*

The Pleistocene Colonization of the New World, ed. N. G. Jablonski, 59–92. San Francisco: California Academy of Sciences.

Green, J. S. 2010. Feasting with foam: ceremonial drinks of cacao, maize, and pataxte cacao. In *Pre-Columbian Foodways: Interdisciplinary Approaches to Food, Culture and Markets in Ancient Mesoamerica*, eds. J. Staller and M. Carrasco, 315–343. New York: Springer.

Hall, G. D., et al. 1990. Cacao residues in ancient Maya vessels from Rio Azul, Guatemala. *American Antiquity* 55:138–143.

Henderson, J. S., and Joyce, R. A. 2006. In *Chocolate in Mesoamerica: A Cultural History of Cacao*, ed. C. L. McNeil, 140–153. Gainesville: University Press of Florida.

Henderson, J. S., et al. 2007. Chemical and archaeological evidence for the earliest cacao beverages. *Proceedings of the National Academy of Sciences USA* 104:18937–18940.

Hodges, G. 2015. The first American. *National Geographic* 227:124–137.

Hurst, W. J., et al. 1989. Authentication of cocoa in Maya vessels using high-performance liquid chromatographic techniques. *Journal of Chromatography* 466:279–289.

―――――. 2002. Archaeology: cacao usage by the earliest Maya civilization. *Nature* 418:289–290.

Jennings, J., et al. 2005. "Drinking beer in a blissful mood": alcohol production, operational chains, and feasting in the ancient world. *Current Anthropology* 46:275–304.

Joyce, R. A., and Henderson, J. S. 2010. Forming Mesoamerican taste: cacao consumption in Formative Period contexts. In *Pre-Columbian Foodways: Interdisciplinary Approaches to Food, Culture and Markets in Ancient Mesoamerica*, eds. J. Staller and M. Carrasco, 157–173. New York: Springer.

McNeil, C. L., ed. 2006. *Chocolate in Mesoamerica: A Cultural History of Cacao*. Gainesville: University Press of Florida.

Prufer, K. M., and Hurst, W. J. 2007. Chocolate in the underworld space of death: cacao seeds from an early Classic mortuary cave. *Ethnohistory* 54:273–301.

CHAPTER 8: *CHICHA*

Blake, M. 2015. *Maize for the Gods: Unearthing the 9,000-Year History of Corn.* Berkeley: University of California.

Cutler, H. C., and Cardenas, M. 1947. Chicha, a native South American beer. *Botanical Museum Leaflet, Harvard University* 13:33–60.

Goldstein, D. J., and Coleman, R. C. 2004. *Schinus Molle* L. (Anacardiaceae) *chicha* production in the central Andes. *Economic Botany* 58:523–529.

Hastorf, C. A., and Johannessen, S. 1993. Pre-Hispanic political change and the role of maize in the central Andes of Peru. *American Anthropologist* 95:115–138.

Mann, C. C. 2005. *1491: New Revelations of the Americas before Columbus.* New York: Knopf.

Moseley, M. E. 2001. *The Incas and Their Ancestors: The Archaeology of Peru.* New York: Thames & Hudson.

Moseley, M. E., et al. 2005. Burning down the brewery: establishing and evacuating an ancient imperial colony at Cerro Baúl, Peru. *Proceedings of the National Academy of Sciences USA* 102:17264–17271.

Smalley, J., and Blake, M. 2003. Sweet beginnings: stalk sugar and the domestication of maize. *Current Anthropology* 44:675–703.

Staller, J. E. 2016. *Maize Cobs and Cultures: History of Zea mays.* Berlin: Springer.

Staller, J. E., Tykot, R. H., and Benz, B. F., eds. 2006. *Histories of Maize: Multidisciplinary Approaches to the Prehistory, Linguistics, Biogeography, Domestication, and Evolution of Maize.* Amsterdam: Elsevier Academic.

Wilson, A. S., et al. 2013. Archaeological, radiological, and biological evidence offer insight into Inca child sacrifice. *Proceedings of the National Academy of Sciences USA* 110:13322–13327.

CHAPTER 9: WHAT NEXT?

Bruman, J. H. 2000. *Alcohol in Ancient Mexico.* Salt Lake City: University of Utah.

Byers, D. S., ed. 1967. *The Prehistory of the Tehuacan Valley.* Vol. 1: *Environment and Subsistence.* Austin: University of Texas.

Flannery, K. V., ed. 1986. *Guila Naquitz: Archaic Foraging and Early Agriculture in Oaxaca, Mexico.* Studies in Archaeology. Orlando, FL: Academic.

Lappe-Oliveras, P., et al. 2008. Yeasts associated with the production of Mexican alcoholic nondistilled and distilled Agave beverages. *FEMS Yeast Research* 8:1037–1052.

Needham, J. 1980. *Science and Civilisation in China.* Vol. 5: *Chemistry and Chemical Technology,* Part 4: *Spagyrical Discovery and Invention: Apparatus, Theories and Gifts.* Cambridge: Cambridge University.

Serra, M. C., and Lazcano Arce, C. 2010. The drink Mescal: its origin and ritual uses. In *Pre-Columbian Foodways: Interdisciplinary Approaches to Food, Culture and Markets in Ancient Mesoamerica Pre-Columbian Foodways,* eds. J. Staller and M. Carrasco, 137–156. New York: Springer.

Valenzuela-Zapata, A. G., et al. 2013. "Huichol" stills: a century of anthropology—technology transfer and innovation. *Crossroads* 8:157–191.

Zizumbo-Villarreal, D., et al. 2009. Distillation in western Mesoamerica before European contact. *Economic Botany* 63:413–426.

———. 2012. The archaic diet in Mesoamerica: incentive for *milpa* development and species domestication. *Economic Botany* 66:328–343.

INDEX

Note: Page numbers in *italics* refer to figures and illustrations.

Abydos, Egypt, 91, 92
  see also Scorpion I tomb
acetaldehyde, 6, 10
achiote, 190, 199
additives. *see specific types*
ADH (alcohol dehydrogenase), 6,
  13–14, 22
Africa, human migration from, 57,
  209
agave, 185, 244, 246, 248
alcohol
  animal attraction to, 8–9
  as energy source, 6–7, 8, 13–14
  medicinal uses and benefits, 15
  mind-altering effects, 9, 14, 16–17,
    32, 164, 215
  occurrence in nature, 6–12, 18
Alcohol and Tobacco Tax and
    Trade Bureau (TTB), 45–46, 74,
    93, 96, 168, 198
alcohol dehydrogenase (ADH), 6,
    13–14, 22
alcoholism, genetic susceptibility
    to, 11
Alexander the Great, 27
Almendros-López, Laura, 243–44
Amanita muscaria (fly-agaric),
    180–81

Amazonian jungle beverages,
    223–24
amphoras
  Canaanite jars, 62, 123–24, 126–
    27, 128
  compared to wood barrels, 163
  Etruscan wine amphoras, 131, 148
  Mediterranean shipwrecks, 126,
    131, 148
amylases, 69–70
Anasazi, 109
Anatolia, 27, 34, 42
ancho chile, 198, 199, 200
Anchor Steam Brewery, 35
Ancient Wine (McGovern), xxii, 138
Anderson, Bengt, 102
Angostura bitters, 136
Animals Are Beautiful People (film),
    8–9, 23
animals, attraction to alcohol, 8–9
anise, 41, 42
annatto, 190, 199, 200, 221
Anyang, China, 64, 70
Apache Indians, 109
Apis mellifera, 5, 198
apples, 168
aquavit, 158, 163
Areni, Armenia, 94

Arketyp, 167
arrowleaf elephant ear plant, 224
Artemisia, 70, 71, 97, 133, 149
artemisinin, 70–71, 102
Ashgrove, 153, 158
Asia, human migrations, 58–59
Askinosie Chocolate, 197
Aspergillus, 71, 72
aspirin (acetylsalicylic acid), 101,
    168, 213
Astrocaryum standleyanum, 10
Asturias, Spain, 150
Australia, 57, 239
Australopithecus afarensis, 12
Avilés, Anacleta, 221–22, 228
Aztecs, 183–84, 189–90, 193–94,
    197–99, 246–48

Baal, 121, 124
baboons, 8–9
The Bacchae (Euripides), 124
bacteria, alcohol intolerance, 6
balm (*Melissa*), 58, 97
Bamberg, Germany, 151–52
Banpo, China, 61
Baq`ah Valley, Jordan, 154
Barbaresco, Italy, 138, 139
Barcelona, Spain, 149–50
barley
    bread-making, 35
    in China, 60
    in Egyptian beverage residues,
        108
    in *Etrusca,* 134, 135
    at Godin Tepe, 60
    in Greek *kykeon,* 130
    in *Midas Touch,* 44
    in modern European beers, 20
    in Phrygian grog, 32
    at Roquepertuse, France, 149
barley beverages. *see specific types*

barley malt
    malting process, 104, 149, 151–52
    Reinheitsgebot, 46, 239–40
barrels, 21, 24, 135, 162–63, 169–70
Başman, Mehmet, 48
Bastianich, Joe and Lidia, 133
Batali, Mario, 133
BATF (Bureau of Alcohol, Tobacco,
    and Firearms), 45
Bats'ub Cave burial, Belize, 189–90
Bavaria, author's travel in, 37–39
beakers, 153, 159
beer-making
    heating with hot rocks, 152, 161
    mashing, 21, 92, 104–5, 219, 220,
        228
    see also malt and malting; sac-
        charification; *specific types of
        beer*
beers. *see specific types*
beerstone (calcium oxalate), 32–33,
    38
beeswax, 32, 66, 156, 160
Beirut, Lebanon, 122, 123, 127–28
Belgian beers, 21, 40, 152, 166,
    169–70
Belize, 188, 189
Beowulf, 164
Beringia, 179
bertam palm (*Eugeissona tristis*),
    9–10
Beverage Alcohol Manual (BAM), 46
beverage re-creations
    Chateau Jiahu, 73–77
    Chicha, 227, 228–30
    Etrusca, 135–39
    Kvasir, 165–71
    methods, general, xxviii–xxxi,
        242–43
    Midas Touch, 43–44, 241
    Ninkasi beer, 35–36, 39, 44

pepper tree berry wine, 228
   Spanish grog, 150
   Stuttgart "Celtic beer," 152
   Ta Henket, 23, 87–88, 102–5,
      106–7, 108–9
   Theobroma, 196–201
   Two-Rabbit Mezcal, 249
   Two-Rabbit Mezcal Fruta, 249
   Two-Rabbit Pulque, 244–46,
      248–50
Bingham, Hiram, 217
birch-bark bucket, Egtved (Denmark) burial, 159–60
birch sap, 155, 156–57, 160–61, 163,
   167, 168, 171
bird-bone flutes, 64, 65
birds, intoxication, 7, 9
Birka, Sweden, 162
Birra Baladin, 133, 136
Birra del Borgo, 133, 135, 136
bitters, 136, 138, 163
bitter vetch, 42, 149
Biver, Nicholas, 3
black pepper, 161
blood
   associations with beverages, 95,
      189, 190, 199, 221
   consumption of, 28
   symbol for reconciliation, 165
boats
   Byblos Ships, 123, 127, 147
   fermentation canoes, 245–46
   funerary ships of pharaoh Khufu,
      122–23
   see also shipwrecks
bog cranberries, 155, 160, 166
bog myrtle (*Myrica gale*), 20, 155,
   158, 160–61, 163, 167
bog sites and artifacts, 164, 181
boldo, 182
bouza, 108

braggot, 40, 136
bread
   barley, 35
   in Egypt, 92, 103, 104–5, 107–8
   Mesopotamian beer made from,
      108
   Ninkasi's "bread-beer," 39
   Russian *kvass* made from, 39, 157
   smørrebrød, 158
"Brew Masters" (TV show), 102
bronze vessels
   Chinese, 59, 65, 70
   Etruscan, 132, 134–35
   Hochdorf (Germany) tomb, 151
   Midas Tumulus, 28, 29, 30, 47–48
   Roman, 159
   strainer-cups, 156, 158–59
   strainers, 158–59, 160–61, 162, 167
broomcorn millet, 59, 60
bulrush (*Scirpus*), 89, 90, 91, 182, 211
Bureau of Alcohol, Tobacco, and
   Firearms (BATF), 45
"Burton Baton and the Legend of
   the Ancient Ale" (short film),
   103
Byblos, Lebanon, 123, 127, 147

cacao beverages
   additives, 190, 191, 198
   among the Aztecs, 183, 189, 190,
      193–94
   associations with blood, 189, 190,
      199
   from cacao beans, 191, 192, 193–94,
      195, 197, 223
   from cacao pulp, 191–92, 195, 197,
      223
   cylindrical jars for, 186, 193–94,
      195
   as elite drinks, 184, 189, 190, 216,
      245

cacao beverages (*continued*)
  frothing and foaming, 191, 193–95, 196, 200
  honey in, 190, 198
  pottery vessels, 184, 185–86, 187, 192–93
  Puerto Escondido, 184, 187–88, 192, 195–96, 197
  "teapots" for, 188, 192–95, 220
  Theobroma re-creation, 196–201
cacao (*Theobroma cacao*), 183–84
cactus, 221, 224, 226
caffeine, 10–11, 186–87, 188, 196, 226
Calabrese Montenuovo, 147
Calagione, Mariah, 137
Calagione, Sam
  brewer-shaman, 17
  Chateau Jiahu, 73–75, 77, 87, 227
  Chicha, 227, 228–29
  in Egypt, 102, 105–6, 107–8
  Etrusca, 133, 137–38
  extreme fermented beverages, 20, 22–23, 33, 239–42, 251
  Kvasir, 166, 168–70
  Midas Touch, 39, 41, 43–50, 87, 239
  plum braggot, 40
  pulque, 244–46, 248–49
  Sah'tea, 161
  sahti, 20, 152, 161
  salivating red Peruvian corn, 207
  Ta Henket, 23, 109–10
  Theobroma, 196–97, 199–200
calcium oxalate (beerstone), 32–33, 38
Canaanites
  Canaanite jars, 62, 123–24, 126–27, 128
  in Crete, 129–30
  in Cyprus, 128
  Egyptian wine industry and, 95–96, 121

  funerary ships of pharaoh Khufu, 122–23
  Uluburun shipwreck, 125–27, 239
  wine culture, 121, 122, 124–25, 128, 131, 147
  wine trade with Egypt, 94–95, 96, 121
Canning, Stephen, 170
Canterbury Tales (Chaucer), 40
Cantillon Brewery, 138
caraway, 158
Cardenas, Juan, 218, 220, 222, 223
Carlsberg beer, 157
Carmignano, Italy, 134
carrot, 152
Carthage, 130
Casa Baladin, 137, 166
Casale Marittimo, Italy, 132, 134
Casa Nocera, Italy, 134
Catalonia, Spain, 149–50
Catching Fire (Wrangham), 12
Caucasus, 57, 129
cauldrons
  in Cyprus, 128
  in Italy, 132
  from Midas Tumulus, 28, 30, 34, 36, 128
  at northern European sites, 151, 156, 162
Cavalieri, Duccio, 136–37
Cedar of Lebanon, 123, 125
Celtic beverages, 148–50
Celtic people, 131, 133, 148, 150–51, 162
Cerro Baúl, Peru, 227–28
chamomile, 91, 106, 108
champagne from Baltic Sea shipwreck, 23–24, 239
chanterelle mushrooms, 155
Chateau Jiahu
  experimental archaeology, 76

homebrew recipe, 78–80
  label, 55, 75–76
  meal pairing, 80–84
  re-creation, 73–77
Chaucer, Geoffrey, 40
chemical analyses. *see* residue
    analyses
Cheng Guangsheng, 73, 76, 80
chewing. *see* mastication
chicha
  chicha de jora, 219, 221, 228
  Chicha homebrew recipe, 230–33
  chicha huyro, 222
  Chicha re-creation, 227, 228–30
  chicherias, 218, 220
  corn-based, 211, 216–21, 222,
    224–26
  drinking vessels for, 225, 227
  fruit-based, 182, 221–22, 227–28
  manioc-based, 224
  mushroom-based, 182
  potato-based, 182, 222
  production methods, 219–20
chiles
  ancho, 198, 199, 200
  in cacao beverages, 198–99
  in *Theobroma* re-creation, 198
Chimay Grande Réserve (Blue),
    40
chimpanzees, 10, 11
Chinese beverages
  beer, 62, 63, 65, 69–70, 72
  Mijiaya brewery, 60
  wine, 66, 67–68
  Xi'an tomb beverage, 60
  see also Chateau Jiahu; Jiahu
Chinese date (*Zizyphus*), 59, 60, 90
Chinese pottery, 61, 62–63
chocolate, 183–84, 186, 188, 189–97,
    198–99, 223
  see also cacao; cacao beverages

Christofidou-Solomidou, Melpo,
    102
chrysanthemum, 68, 74
Ciliegiolo, 147
Cimmerians, 27–28
clay seals and stoppers, 98–99
cloudberries, 171, 180
clover, 60, 160, 168
Clovis First theory, 209–10
coca tea, 220
Codex Magliabechiano, 237, 247
Colha, 188
Colima, Mexica, 243–44, 245
Colunga-GarcíaMarín, Patricia,
    243–44, 245
comets, 3–4
Compendium of Materia Medica
    (Li), 71, 73
coriander, 58, 97, 106
corks, 46–47, 148, 242
corn (*Zea mays,* maize)
  domestication of, 190, 214–16
  production, current statistics, 214
  remains in caves, 211–12
  sprouting and malting, 198, 216,
    219
  stalks as juice source, 212
  in *Theobroma* re-creation, 198
  see also chicha
corn beer. *see chicha*
cowberries, 160
Crete, 129–30
Cuzco, Peru, 217, 220–22, 224–26,
    228
cylinder seals, 98–99, 125
Cyprus, 127–28

Dabove, Lorenzo, 138
Danube, 151, 162
Debye, Peter, 37
deer penis, 106

Delee, Floris, 102, 110
Denmark, Danish sites
  Copenhagen, 157–58, 168
  Egtved, 159–61, 168, 169, 170
  Juellinge, 159, 160, 162, 168
  Kostræde, 158–59, 160–61, 162
  Nandrup, 158, 159, 160
digestives, 163
"Digging for Drug Discovery" (D3)
  project, 70, 100–102
Diodorus Siculus, 150
Dionysius of Halicarnassus, 150
Dionysus, 29, 124
distillation, 152, 220, 243–46, 249–50
di Vincenzo, Leonardo, 133, 134, 135,
  136, 138
Djibouti, palm wine in, 91
Dogfish Head Craft Brewery
  motto, 241
  Shelter Pale Ale, 40, 43, 49
  yeast library, 22
  see also beverage re-creations
dom palm fruit (Hyphaene thebaica),
  91, 106, 108, 109, 110
Drake, Frances, 122
Dreyer, Günter, 91, 93
drinking vessels
  Assyrian, 34
  beakers, 153, 159
  for cacao beverages, 184, 185–86,
    187, 192–93
  for chicha, 225, 227
  Chinese, 59, 65
  drinking horns, 34, 125, 128, 151,
    171
  Etruscan, 134–35
  Greek, 125
  Hochdorf (Germany) tomb, 151
  Mesoamerica, 184, 185–86, 187,
    192–93
  Midas Tumulus, 28, 29–30, 31, 34

Phoenician wine sets, 128
  from Scandinavian sites, 159, 162
Drosophila melanogaster, 5, 7, 107
"The Drunkards" at Cholula, 247
The Drunken Monkey (Dudley), 10
Drunken Monkey Hypothesis,
    10–12, 15, 87, 213
Duck Mole, 204–5
Dudley, Robert, 10–11
Dunhuang, China, 58
durum wheat, 135–36

early humans
  arrival in Near East, 58
  arrival in the Americas, 179, 209
  hominid diets, 12–14, 210
  migration out of Africa, 57
  Palaeolithic Hypothesis, 15–19, 87
Edgar, Blake, 77
Egtved burial, Denmark, 159–61,
    168, 169, 170
Egypt
  beer in, 92, 103
  bread-making with beer-making,
    92, 103, 104–5, 107–8
  Khan el-Khalili bazaar in Cairo,
    105–7
  medical papyri, 100
  modern bouza, 108
  Nabta Playa, 88, 89, 90
  Ti's tomb at Saqqara, 103–5
  viticulture and winemaking in,
    95–96, 121
  Wadi Kubbaniya, 88, 89, 91, 106
  wine importation from Levant,
    94–95, 96, 121
  see also Abydos, Egypt; Scorpion
    I tomb; Ta Henket
El, 121, 124
el-Amarna, Egypt, 108
El-Deiry, Wafik, 102

elephants, 8
emmer wheat, 104, 108, 149–50
Erickson, Clark, 207, 225, 226, 227, 228–29
Ericsson, Lasse, 166
ethanol, extraterrestrial, 3–4
Ethiopian *tej*, 20
Etruria, Etruscans
  Etruscan grog, evidence for, 132–33, 134–35
  Etruscan grog, re-creation, 135–39
  frescoes, 132
  funerary rituals, 134–35
  Phoenician influence, 130–31, 133, 134–35, 136, 147
  territory and city-states, 132
  wine culture, 131–32, 133, 147, 148
Etrusca
  Etrusca Bronze, 139
  Etruscan grog re-creation, 135–39
  Etrusca Terra Cotta, 138
  Etrusca Wood, 138
  homebrew recipe, 140–42
  introduction, 137–39
  label, 119
  myrrh, 135–36
  yeast, 136–37
Eurasian grape. *see* grape, Eurasian
Euripides, 124
experimental archaeology, 33–37, 39, 76, 244–46
extraterrestrial alcohols, 3–4
extreme fermented beverages
  Cretaceous Dino-Brew, 22–23, 57
  defined, 19
  development of, xxviii–xxxi, 19–22, 240–41
  discovering, xxii–xxv
  future of, 251–52
  methods, general, xxii–xxviii, 242–43

Paleo-Brew, 22, 23–24
  see also specific types
fennel, 42
Fergana Valley, Central Asia, 67
fermentation canoes, 245–46
fermentation in nature, 5–6, 11–12, 18
  see also yeasts
fermented-beverage cultures, 17–18
Fermented Black Beans, 83
Fermented Black Bean Sauce, 82–83
Fermented Daikon or Asian Radish, 84
figs in Scorpion I's wine, 97–98
fire, 12
flutes, 64, 65, 104
fly-agaric (*Amanita muscaria*), 180
Food and Drug Administration (FDA), 45, 74, 108–9, 168, 213
Fourier-transform infrared spectrometry (FT-IR), xxv, 31, 156, 185
foxtail millet, 59
frankincense, 100, 134
fruit
  berries in *Kvasir* re-creation, 166, 170, 171
  in *chicha*, 182, 221–22, 227–28
  dom palm fruit in *Ta Henket*, 106, 108, 109, 110
  in early hominid diets, 12–13, 210
  in *Etrusca*, 135, 136, 139
  hawthorn and grapes in *Chateau Jiahu*, 74
  in *Midas Touch* re-creation, 44
  natural fermentation of, 5–6, 18
  Scorpion I's wine, 97–98
  in *Two-Rabbit* beverage re-creations, 246, 248, 250
fruit fly, 5, 7, 107

funerary rituals
  Celtic, 151
  China, 189
  Egyptian, 91–92, 121
  Etruscan, 134–35
  Maya, 189
  Near East, 29, 30–31, 91
fungi
  hallucinogenic mushrooms, 180, 199, 247
  for mold saccharification, 69–72
  in Scorpion I jars, 99–100
  see also yeasts
funnels, 60, 130

Gaja, Angelo, 138–39
Gaja winery, 138
gas chromatography-mass spectrometry (GC-MS), xxv–xxvi, 4, 31, 66, 96–97, 148, 188, 190
Gaul, Gauls, 135, 148
Gaza, Palestine, 94, 121
General History of the Things of New Spain (Sahagún), 190, 193, 246
genetics
  alcohol consumption and, 7, 11, 18
  DNA analysis, 5, 99, 136
  Saccharomyces cerevisiae, 5, 6, 22, 99
Genó, Spain, 149–50
gentian root, 136
Gentius, 136
Gerhardt, Mike, 73–74
Giaconne, Luca, 138
Giza, Egypt, 103, 108
Glenfiddich distillery, 153
glycolysis, 5
Göbekli Tepe, Turkey, 39
Godin Tepe, Iran, 60
Golden Hind, 122
Goldstein, David, 227, 228–29

González-Zozaya, Fernando, 243–44
Gordias (king), 27, 29, 41–42
Gordion, Midas Tumulus, 27–31
Gotlandsdryka, 155
Gotland sites, Sweden, 155–57
gourds, 212–13
grape, Eurasian (*Vitis vinifera*)
  Calabrese Montenuovo, 147
  in China, 67–68
  DNA sequencing, 5
  domestication, 67
  in Egypt, 93, 96, 121
  in France, 148, 149
  in Italy, 132–33, 134–35, 147
  Muscat grapes, 41, 44, 74, 136
  in Myrtos, Crete, 129–30
  in Scandinavia, 156, 160–63
  in Turkey, 32
  see also wine
grapes
  American varietals, 67
  Chinese varietals, 67
  domestication of, 67
  in Jiahu grog, 66
  for Jiahu grog re-creation, 74
  in *Midas Touch* re-creation, 44
  as tartaric acid source, 32, 66, 93–94, 126, 148, 156
  see also grape, Eurasian
grasses, domestication, 59
Great Lakes Brewing Company, 35
Great Pyramid, Giza, Egypt, 106, 122
Great Wall of China, 58
Greece, Greeks
  cauldrons from northern European sites, 151, 162
  Crete, 129–30
  in Italy, 125, 130–31
  kykeon, 130
  retsina, 96

Grilled and Braised Pork Neck, 143–44
gruit, 20, 33, 163, 166, 170, 240

Hajji Firuz, Iran, 5
Hall, Gretchen, 166
Hamblett, Graham, 249
Handbook of Prescriptions for Emergency Treatment (Ge), 71
Han Dynasty, 60, 189–90
Hartung, Ulrich, 93
Hasselqvist, Jörgen, 166
Hathor, 89–90, 91
Havor, Sweden, 155–57, 158–59, 162, 167
Hawass, Zahi, 103
Hawn, Tim, 166, 168, 248, 250
hawthorn (*Crataegus*), 46, 66, 67, 68–69, 74
hazelnuts, 132, 134, 136, 139
heather (*Calluna vulgaris*), 153
hemp, 60
Henderson, John, 183, 184, 185, 187, 191, 196
Henkin, Josh, 225
herbs, herbal additives
    annatto in *Theobroma*, 199, 200, 221
    Chinese medicine, 70–71
    Chinese *qu*, 70
    in gruit beer, 20, 33, 163, 170, 240
    in *Kvasir* re-creation, 167, 168
    medicinal plants from Mediterranean basin, 148–49
    saffron in *Midas Touch*, 43–44
    Scorpion I's wine, 97, 100, 102
    za'atar and chamomile in *Ta Henket*, 106, 108, 109, 110
Hero Twins, 216–17
The Hershey Company, 185
Hetherington, Nigel, 107–8

high-performance liquid chromatography (HPLC), 31, 185, 188
Hilazon Tachtit, Israel, 64–65
Hochdorf sites, Germany, 150–51, 153, 156, 162, 167
hog plum, 211, 245, 248
holly (*Ilex*), 187
Homer, 27, 42
hominid diets
    alcohol consumption and, 11, 13–14
    fruit in, 12–13, 210
    tasting and testing for palatability, 212–15
Honduras sites. *see* Puerto Escondido, Honduras
honey
    in braggot, 40, 136
    in cacao beverages, 190, 198
    in *Chateau Jiahu* re-creation, 74–75
    chimpanzees and, 11
    in China, 72–73
    in Etruscan grog, 132, 135, 136
    in *Etrusca* re-creation, 136
    in Greek *kykeon*, 130
    in Jiahu Neolithic grog, 66, 72–73
    in *Kvasir* re-creation, 167, 168, 170
    medicinal and nutritional benefits, 73
    in *Midas Touch* re-creation, 32, 44
    in Midas Tumulus Phrygian grog, 32, 36–37
    natural fermentation of, 11–12, 18
    in Ninkasi beer, 35–36
    in Nordic grog, 153–54, 160, 164
    properties of, 7, 164
    in *Theobroma* re-creation, 198, 199, 200
    Turkish red pine honey, 36–37
    yeast in, 32
    see also honey mead

honeybee, 5, 7, 12, 73, 198
honeydew, 37
honey mead
 in braggots, 40
 from Danish sites, 160
 evidence from Scottish sites, 153
 Hochdorf (Germany) tomb, 151
 in Jiahu Neolithic grog, 66,
  72–73
 in Midas Tumulus Phrygian grog,
  36
 natural occurrence, 11–12, 18
 in Nordic grog, 153–54, 160, 164
 in Norse mythology, 164–65
 in Sweden, 154–55
 see also honey
hops (*Humulus*)
 bittering agent, 33, 36
 Iron Age, 133, 136, 152
 Reinheitsgebot, 19–20, 46, 163,
  239–40
 required, in re-created brews, 167,
  198, 228
hormetic effect, 11, 213
Horowitz, Pam, 42, 52
howler monkeys, 10–11
Huilliche people, 182
Hurst, Jeff, 185–86, 188, 189, 192, 193,
  195

Ikonen, Juha, 161
Iliad (Homer), 27, 42, 125
I Li (*Book of Conduct*), 65
Imhotep, 103
Inca, *chicha* among, 217–19, 224–26
insects, as yeast transporters, 69,
  107
Inside Passage, 179–80
intoxication of animals, 8–9
Iran, Iranian sites, 5, 32–33, 60
isotope studies, 66

Jackson, Michael, 39–40, 138, 157
jade, 189–90
Jiahu
 beverage re-creation, 73–77
 beverage residue analysis, 66–67
 crane bone flutes, 64, 65
 pottery jars, 61, 63
 rice at, 63, 79
 tortoise shells, 63, 64
Jordan, 154
Jordan Valley, 58, 94
Joyce, Rosemary, 184, 191, 192, 196
Juellinge burial, Denmark, 159, 160,
  162, 168
jujube (*Zizyphus*), 59, 90
junco reed, 182
juniper, 30, 155, 160–61, 163

Katz, Sol, 35
Khan el-Khalili bazaar in Cairo,
  105–7
Khufu, 122–23
Kition, Cyprus, 128
Koch, Eva, 158
Kostræde, Denmark, 158–59, 160–
  61, 162
kraters, 133, 134, 162
Kvasir
 Arketyp label, 167
 homebrew recipe, 172–74
 label, *145,* 169
 Nordic grog re-creation, 165–71
kvass, 39, 157, 169
kykeon, 130

La Birreria brewpub, 133
La Bottega brewpub, 134
lactase deficiency, 209
lambic beers, 21–22, 70, 152, 166,
  169–70
L'Anse aux Meadows, Canada, 171

Lattara (Lattes), France, 148–49
Lauer, Matt, 47–48
Lebanon, Lebanese sites
    Byblos, 123, 127, 147
    forests as shipbuilding resource,
        123
    see also Canaanites
Leeuwenhoek, Antonie van, 17
Lehner, Mark, 103
lentils, 41–42
Lerman, Caryn, 101
Levant, wine trade with Egypt,
        94–95, 96, 121
Liangchengzhen, China, 61
Li Ji (Book of Records), 65
lime tree (Tilia cordata), 153, 160
lingonberries, 160, 166, 170, 171, 180
Linnaeus, Carl, 184
liquid chromatography tandem
        mass spectrometry (LC-MS-
        MS), xxvi, 31, 93, 126, 148, 156
lotus, 73, 75, 109
Lucy, 12
luo, 68

Mabud, Abdul, 93
Machu Picchu, Peru, 217–18
maize. see corn
Malaysian tree shrew, 9–10
malt and malting
    barley, 104, 149, 151–52
    corn, 198, 216, 219
    process, 104, 149, 151–52, 219
    Reinheitsgebot, 46, 239–40
    rice, 69
    saccharification, 69
    see also barley malt
manioc (cassava), 223–24, 226
manzanita, 179
maple syrup, 157, 240
Mapuche people, 182

mashing, 21, 92, 104–5, 219, 220, 228
mastication
    for chicha, 216, 219, 222, 225, 226,
        229
    fibrous plants, 210
    quids, 181–82, 211–12, 214, 215, 229,
        245–46
    rice, 69
    saccharification by, 69, 72, 74
    sorghum, 90
maté, 187
Maya
    chocolate vessels, 186
    maize god, 216–17
    modern Lacandón Maya, 245
    "teapots" for cacao beverages, 188,
        192–95, 220
Mayahuel, 248, 249
Maytag, Fritz, 35
Mazza, Jim, 169
McGovern, Doris, 45, 80, 109, 127–
        28, 154, 180, 192
McGovern, Pat (photograph), 207
mead. see honey mead
meadowsweet (Filipendula vulgaris),
        20, 46, 153, 160, 163, 167, 168
medicinal beverages, plant addi-
        tives, and chemical compounds
    alcohol, general, 15
    artemisinin, 70–71, 102
    aspirin (acetylsalicylic acid), 101,
        168, 213
    bitters and digestives, 163
    China, 68, 70–71, 106
    "Digging for Drug Discovery"
        (D^3) project, 70, 100–102
    diterpenoids and triterpenoids,
        96, 102
    Egypt, 100, 101–2
    herbs from Mediterranean basin,
        148–49

medicinal beverages, plant additives, and chemical compounds (*continued*)
    honey, 73
    Mexico, 214, 247
    Phrygian grog, 49
    quinine, 101
    Scandinavia, 157, 163
    South America, 101, 213–14
    tree saps and resins, 100
    wormwood/mugwort family, 70–71
    see also specific plants and compounds
Mendoza, Nilo, 221–22, 228
Mesa Verde, 109
Mesoamerica. *see specific topics*
Mesopotamian beer, 38, 39, 108
    see also Ninkasi beer re-creation
Metamorphoses (Ovid), 29
Meussdoerffer, Franz, 39
Mexico
    teosinte and maize domestication, 190
    see also Aztecs; cacao beverages; Maya
mezcal, 244, 245, 246, 249–50
Midas (king), 27, 29, 41–42
Midas Touch
    awards, 47, 49
    commercial production and sales, 45–49
    experimental archaeology, 33–37, 39
    homebrew recipe, 50–52
    label, 25, 46
    meal pairing, 52–53
    re-creation, 43–44, 241
Midas Tumulus, Gordion, Turkey, 27–31

Midas Tumulus Phrygian grog
    chemical analysis, 31–33, 36
    experimental archaeology, 33–37, 39
    proposal for re-creating, 40–41
    residue in drinking vessels, 30–33, 36, 42, 43
    see also Midas Touch
Mijiaya, China, brewery, 60
Miller, Naomi, 42
millet
    in Africa, 90
    beverages, 17, 62, 65, 189
    in China, 59, 60
    Lattara, 149
mint (*Mentha*), 97, 149, 150
Mirzoian, Armen, 93–94
mold saccharification, 69–72
Monascus, 70, 72
Monk's Café, 40
monoterpenes, 97
Monte Albán, Italy, 192, 194
Montefortini Tumulus, Italy, 134
Monte Verde, Chile, 181–82, 183, 184, 210
Montezuma, 183, 198
mugwort (*Artemisia vulgaris*), 133, 149–50, 152
Murlo (Poggio Civitate), Italy, 132
Muscat grapes, 41, 44, 74, 136
mushrooms, 155, 180–81, 182, 199, 247
Musso, Teo, 133, 134, 135, 137–38
Mycenae, Greece, 125
myrrh, 100, 134, 135, 136
Myrtos, Crete, 129–30

Nabta Playa, Egypt, 88, 89, 90
Nandrup burial, Denmark, 158, 159, 160

Narmer, 96
Near East
    earliest barley beer vessel, 60
    human arrival, 58
    see also specific peoples and sites
Nebbiolo, 138
Needham, Joseph, 243
Nefertiti's nip, 108
Nestor's cup, 125, 130
neurotransmitters, 10, 14
New World, human arrival and
    migrations, 179–80, 209
Nicosia, Cyprus, 128
Nielsen, Poul Otto, 168
Nile, 89–90, 93, 95, 107, 121
    see also Egypt
Ninkasi, 35
Ninkasi beer re-creation, 35–36, 39,
    44
Nordic grog
    birch sap, 156–57, 160–61, 163, 167,
        168, 171
    in Denmark, 158–61, 162
    honey in, 153–54, 160, 164
    re-creation, 165–71
    resinated wine in, 156, 160,
        161–63
    in Scotland, 152–53
    in Sweden, 155–57
Norse mythology, mead in, 164–65
North America, human arrival,
    179–80, 209
Nylén, Erik, 155–56
Nynäshamns Ångbryggeri, 166

oak barrels, 21, 24, 135, 162–63,
    169–70
Oaxaca, Mexico, 192, 194
Odin, 164–65, 167
Ohalo II, Israel, 59

Oliver Twist Pub and Restaurant,
    166
Olmecs, 184
Ometochtli (Náhuatl, "Two-Rabbit"),
    248, 249
Orkney Islands, Scotland, 153
Osiris, 91, 121
Otter Creek Brewery, 73
Ottosen, Christopher, 168
Ottosson, Magnus, 154
oyamel or sacred fir tree (Abies reli-
    giosa), 245

Palaeolithic Hypothesis, 15–19, 87
Palermo Stone "Annals" of the Old
    Kingdom, 123
palms
    Americas, 223
    Astrocaryum standleyanum, 10
    bertam palm (Eugeissona tristis),
        9–10
    dom palm fruit (Hyphaene thebaica),
        91, 106, 108, 109, 110
    palm wine, 9–10, 91
Panspermia theory, 3–4
Papazian, Charlie, 77
parota or devil's ear tree (Enterolo-
    bium cyclocarpum), 245
Past Preservers, 107–8
peat bogs. see bog sites and artifacts
Penn Museum
    beer tastings, 39
    Egyptian excavation, 88
    Gordion excavation and exhibits,
        27, 28–30
    launch of Uncorking the Past, 228
    Midas funerary feast re-creation,
        40, 41–43, 52, 241
    Ninkasi re-created beer, 35–36,
        44

peppers
    black pepper, 161
    poblano pepper, 198
    see also chiles
pepper tree berries (*Schinus molle*),
    221, 227
Peru, Peruvian sites
    Cerro Baúl, 227–28
    chicha among the Inca, 217–19,
        224–26
    Cuzco, 217, 220–22, 224–26,
        228
    Machu Picchu, 217–18
    modern fermented beverages,
        222–24
Peruvian ceviche, 234–35
Peters, Tom, 40
Phoenicians, Phoenician sites
    beyond Gibraltar, 130
    central and western Mediterra-
        nean, 130–31
    in Crete, 130
    in Cyprus, 128
    influence on Etruscans, 130–31,
        133, 134–35, 136, 147
    shipwrecks, 131
    spread of Phoenician alphabet,
        124, 131
    wine culture, 125, 130, 131, 133
Phrygian grog. *see* Midas Tumulus
    Phrygian grog
Phrygians, 27–28, 42
Picanteria "La Wally," 221
Piñarreal, Susana, 223
pine resin, 96, 145, 163
Piozzo, Italy, 137, 138
Pisaq, Peru, 218
pisco, 220
Pithekoussai, Italy, 125
Pizarro, Francisco, 217

Pliny the Elder, 124, 149
poblano pepper, 198
Pombia, Italy, 133
pomegranate, 132, 134, 136, 139
popcorn flower, 199
Popol Vuh, 216
pors. see bog myrtle
potato (*Solanum*), 182, 222
pottery
    Catalonia, 149, 150
    China, 60, 61, 62–63
    clay seals and stoppers,
        98–99
    at Godin Tepe, 60
    Jiahu, 61, 63
    Mesoamerica, 184, 185–86, 187–
        88, 192–93, 195–96, 212
    Scorpion I tomb, 92–93, 98
    from Scottish sites, 153
    Tell el-Fukhar, 154, 158
    see also amphoras; drinking
        vessels
Potts, Ben, 168, 169–70
Pramnian wine, 130
prickly pear cactus (*Opuntia soeh-
    rensii*), 221, 245, 246
primates, alcohol consumption,
    9–11
Proconsul, 12
psychoactive mushrooms, 180, 199,
    247
ptyalin (diastase), 69, 210
Puerto Escondido, Honduras, 184,
    187–88, 192, 195–96, 197
pulque
    alcohol content, 244
    canoe fermentation, 245–46
    experimental archaeology,
        244–46
    modern popularity, 248

production and use by Aztecs,
246–48
re-creation, 244–46, 248–50

Q'enko, Peru, 218
quids, 181–82, 211–12, 214, 215, 229,
245–46
qu (mold cake), 70, 73
Qurikancha, Peru, 224–25

Ra, 89–90
Rabbit Stew, 256–57
raisins, 44, 97, 136
Ramat David, Israel, 129
Rauchbier, 152
recipes
Chateau Jiahu homebrew, 78–80
Chicha homebrew, 230–33
Duck Mole, 204–5
Etrusca homebrew, 140–42
Fermented Black Beans, 83
Fermented Black Bean Sauce,
82–83
Fermented Daikon or Asian
Radish, 84
Grilled and Braised Pork Neck,
143–44
Kvasir homebrew, 172–74
Midas Touch homebrew, 50–52
Peruvian ceviche, 234–35
Rabbit Stew, 256–57
Spicy Barbecued Lamb and
Lentil Stew, 41–42, 52–53
Spicy Tofu, 81–82
Ta Henket homebrew, 110–13
Theobroma homebrew, 201–3
24-hour Gravlax, 175–76
Two-Rabbit Pulque homebrew,
252–55
Whole Roasted Goose, 114–17

red-crowned crane, 64
Reinheitsgebot, 19–20, 21, 45–46, 49,
163, 239–40
residue analyses
Capacha distillation jars, 244
el-Amarna beer, 108
Hochdorf (Germany) tomb, 151
instruments and techniques,
xxv–xxvi
Jiahu beverage, 66–67
Maya chocolate vessels, 186, 188,
192, 195–96
Midas Tumulus, 31–33, 36, 42, 43
Myrtos wine, 129
Nordic grogs, 153, 156–57, 160–61
Scorpion I tomb, 93–95, 96–97, 99
Uluburun shipwreck Canaanite
Jars, 126–27
resinated beverages
Etruscan grog, 133, 134–35, 148
Myrtos wine, 129
in Nordic grog, 156, 160, 161
Scorpion I's wine, 96–97, 126
Uluburun shipwreck, 126
retsina, 96
Rhizopus, 70
Rhum (Inner Hebrides), Scotland,
153–54
rice
domestication of, 63, 71
malting, 69
saccharification methods, 69–72,
74
rice beer
in Jiahu Neolithic grog, 66, 69
in modern China, 21, 62
of Shang Dynasty, 70, 72
Río Azul, Guatemala, 186–87, 188,
193
Romany, Ramy, 102–3, 105–6

Rome, Romans
attitudes toward Celtic beverages,
149, 150
conquest of Etruria, 132
drinking vessels in northern
Europe, 156, 159
wine culture, 150
Roquepertuse, France, 149
rosemary, 20, 148, 149–50

saccharification
mastication as method for, 69,
72, 74
mold saccharification, 69–72
rice, 69–72, 74
sprouting and, 69
see also malt and malting; mastication; saliva
Saccharomyces bayanus, 6, 22, 137
Saccharomyces carlsbergensis (S. pastorianus), 137
Saccharomyces cerevisiae
fermentation, 6, 22
genetics, 5, 6, 22, 99
hybridization with S. bayanus, 137
saffron, 41, 43–44, 46
Sagan, Carl, 3
sage (Salvia), 97
Sagittarius B2N, 3
Sahagún, Bernardino de, 190, 193–
94, 246, 247
Sahel, 90
sahti, 20, 152, 161
sake, 72
Salamis, Cyprus, 128
saliva
corn and, 207, 215, 216, 222, 225–
26, 227–29
enzymes in, 18, 69, 210, 212
fruit and, 165

rice and, 69
for saccharification, 69
tubers and, 90–91, 222
see also mastication
Salone del Gusto in Torino, 137–38
Samuel, Delwen, 108
Sangiovese, 147
San Miguel brewery, 150
San Pedro cactus, 224, 226
sapote, 198, 199
Sargon II palace, 34
savory (Satureja), 97, 106
Schmitt-Kopplin, Philippe, 24
Scorpion I tomb
beverage residue analysis, 93–95,
96–97, 99
contents and structure, 91–92
pottery beer jars, 92
wine and wine jars, 92–95, 98–99,
100, 121, 126, 129
Scotch whisky, 152, 153–54
Scotland, Scottish sites, 152–53
Scythians, 27–28
Sekhmet, 89
Selders, Bryan, 108, 228
senna (Cassia), 97
shamans, shamanic ritual, 17, 64, 65,
90, 180–81, 189
Shang Dynasty, 60, 64–65, 68,
69–70, 72, 76
Shaoxing rice wine, 80
shi ancestor ritual, 65
Shihuangdi, 59
shipping, shipbuilding. see boats
shipwrecks
amphoras from, 126, 131, 148
Canaanite Uluburun wreck, 125–
27, 239
champagne from Baltic Sea shipwreck, 23–24, 239

Etruscan *Grand Ribaud F* wreck, 148

Phoenician, 131

Shizitan, China, 59

Siberia, 179, 180–81

Silenus, 29

Silk Road, 58, 129

Sinai Peninsula, 57, 121

situlae (buckets), 29, 34, 46

small-leaved lime tree (*Tilia cordata*), 153, 160

smørrebrød, 158

Snefru, 123

Soconusco, Mexico, 184, 195–96, 197

solid-phase microextraction (SPME), 96, 148, 156

Somalia, 91, 135

sorghum and sorghum beverages, 17, 62, 90

Sori San Lorenzo vineyard, 138–39

Sori Tildin vineyard, 138–39

South America. *see specific topics*

Spain, Spanish sites, 149–50

Spicy Barbecued Lamb and Lentil Stew, 41–42, 52–53

Spicy Tofu, 81–82

Spinnakers, 180

sprouting and malting
  barley, 104, 149, 151–52
  corn, 198, 216, 219
  rice, 69
  saccharification, 69

Squadrilli, Luciana, 134

Steinbier, 152

Stella beer, 106

Stew, Spicy Barbecued Lamb and Lentil, 41–42, 52–53

Stika, Hans-Peter, 150, 151–52

strainers and strainer-cups, 156, 158–59, 160–61, 162, 167

Strange, John, 157

strawberries, 179, 221, 228, 229

straws and drinking-tubes, 32–33, 72, 187, 225

Stuttgarter Hofbräu brewery, 152

Sumerian beer, 35–36

Šuppliluliuma, 43

Suro-Piñera, David, 244

Sweden, Swedish sites, 154–57, 162, 166–68

sweet gale. *see* bog myrtle

sweet potato, 222, 224

Szamatulski, Tess and Mark, 41

Ta Henket
  homebrew recipe, 110–13
  introduction and sale, 109–10
  label, *85,* 108
  re-creation, 23, 87–88, 102–5, 106–7, 108–9

Taklamakan Desert, Central Asia, 58

Tamaulipas, Mexico, 211

Tarquinia, Italy, 132

tartaric acid
  amphoras from Lattara, 148
  Canaanite Jars from Uluburun shipwreck, 126
  grapes as source, 32, 66, 93–94, 126, 148, 156
  Havor residue, 156
  identification techniques, 31, 93, 148, 156
  in Jiahu beverage, 66
  in Midas Tumulus beverage, 32
  Nordic grog, 156, 160
  Scorpion I tomb residues, 93, 94

tea, 161, 220

"teapots" for cacao beverages, 188, 192–95, 220

Tehuacán Valley, Mexico, 211
tej, 20
Tell Bazi, Syria, 38
Tell el-Fukhar, Jordan, 154, 158
Tenochtitlán, Mexico, 183, 193, 248
teosinte (*Tripsacum*), 214–15, 216, 226
tequila, 244, 249, 250
terebinth resin, 96, 126
terpenes and terpenoids, 42, 96, 97, 102
a-terpineol, 42, 97
Theobroma
    homebrew recipe, 201–3
    label, 177, 199
    re-creation, 196–201
Theobroma cacao. see cacao
theobromine, 11, 186–87, 188, 191, 196, 213, 226
thyme (*Thymus/Thymbra*), 42, 58, 97, 102, 148, 149–50
Ti's tomb at Saqqara, Egypt, 103–5
tiswin, 109
Today Show, 47–48
tortoise and turtle shells, 63, 64, 68, 189
trade routes
    amber trade, 161–62
    Canaanite and Phoenician trad-
        ers, 121–22
    Greek traders, 130–31
    Silk Road, 58, 129
tree saps and resins
    birch sap, 155, 156–57, 160–61, 163, 167, 168, 171
    in *Kvasir* re-creation, 167, 168, 171
    medicinal uses of, 100
    myrrh, 100, 134, 135, 136
    pine resin, 96, 148, 163
    terebinth resin, 96, 126
    for wine preservation, 96, 126

tree shrew, Malaysian, 9–10
TTB (Alcohol and Tobacco Tax and
    Trade Bureau), 45–46, 74, 93, 96, 168, 198
Tuborg beer, 128
Turfa, Jean, 131–32
Tutankhamun's tipple, 108
24-hour Gravlax, 175–76
Two-Rabbit Mezcal, 249
Two-Rabbit Mezcal Fruta, 249
Two-Rabbit Pulque
    homebrew recipe, 252–55
    re-creation, 244–46, 248–50

Ultima Thule, 152, 168–69
Uluburun shipwreck, 125–27, 239
Uncorking the Past (McGovern), xxii, 77, 228
Underhill, Anne, 61
Uppsala, Sweden, 154–55

van Roy, Jean, 138
Verucchio, Italy, 132
Vikings, 155, 164, 171, 179
vinegar, 24, 32, 96, 98
Vin Santo, 137
Visby, Sweden, 155
Vitis amurensis, 67
Vitis vinifera. see grape, Eurasian
Vix, France, 162
Vouillamoz, José, 147

Wadi Kubbaniya, Egypt, 88, 89, 91, 106
Wang, Changsui, 61–62
Wari, 227–28
water lily (*Nymphaea*), 91, 109
Wendorf, Fred, 89
wheat
    domestication, 59
    durum wheat, 135–36

emmer wheat, 104, 108, 149–50
  at northern European sites, 152,
    160
Whole Roasted Goose, 114–17
William Grant and Sons, 153–54
wine
  in Jiahu grog, 66
  in Midas Tumulus Phrygian grog,
    32
  palm wine, 9–10, 91
  preservation and sealing tech-
    niques, 98–99
  from Scorpion I tomb, 92–95,
    98–99, 100
  in Sumerian beer recipe, 36
  see also grapes; resinated
    beverages
wine culture
  Canaanite/Phoenician, 121, 122,
    124–25, 128, 133, 147
  diffusion of, 95, 121, 124–25
  Etruscans, 131–32, 133, 147, 148
  grape wine as prestige beverage,
    95
  Romans, 150
wine grape. *see* grape, Eurasian
women, mastication for
  beverage making
  chicha, 216, 219, 222, 225, 226,
    229
  rice, 69

in Siberia, 181
  sorghum, 90
wooden barrels, 21, 24, 135, 162–63,
  169–70
World Science Festival, 169, 244, 250
wormwood, 71, 133
wort, 21, 35, 69, 74, 105, 152, 161

Xi'an, China, 59–61, 67–68

yarrow, 159, 163, 167
yeasts
  alcohol tolerance, 6
  DNA in Scorpion I jars, 99, 136
  Etrusca, 136–37
  in honey, 32
  insects as transporters, 69, 107
  for *Kvasir*, 167
  New World *chicha*, 220
  for *Ta Henket*, 107, 108
  see also Saccharomyces
Yellow Emperor Huangdi, 75
yerba-maté, 187

za'atar, 106, 108, 109, 110
Zarnkow, Martin, 38–39
Zhang, JuZhong, 62
Zhang Qian, 67–68
Zizumbo-Villarreal, Daniel, 243–
  44, 245
Zymomonas mobilis, 246